The publisher and the University of California Press Foundation gratefully acknowledge the generous support of the Ahmanson Foundation Endowment Fund in Humanities.

Soldiering through Empire

AMERICAN CROSSROADS

Edited by Earl Lewis, George Lipsitz, George Sánchez, Dana Takagi, Laura Briggs, and Nikhil Pal Singh

Soldiering through Empire

RACE AND THE MAKING
OF THE DECOLONIZING PACIFIC

Simeon Man

UNIVERSITY OF CALIFORNIA PRESS

University of California Press, one of the most distinguished university presses in the United States, enriches lives around the world by advancing scholarship in the humanities, social sciences, and natural sciences. Its activities are supported by the UC Press Foundation and by philanthropic contributions from individuals and institutions. For more information, visit www.ucpress.edu.

University of California Press
Oakland, California

Library of Congress Cataloging-in-Publication Data

Names: Man, Simeon, author.
Title: Soldiering through empire : race and the making of the decolonizing Pacific / Simeon Man.
Description: Oakland, CA : University of California Press, [2018] | Series: American crossroads ; 48 | Includes bibliographical references and index.
Identifiers: LCCN 2017034917 (print) | LCCN 2017040995 (ebook) | ISBN 9780520959255 (ebook) | ISBN 9780520283343 (cloth : alk. paper) | ISBN 9780520283367 (pbk. : alk. paper)
Subjects: LCSH: Vietnam War, 1961–1975—Participation, Filipinos. | Vietnam War, 1961–1975—Participation, Korean. | Vietnam War, 1961–1975—Participation, Asian Americans. | Pacific Area—History—20th century. | United States—History, Military—20th century. | Imperialism—History—20th century.
Classification: LCC DS558 (ebook) | LCC DS558 .M33 2018 (print) | DDC 959.704/340973—dc23
LC record available at https://lccn.loc.gov/2017034917

26 25 24 23 22 21 20 19 18 17
10 9 8 7 6 5 4 3 2 1

For my parents

CONTENTS

ILLUSTRATIONS

ACKNOWLEDGMENTS

I could not have written this book without the support of many generous people. First, I thank my teachers in the American Studies program at Yale, where this project got its start. I am most grateful to have learned so much from Mary Lui. Mary contributed more to this book and to my growth as a scholar than anyone else. She read drafts carefully and offered critical feedback at every stage, and has been a source of genuine encouragement throughout the process. She is the best model for the kind of generous scholar and mentor that I hope to be. Thanks to my dissertation co-chair, Matthew Frye Jacobson, for his enthusiasm for this project and his sharp interventions, professional advice, and generous spirit. Thanks to Michael Denning for helping me think outside the disciplines and for encouraging me to find my voice as a writer. I learned from a remarkable group of faculty members in those years. Thanks to Stephen Pitti, Alicia Schmidt Camacho, Lisa Lowe, Joanne Meyerowitz, Seth Fein, and Hazel Carby. None of this would have been possible without Moon-Ho Jung, who first introduced me to Asian American history and encouraged me to go to graduate school. Moon taught me the nuts and bolts of doing archival work, and taught me to never settle for the easy answer. I'm grateful to have him as a mentor and an ally.

An Andrew W. Mellon Postdoctoral Fellowship allowed me to spend two years at Northwestern University in the American Studies and Asian American Studies programs. Thanks to Ivy Wilson and Carolyn Chen, the two program directors, for making my time so enriching and productive. Numerous people improved my work through conversations and commenting on early drafts of my writing. Thanks to Kathleen Belew, Martha Biondi, Gerry Cadava, Joshua Chambers-Letson, Daniel Immerwahr, Sylvester Johnson, Jinah Kim, Andrew Leong, Beth Lew-Williams, Linde Murugan,

Shalini Shankar, Nitasha Sharma, Liz Son, Ji-Yeon Yuh, and James Zarsadiaz. The manuscript workshop Carolyn organized for me came at a critical time in my revision process. I thank Mark Philip Bradley, Jodi Kim, and Ji-Yeon Yuh for their careful reading and generous engagement with the book's first draft. Mike Amezcua and Mireya Loza are two of my favorite people who made Chicago feel a little more like home. Thanks to Cheryl Jue and Greg Jue for the good company. I was fortunate to have spent one year at the University of Southern California as a Postdoctoral Scholar in the Humanities in the Department of American Studies and Ethnicity. Conversations with Jih-Fei Cheng, Sarah Fong, Jenny Hoang, Neetu Khanna, Lon Kurashige, Joshua Mitchell, Viet Nguyen, and Nic John Ramos made my time at USC an enjoyable one. Deep thanks to Nayan Shah for his mentorship and generous support.

My current colleagues in the History Department at UC San Diego have been incredibly supportive. Special thanks to Luis Alvarez, Bob Edelman, Claire Edington, Denise Demetriou, Jessica Graham, Mark Hanna, Cathy Gere, Dave Gutierrez, Todd Henry, Nancy Kwak, Wendy Matsumura, Dana Murillo, Pamela Radcliff, Nir Shafir, Matthew Vitz, and especially Natalia Molina and Danny Widener for their camaraderie and advice. The incredible staff in our department made much of this work possible. Thanks to Sarab Aziz, Joan Bahrini, Susan Bernal, Sally Hargate, Andy Liedholm, Amber Rieder, Leah Tamayo-Brion, and Susan Winchester. It has been a joy to work with and learn from Yen Espiritu. Yen welcomed me to the Critical Refugee Studies Working Group, and I've benefited from conversations with group members Mohamed Abumaye, Rawan Arar, Lisa Ho, Alexis Meza, Linh Nguyen, Davorn Sisavath, and Jael Vizcarra; I thank them for their rigorous comments on one of my chapters. My writing group kept me focused during the academic year; thanks to Claire Edington, Jessica Graham, Jin-Kyung Lee, Wendy Matsumura, and Abbie Yamamoto for their invaluable feedback. Colleagues and friends beyond my department and institution have enriched my time in San Diego. Thanks to Patty Ahn, Victor Betts, Jody Blanco, Erica Cho, Josen Diaz, Erin Glass, Lilly Irani, Aftab Jassal, Dredge Kang, Hoang Nguyen, Yumi Pak, Joseph Ramirez, Erin Suzuki, and Kamala Visweswaran. Ash Kini is as solid as they come and is dearly missed in San Diego. Saiba Varma, thank you for being my unfailing tennis partner, and for always being up to do fun things.

Numerous people have offered timely encouragement and helped sharpen my thinking and arguments over the years. Thanks to Eiichiro Azuma, Keith

Camacho, Chris Capozzola, Kornel Chang, Andrew Friedman, Tak Fujitani, Irene Garza, Cindy I-Fen Cheng, Jenny Kelly, Paul Kramer, Julia Lee, Jana Lipman, Allan Lumba, Liz Mesok, Mark Padoongpatt, Chris Patterson, Vicente Rafael, Chandan Reddy, Seema Sohi, Colleen Woods, and David Yoo. Nikhil Singh believed in this project long before I saw what it was, and has been an unstinting supporter since I started this journey. I'm grateful for my coconspirators at Yale who sustained me through graduate school, including Mike Amezcua, Megan Asaka, Ryan Brasseaux, Karilyn Crockett, Zane Curtis-Olsen, Hong Liang, Deborah March, Uri McMillan, April Merleaux, Ana Minian, A. Naomi Paik, David Stein, Tim Retzloff, Quan Tran, and Susie Woo. Thank you, Jessie Kindig, for our many conversations that helped shape the core of this book, and for your sharp editorial eye. I would not have survived graduate school were it not for Monica Muñoz Martinez, whose generosity and brilliance never ceases to amaze me. Sam Vong, thank you for being one of my staunchest critics and supporters, and for being a good friend.

I'm grateful to the many individuals who shared their personal stories with me. Although many of them did not make it into the book, I thank them for their time and willingness to trust me with their stories. Thanks to Jim Albertini, James Arima, Dale Borgeson, Ray Burdeos, Doug Chin, Ed Greevy, Richard Kim, Kenji Kudo, Lee Lagda, Chalsa Loo, Sharon Maeda, Stanford Masui, Allan Miller, Ken Mochizuki, Toshio Nakano, Vincent Okamoto, Josefina Pablo, Hugh Paik, Alan Sugiyama, Yuzo Tokita, Mayumi Tsutakawa, Henry Wadahara, Bob Watada, John Witeck, Mike Wong, Keith Yamaguchi, Mike Yanagita, Richard Yee, and Teruo Yorita. Many thanks to Kathy Masaoka, Mike Nakayama, and Nick Nagatani.

Research for this book would not have been possible without the help of many people who guided me to the right sources. Thanks in particular to the archivists and staff at the Hawai'i State Archives, the National Archives and Records Administration in College Park, the Hoover Institution, the Bancroft Library, and the U.S. Army Military History Institute. Thanks especially to Dore Minadotani at the University of Hawai'i at Manoa Library for her patience and expert guidance.

Generous financial support from UC San Diego's academic senate and the Hellman Foundation provided funds to complete this book. Thanks to Niels Hooper, my editor, for his enthusiasm and incredible patience in shepherding this project. It was a pleasure working with Bradley Depew and the staff at University of California Press. Kornel Chang, Moon-Ho Jung, and George Lipsitz gave the manuscript a thorough read and offered incisive comments and generative critiques that guided my revisions. I especially thank George for helping me expand my conception of what this book could be, and for pushing me to articulate the stakes of my project. Thanks to Anthony Chiffolo, my copyeditor, and to David Lobenstine and Zoë Ruiz, whose crucial interventions at the final stage of my revisions made this a better book.

I dedicate this book to my parents, Yvonne Tam and John Man. Thank you for encouraging me to find my own path and for always reminding me to stay grounded and true to myself. I'm eternally grateful for your love and support and for making everything possible. Moses Man has been my anchor and source of guidance my entire life. I thank him, Son Nguyen Man, and Caleb Man who came into this world as I finished the book, for bringing so much joy into my life. Edward Choi endured the writing of this book more than anyone else; words cannot express my gratitude to him. My grandmother, Chan Sau-Yuk, is the strongest person I know. I miss her laughter, wit, and beautiful spirit.

ABBREVIATIONS

AVF	All-Volunteer Force
AAPA	Asian American Political Alliance
AFP	Armed Forces of the Philippines
AMMO	Asian Movement for Military Outreach
CCD	Civil Censorship Detachment
CIA	Central Intelligence Agency
DOD	Department of Defense
ECCOI	Eastern Construction Company, Incorporated
EDCOR	Economic Development Corps
FTA	Free the Army (Antiwar Troupe)
FOA	Foreign Operations Administration
JACL	Japanese American Citizens League
JACS	Japanese American Community Services
JCI	Junior Chamber International
JUSMAG	Joint U.S. Military Advisory Group
KM	Kabataang Makabayan
KATUSA	Korean Augmentation to the U.S. Army
KDP	Katipunan ng mga Demokratikong Pilipino (Union of Democratic Filipinos)
KMAG	U.S. Military Advisory Group to the Republic of Korea
MDAP	Mutual Defense Assistance Program
MDM	Movement for a Democratic Military

NCRCLP	National Committee to Restore Civil Liberties in the Philippines
NLG	National Lawyers Guild
NLF	National Liberation Front
PCS	Pacific Counseling Service
PTSD	Post-traumatic Stress Disorder
PHILCAG	Philippine Civic Action Group
PVL	Philippine Veterans Legion
ROK	Republic of Korea
SCAP	Supreme Commander of the Allied Powers
USAID	U.S. Agency for International Development
USOM	U.S. Operations Mission
VVAW	Vietnam Veterans Against the War
VNA	Vietnamese National Army
VVL	Vietnamese Veterans Legion

Introduction

"DO YOU WANT TO JOIN THE ARMY, or do you want to go to jail?" Nick Nagatani and Mike Nakayama had heard this line many times. The two teenagers grew up in the West Los Angeles neighborhood of Crenshaw in the 1960s as the Vietnam War was pushing into the public consciousness. They were Sansei, born in the United States with Japanese grandparents. Their neighbors were nearly all black and Japanese American, and nearly all working class. Crenshaw reaped little of the state and federal resources that made cities desirable for capital investments; its streets, and the worldviews of its residents, were shaped by organized neglect. Nagatani and Nakayama remembered the time as one of widespread disaffection. The teenage boys around them joined gangs, got into fights, and took drugs. And again and again, these young men were arrested, brought before a judge for their petty crimes, and asked the question: "army or jail?" To most it was an easy choice. To some it was an opportunity. Before ever having to answer the question before a judge, Nagatani and Nakayama weighed their options and made their decisions: they chose war. In 1967, the pair enlisted in the Marines and traveled halfway around the world to South Vietnam. They saw it as "one of the options for getting out," a chance to make something of their lives.[1]

This brutal quandary—prison or war—had confronted the previous generation of young men, too. In 1943, thousands of young Nisei men in concentration camps were offered the choice between joining the army or remaining imprisoned in their own country.[2] Fighting in the 442nd Regimental Combat Team—the segregated Japanese American unit—many thought, would prove their loyalty to a nation that had deemed them untrustworthy because of their race. For some, the gamble seemed to pay off. As the United States figured out the logistics of occupying Japan in the months after the war, Nisei linguists earned the unofficial title of "ambassadors of the American army."[3] The military had offered them a route to secure their belonging in the nation and, in the process, to redeem American democracy. Those who refused the opportunity (which, by 1944, became a mandatory order) to join the army—the so-called "no-no boys" and draft resisters—remained vilified and relegated to prison.

Although Nagatani and Nakayama's decision certainly differed from the one that Japanese internees faced during World War II, it was a difference in degree, not in kind. In the 1960s, Asians in the United States were no longer deemed a racial enemy of the state. But as Nagatani and Nakayama's coming-of-age experiences attest, formal inclusion as citizens did not exempt them from the racism of American capitalism. If anything, one fueled the other. Like African Americans, Latinos, and indigenous peoples whose histories of theft and dispossession had made them surplus in the political economy, consigned to low-wage and informal sectors of the labor market, Asians were given a choice that was no choice at all: to serve the needs of the state or be criminalized or contained, or be killed. While many did choose to go to war, others—Muhammad Ali most famous among them—chose prison and reminded the world that the choice to kill or be killed was above all a call to action. This is a book about the choices people made under extraordinary circumstances, and how, in the process, they acquired a worldliness that allowed them to imagine themselves as part of a wider community, and how they imagined a world that was not built upon state violence. For Nakayama, seeing death all around him in Vietnam prompted him to see the life all around him: "You become more human; they [the Vietnamese] became more human to me."[4]

The role of race in the decades after World War II was defined by paradox. During these years, the disavowal of formal, state-sanctioned racism occurred alongside a series of wars in which race was the unspoken subject. Starting in the late 1940s, racial liberalism took hold, a vision of government in which racial minorities would bear the rights of citizenship free from discrimination and extralegal violence; over the next two decades, civil rights legislation and immigration reform hastened the end of legal segregation and immigration exclusion.[5] Liberals touted mixed-race neighborhoods like Crenshaw as a success story of postwar integration.[6] Revisionist narratives of the United States as a "nation of nations" were ascendant in the political culture.[7] Yet in this era, the U.S. government modernized the infrastructures of national security—the border patrol, the military, the criminal justice system—

expanding its capacity to criminalize and make war on particular people at home and abroad. Seen through a prism of domestic civil rights progress, these dueling impulses of "inclusion" and "exclusion" seem contradictory, a failure on the part of the United States to live up to its promise of racial equality. It is only by taking a more expansive view that they make sense together.

I believe that the choice between prison and war did not only reflect the austerity of racialized life in the United States; rather it was a governing logic that emerged in the post–World War II age of decolonization around the globe. The bipolar divide between communism and liberal democracy that structured U.S. global politics after 1945 indeed produced new categories of differences that at first glance do not appear to be rooted in race. As the United States sought to uphold liberal democracy and defeat communism, Asians became cast as either "good" or "bad," those whose lives were deemed worthy and productive under capitalism and those cast as its perpetual others. These "bad" Asians—the communists, political agitators, labor radicals, and "Viet Cong"—were monitored, jailed, tortured, or killed. Undergirding racial liberalism and its mandate of national inclusion, then, was an ongoing war against a new enemy, a communist menace that was also a racial menace, whose differentiation and expulsion from the national community was achieved in tandem through state violence.[8]

Soldiering through Empire: Race and the Making of the Decolonizing Pacific centers the role of Asians in the making of U.S. global power after 1945. If "bad" Asians were the targets of seemingly endless war, the "good" ones served a similarly utilitarian purpose: they were channeled into the military. As the end of World War II marked the end of formal colonial rule in Asia, thousands of young, able-bodied men joined the armed forces of their newly independent nations. This occurred in South Korea, Taiwan, the Philippines, and other countries where American military advisers helped transform the fledgling armies into modern institutions for nation building. Men and women in these countries also found opportunities as civilian contractors and counterinsurgency agents for the U.S. military and the Central Intelligence Agency (CIA) in the 1950s and 1960s. This book follows the labor circuits of these Asian soldiers and military workers as they navigated an emergent Pacific world in the middle decades of the twentieth century. Like the Nisei soldiers of World War II, these were "good" Asians who represented American democracy for the age of decolonization. Although these individuals were motivated by their own personal desires, ranging from the search for economic security to the lure of travel, their desires and their labor were inextricably intertwined with the spread of U.S. empire.

The story of these Asian soldiers remains largely untold. In the 1950s, nearly one hundred thousand military personnel from South Korea, Taiwan, the Philippines, and South Vietnam traveled to the United States for military training.[9] A decade later, at the peak of the U.S. war in Vietnam, around six thousand Filipino soldiers and fifty thousand South Korean soldiers and marines were deployed to South Vietnam annually to assist the U.S. military. These men are mostly remembered within the confines of their own country's military chronicle. As such, in almost all cases, they have been rendered either as minor actors in the history of postcolonial national development or, as in the case of South Koreans in Vietnam, as an exception to the dominant narrative of South Koreans as victims of communist aggression.[10] Where they are acknowledged in U.S. history—notably the South Koreans and Filipinos who fought in Vietnam—they have been described, and just as quickly dismissed, as mercenaries of an otherwise American-centered war.[11] In short, nationalism has consigned these subjects to history's silences. Yet when brought together within one analytical frame, these subjects tell us much about how citizens experienced their nation's aspirations for development and modernity, and how these aspirations were integral to the making of the U.S. empire.

By writing Asian soldiers and military workers into the history of the United States' post-1945 global ascendency, what can seem like a contradiction about the entanglements of race and empire becomes less confounding: the expansion of the United States's capacity to criminalize and make war in the second half of the century has functioned through, not in spite of, its proclaimed commitment to racial equality and democracy. Racial liberalism was never just about the U.S. government's mandate to incorporate racial minorities into the nation—a mandate that occasionally gets forestalled or derailed by the government's dueling commitment to war. Instead, war was the terrain upon which racial liberalism unfolded and gained traction.[12] As the United States secured its global dominance after World War II, it relied both on a growing military apparatus and on assertions of its moral authority as an inclusive, even liberating, empire. Asians, I argue, were central to this imperial project. By "Asians" I mean both Asian Americans—those legally and culturally defined as U.S. citizens—and citizens of South Korea, the Philippines, and other countries and territories whose postcolonial trajectories were entwined with the United States. In the stories we tell, Asians and

Asian Americans too often occupy separate parts of the narrative. Here, they emerge together as racialized subjects of the U.S. empire. Soldiering through empire, for Asians and Asian Americans, became one means by which they negotiated their relationship to the nation and, as we shall see, imagined and pursued other affinities in the age of decolonization.

THE DECOLONIZING PACIFIC

The Pacific world these Asian soldiers traversed was the product of overlapping histories of imperial expansion and rivalries. Beginning in the seventeenth century, European powers vied for dominance in the region, establishing commercial trade routes that enriched and expanded their respective empires. As the Spanish, Dutch, Portuguese, French, and British staked their territorial claims across Asia and the Pacific Ocean, islands and nations fell under their domains. By the late nineteenth century, other rising powers, notably the United States and Japan, had joined the imperial competition. The United States seized the Philippines, Guam, Cuba, and Puerto Rico from Spain in 1898; around the same time, Japan annexed Taiwan, Kwantung, and Korea, following its earlier annexation of Hokkaido (in 1869) and Okinawa (in 1879). The South Pacific Mandate after World War I expanded the Japanese empire into the former German possessions of the Marianas, Caroline Islands, and Marshall Islands. In time, Japan came to justify its expansionist policies in the name of pan-Asian unity, and as a means to counter Euro-American imperialism and the attendant rumblings of white racial supremacy. These imperial projects wrought devastation, fundamentally restructuring each dominated society along the racialized demarcations of the colonizer and colonized. At the same time, they prompted cultures of collaboration and resistance among the colonized as they sought to negotiate, and at times challenge directly, the terms of colonial rule.[13]

World War II marked a rupture in the spread of Western colonialism. Between 1941 and 1945, Japanese forces besieged the Euro-American empires in Southeast Asia and the Pacific Islands; unlikely alliances between the colonized and the colonizers were momentarily forged. The expansion of Japanese militarism intensified anticolonial resistance in Malaya, the Philippines, Vietnam, Korea, and elsewhere. At the end of the war, as European powers sought to regain control of their colonies from the ruins of the shattered Japanese empire, they encountered emboldened nationalists for whom independence seemed at long last a reality. Anticolonial revolts across the next decade and beyond spelled the demise of Western colonialism in Asia; the Philippines, India, Malaya, Indonesia, Korea, and Vietnam all secured formal independence.[14] Another world seemed on the horizon.

Decolonization, however, was disorderly and fraught with difficulty, for formal independence hardly ushered in sustainable democracies in a postimperial world. Instead, throwing off the colonizer's yoke was merely the beginning of an ongoing political project to secure more substantive freedoms beyond the moment of independence.[15] As the second half of the twentieth century went on, people who had spent much of their lives fighting the oppression of a single colonizer found themselves confronting a new and more complex imperial power. This was a murkier empire, one that projected an intention to spread freedom and liberate people from oppression, yet embraced some of the same repressive tactics of the Japanese empire.

The United States emerged from World War II as an undisputed world power, with a preponderance of military might and economic influence.[16] The new U.S. empire did not seek hegemony merely through colonial possessions, as it had done in the nineteenth century, but instead through two seemingly less coercive means. The first was domination of the global economy, in which the government enacted policies to foster capitalism as the basis for an integrated "free world." The second was militarization, a broad and evolving concept that included short occupations, the maintenance of bases, and the stationing of military advisory groups. Insofar as the military was needed to make the world safe for capitalism, the two went hand in hand. Asia and the Pacific became the site of this renewed onslaught. As country after country declared their independence, the United States rushed in to establish bilateral relations to keep them within the capitalist orbit. This "hub-and-spokes" system, in which each state was informally tied to all the others through their economic dependence on the United States and other core industrial nations, created a new map of empire.[17] It would be wrong to suggest this new U.S. empire was any less territorial than the colonial empire of the past. In addition to maintaining informal influence over this network of states, the United States also continued to administer formal control over the Pacific Islands, including Guam, the Northern Marianas, the Marshall Islands, and Okinawa, as part of its expanding empire of bases for military deployment and weapons testing.[18]

The United States's post-1945 empire essentially reanimated old colonial dynamics in the region. By the early 1950s, Japan, under American aegis, had

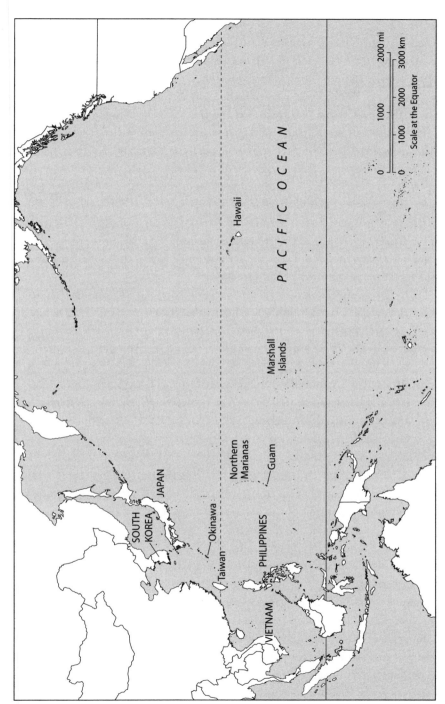

FIGURE 1. Asia and the Pacific. (Map by William L. Nelson.)

revived its industrial capacity to produce export goods, part of a broader scheme by the United States to transform Japan into an engine of capitalist development in Asia.[19] U.S. dominance in the region depended on securing Japan as a "subempire," or a surrogate of U.S. power; and war became vital to this effort.[20] Since World War II, the United States has been at war continuously. The Korean War (1950–53) and the Vietnam War (1954–73) were instantiations of what historian Thomas McCormick called a "Rimlands War," to secure the extractive economies of Northeast and Southeast Asia and to ensure Japan's place as a proxy for U.S. control. They were the start of a permanent war in U.S. culture that set into motion a range of military and economic activities across the Pacific including offshore procurement, the building of infrastructure, the training of armed forces, and the mobilization of civilian workers. These wars, fought in the name of anticommunism, "liberated" these countries to make them functional within the global economy and accessible to free markets and free trade.

Throughout this book we'll refer to these overlapping efforts as the "decolonizing Pacific," a term that names the historical conjuncture when anticolonial movements in the United States, Asia, and the Pacific became intertwined with the U.S. militarization drive to secure the global capitalist economy. The decolonizing Pacific is not a fixed temporal or geographic construct but a methodology for explaining the convergent forces that animated the U.S. empire after 1945. At its core, it explains how decolonization was not antithetical to the spread of U.S. global power but intrinsic to it. Over the last half-century, the United States has been an increasingly vocal proponent of democracy and equality; yet this commitment has simultaneously worked to legitimate and obscure U.S. state violence. Here we will explore the ways that racial liberalism was materially enacted through the functional expansion of the U.S. military in Asia and the Pacific. Time and again, U.S. state officials declared their support of an "Asia for Asians"— the racialist language propagated by the Japanese empire during World War II—to pursue capitalist integration under the banner of anticolonialism and antiracism.

Here was a new racial order taking shape, in which the government's disavowal of racism and nominal support for anticolonial sovereignty gave rise to new forms of state violence against insurgents, communists, and a growing group of people marked for permanent exclusion from the "free world." The term "race war" is useful for explaining this emerging relationship of U.S. imperial governance in the post–World War II era, in which preexisting forms of racism and extant colonial relations were recalibrated to justify war in inclusionary terms.[21] Black anticolonial thinkers such as Cedric Robinson and W. E . B. Du Bois were among the most incisive critics of the cold war as an ongoing imperial race war against the "darker peoples" of the colonial world.[22] Even as race as a category of differentiation appears to recede in significance in the age of global decolonization, "war," Du Bois reminded us in 1953, "tends to become universal and continuous, and the excuse for this war continues largely to be color and race."[23] War, in other words, was central to reproducing U.S. race relations and making its attendant violence normal in the face of a rapidly changing post-1945 world.

At the same time, the U.S. militarization of Asia and the Pacific made other forms of decolonization—namely, the realization of freedom and self-determination beyond the nation-state form—a permanently suspended and incomplete project.[24] Thinking through the decolonizing Pacific thus also forces us to reckon with what's left, of what remains from a truncated attempt at liberation. As militarization foreclosed particular forms of postcolonial sovereignty in the region, the dreams and aspirations of the formerly colonized did not end but were channeled elsewhere. The military became a vehicle that conveyed these desires. People were drawn to the military, enticed by the prospects of steady pay and economic mobility. Some saw joining the armed forces as a way to overcome the racial degradations of colonialism by embodying a martial masculinity. Still others, insistent that a different world was yet possible, renewed their insurgent calls for decolonization, connecting the fates of one place to another in a global project to unite what many were now calling the Third World. At times, these competing aspirations—of fighting the U.S. empire and finding a place within it—were surprisingly aligned.

We will investigate these aspirations and their resulting efforts as they unfolded through one of the most influential liberation struggles of the post–World War II era: the Vietnam War. The Vietnam War, in this study, is not simply a battleground in the emerging cold war between the United States and the Soviet Union but, borrowing from geographer Derek Gregory, "an event in which multiple geographies coalesced and multiple histories condensed."[25] The Vietnam War was more than just a war between world powers, a contest between two ideological systems; rather, in this war, the legacies of multiple colonialisms converged and were fought over by the soldiers and workers on the ground. From the perspective of the decolonizing Pacific, we can see the Vietnam War as a globe-spanning moment, one that mobilized various decolonizing nations and territories, including South Korea, the Philippines, Okinawa, Guam, and Hawai'i, among others. For these islands and nations in the midst of transition from formal colonial rule, the fates of their political projects were determined by the intensity of their involvement in the war. Across the two decades of the U.S. war in Vietnam, the dreams and aspirations of the colonized were mobilized, thwarted, and, in many cases, destroyed with those who perished in the fighting.[26] The decolonizing Pacific, in short, is about the dreams of anticolonial liberation cut short and coopted into the U.S. imperial project, and the struggles to imagine a new humanity that came in its wake.

THE WORK OF SOLDIERING

The making of the decolonizing Pacific required particular kinds of workers, and the United States, over two and a half decades, mobilized tens of thousands of them from across Asia and the Pacific. These numbers include those who were enlisted into the armed forces of their own countries—the Filipino, South Korean, Taiwanese, and South Vietnamese soldiers who were tasked with arming and defending their countries and respective regions from communism. They also include draftees and reservists of the U.S. Army, which doubled in size after 1951 as the permanent war in Asia continued to grow. Others were mobilized in more ambiguous ways, including former guerrilla fighters who had fought in the imperial armies of Japan and the United States, and who then came to serve the CIA's expanding efforts in unconventional warfare. All of these men and women were citizens of their respective countries who, by taking advantage of the work opportunities opened up by the military, emerged as participants in the U.S. empire.[27]

From the stories of these soldiers and workers we are able to see their lives as part of the broader notion of *soldiering*. I examine soldiering as an optic through which the racial and imperial politics of the decolonizing Pacific were forged and became contested. While soldiers and military workers are central to this story, I focus on the policies and representations that constituted them as imperial subjects, and the wider world they helped to shape. Here, "soldiers" refers to those individuals who participated in the conventional armed forces as well as a proliferating category of people whose labor and lives became entwined with the military. Thus, I approach soldiering not merely as military service or a rite of citizenship, but as a form of labor. Seeing soldiering as labor reveals the class basis of war and the fact those who are most likely to fight are most likely to be poor or from the working class.[28] Indeed, few who enlisted in the armed forces or volunteered to fight in the Korean or Vietnam Wars did so out of sheer motivation against communism or for nationalism; instead, most were drawn by economic incentives or otherwise were conscripted into service. For Mike Nakayama and Nick Nagatani growing up in the neighborhoods of Crenshaw, soldiering offered the prospect of a better future.

Soldiering also signals particular kinds of labor that developed in tandem with an evolving U.S. militarism—a range of ideological and affective labors, like the work of befriending and forging intimacy with the population, that proved critical to U.S. counterinsurgency in Asia in this period. Such military power was always both violent and benevolent, and was intrinsically tied to the racialization of Asian soldiers as "free Asians." The Filipinos who were deployed to South Vietnam in the 1950s and 1960s epitomized this category of free Asians; they became agents in the work of winning hearts and minds, who labored to embody a liberal democracy that the South Vietnamese would want to emulate. As "fellow" Asians, U.S. officials believed, these Filipinos could gain the trust of the Vietnamese and cast away their suspicions about American intentions as the United States sought to bring them under the control of the South Vietnamese government.

Highlighting these soldiers in post-1945 U.S. history offers a new vantage point in the study of U.S. empire. First and foremost, soldiering reveals the overlapping dynamics between the formation of postcolonial states in Asia and U.S. imperialism. As South Korea, the Philippines, and South Vietnam emerged as independent nations, they depended on U.S. military and economic aid to ensure their stability. These neocolonial dependencies inextricably bound their respective nation-building projects to U.S. foreign policy objectives, even if leaders of these countries invariably pursued goals that diverged from those of the United States.[29] Soldiers were at the center of this entanglement. Through their various activities—as medics, engineers, technicians, instructors, and combatants—they functioned as intermediaries who, at every step, buttressed their nation and the U.S. empire.[30] As postcolonial nations mobilized the soldiers' desires through the promise of citizenship and national belonging, soldiers performed the tasks that sutured each nation to the vast needs of U.S. capitalism.

A focus on soldiering also disrupts the conventional divisions of U.S. history into "pre-" and "post-," one that posits 1945 as a break from the colonial past and that heralded the "postwar" era in U.S. history. By studying the work of soldiers and military workers, many who participated in the Japanese and U.S. imperial armies during World War II, this book reveals world-making without any such break and showcases people whose labor and desires were merely channeled from one imperial project to another. The empire-building efforts of the United States after 1945 were not a departure from the colonial past but its recalibration. The skills performed by these various subjects reflect the enduring legacies of colonialism, whether from American nursing education in the Philippines or from U.S.-trained guerrilla units during World War II and the Korean War. As we shall see, soldiering amidst counterinsurgency reinvigorated the colonial discourses that lent meaning to the soldiers' activities, transforming them from subjects of the U.S. and Japanese colonial empires into agents of colonial uplift. In the process, soldiering reworked race and colonial relations, enabling the United States to justify its war in Vietnam in the name of antiracism and anticolonialism. Soldiering, therefore, describes the social and cultural processes that made the decolonizing Pacific. Soldiering, seen both as labor and as process, reveals the violence undergirding the project of U.S. liberation and the discursive complexities of U.S. imperial violence, all while allowing us to map the scale of the U.S. empire amidst the terrain of individual life.

Finally, soldiering extends the study of race in Asian American history and elucidates the workings of race within a globe-spanning empire. The exploits of the "all-Nisei" 100th Battalion and 442nd Regimental Combat Team in World War II, created both for their manpower and for their symbolic value as reformed American citizens, have been well documented.[31] These and other soldiers of color demonstrated the U.S. commitment to racial democracy; and indeed their utility expanded after World War II. As the United States ramped up its struggle against communism in the Korean War, the integration of African American troops became an ideological and military imperative.[32] Such efforts have been framed largely within a narrative of cold war civil rights, in which U.S. foreign policy objectives compelled symbolic yet significant reforms.[33] The Asian American "model minority," scholars have shown, emerged during this same time as a figurative bridge between the racism of the past and the ideal of a postracial present. As the civil rights movement exploded, the image of the model minority helped to explain away racial grievances in terms of individual deficiency and cultural pathology within the black community; just as important, the model minority also evidenced the United States's commitment to liberal inclusion for the decolonizing world.[34]

My aim here is to extend the study of Asian Americans and race within a transnational field, but to revise a core proposition: U.S. wars in Asia after 1945, I contend, did not simply form the backdrop for racial minorities to assert their claims to national belonging; rather, those wars were the very ground upon which racial liberalism emerged as a dominant force in U.S. politics. This book argues that race making and war making were deeply entangled, and they were crucial to the U.S. empire and the making of Asian American subjects.[35] In the second half of the twentieth century, the United States mobilized Asian soldiers both for their potential to represent American democracy on the world stage and as particular assets for counterinsurgency. Indeed, the inclusion of Asians into the military proceeded apace of state efforts to eliminate racism in military culture. "We still have Americans who see 'gooks' and 'flips' and 'wily Orientals,'" Edward Lansdale, the famed counterinsurgent and CIA operative, remarked in 1957, "but those who have come to know Koreans and Filipinos and Asians as friends have increased numbers tremendously."[36] Guided by the belief that a more inclusionary and less racist military would help legitimate and bring about the "free world," U.S. officials transformed the culture and infrastructure of the military. The inclusion of Asians into the globalizing U.S. military empire, and their formation as "free Asians" therein, was a manifestation of this imperative.

Racial inclusion, however, did not produce an orderly free world, but its opposite: more violence, more insurgencies. Channeling Asians into the military indeed magnified the global communist menace, whether real or imagined, that such policies sought to contain in the first place. In 1948, when soldiers of the newly minted South Korean Army were called to subdue a peasant rebellion, some refused and turned on their officers. In the late 1960s, Asian American GIs, including Nakayama and Nagatani, came to disavow their role and became advocates of anti-imperialism. These instances of soldiers' revolts were hints of another world on the verge of becoming. By the early 1970s, GIs stationed in Asia and the Pacific were building alliances with base workers and anti-imperialist activists that were short-lived yet remarkable in what they sought to achieve. During this time, some turned to culture to critically reimagine the possibilities for an East Asian modernity not yet arrived, an alternative future that was not predicated on militarized violence. In short, the labor of soldiers was never divorced from the imperial and anti-imperial politics taking shape around them. As these emergent political struggles coalesced around the Vietnam War, they revived memories of the multiple, convergent histories of colonialism in Asia and the Pacific not yet ended, the very conditions of possibility for the colonial present. Soldiering thus necessarily entailed its counterpractice of undoing the violence of empire and reckoning with an unfinished decolonization. The military, this book demonstrates, formed the crucible of imperial encounters and anticolonial resistance that made the decolonizing Pacific into a dynamic site of political struggles.

This is a work of history that attempts to reconstruct a past, however partial and incomplete, that has fallen in the cracks between sweeping histories of the cold war and specific national histories. It is based on archival research across the continental United States, Asia, and the Pacific, as well as oral history with the soldiers, workers, and activists whose lives are the heart of this story. In charting the rise of the decolonizing Pacific, I read across multiple archives to ask how seemingly disjointed histories were imbricated with each other.[37] The U.S. National Archives where I conducted the bulk of the research is an endless trove of documentation about particular events, places, and institutions that were crucial to the post–World War II U.S. empire; the occupations of South Korea and Japan, the U.S. Army's stationing in Hawai'i, and the Vietnam War are each recorded extensively, and yet their connections are not immediately transparent. Thus, I approach the National Archives not merely as a repository of knowledge retrieval about these specific events in specific places, but as a site to apprehend how the government thought about—indeed obsessed about—the subjects who traversed these national and imperial boundaries. In sifting through the official documents, including military histories, records of memorandum, reports of "lessons learned," and surveillance dossiers, I am interested in how state and military officials made sense of the unruly aftermaths of global decolonization, and how they sought to impose order upon a disorderly world, by engineering and controlling the movements of people. I am also interested in how soldiers, workers, and activists navigated through and negotiated these state efforts. At times, these negotiations are legible in the National Archives, registered in the anxieties and concerns of officials. But when official records could not provide answers, I turned to other archives and to oral history, not merely to fill gaps or silences or to put forth a more truthful account based on personal experience, but to ascertain how some of these subjects imagined and pursued another world that the official state archives could only give a hint of, to give shape to, as Lisa Lowe put it, the "'what could have been.'"[38]

The book moves chronologically in six chapters. In the first two, I explain the U.S. efforts to promote and to fortify a vision of "Asia for Asians" through the military in the late 1940s and 1950s. Chapter 1 details the U.S. buildup of the armed forces of South Korea and other allied countries in Asia after World War II; chapter 2 traces the circuits of Filipino paramilitary workers and medics that were crucial to the counterinsurgency in South Vietnam in the 1950s. In both cases, U.S. officials justified these endeavors as part of a broader project of teaching former colonial subjects how to embody freedom and to embark on nation building, and in both cases, they carried unintended consequences. Rather than achieving an integrated "free" Asia, the efforts to create an "Asia for Asians" sowed the seeds of its own unraveling, deepening anticolonial nationalism throughout the region.

The next two chapters examine the escalation of the U.S. ground war in Vietnam in the 1960s from the vantage point of particular countries and territories that were in the throes of a thwarted decolonization. Chapter 3 uncovers the military mobilization and training practices in Hawai'i around the time of its transition to statehood; chapter 4 turns to South Korea and the Philippines and the deployment of their citizens to the war during a period of nationalist upheaval and economic restructuring. As these countries and territory became further embroiled in the U.S. war, their citizens began to comprehend more fully the limits of their sovereignty. They made connections between the imperial violence in Vietnam and state repression at home, and came to articulate a deeper understanding of their own unfinished decolonization that took seriously the question of their governments' complicity in the war.

The last two chapters delve into these emergent radical movements in the closing years of the war. Chapter 5 centers Asian American Vietnam veterans as crucial actors of the Asian American movement in the late 1960s and early 1970s. Their experiences of imminent death in the war, magnified by the military's anti-Asian racism, led them to see the structural violence facing their communities in Los Angeles, the Bay Area, and elsewhere as an intrinsic part of the violence of empire. This perception empowered Asian American veterans to play a unique part in the movement for Third World liberation. Chapter 6 explores the coalitions formed among American GIs and Okinawan, Japanese, and Filipino labor and anti-imperialist activists, at the locations where the intensified U.S. war in Southeast Asia was being waged. Sharing a differential yet entangled relationship to the U.S. military, these subjects forged momentary, fragile alliances that disrupted the war effort and challenged the Japanese and Philippine governments' collusion with the U.S. empire. These movements, forged in the crucible of the decolonizing Pacific, provide a glimpse of another world that's possible. It is ultimately this sense of evasive possibility of a world not yet arrived that is at the core of this book.

To make Asian and Asian American soldiers central to the history of the Vietnam War is not simply to recover the visibility of yet another racial group that has been written out of the war's accounts. Instead, it is to demand that we reckon with the global connections that made their travels possible, and that made the war seem inevitable. The paths of these soldiers were layered upon the sediment of colonialism, race, and empire, laid down again and again across the twentieth century; the desires of these soldiers, individual and collective alike, carry the weight of these histories. These histories, in turn, have been elided by conventional accounts of the cold war and by our scholarly instinct to divide geography and time into discrete fixities.[39] My conception of the decolonizing Pacific is an attempt to widen the analytical frame by engaging with the cold war's forgotten histories and imperial roots. And it is admittedly partial. Rather than seeking comprehensive coverage of the places and people who made the decolonizing Pacific, the book has a different, perhaps more modest, goal: to present a history of Asian Americans and the military in which belonging in the nation was neither a sole determining force nor the end goal. In what follows, I tell a story of Asian Americans soldiering through the U.S. empire after World War II, a history of imperial conscription and the new forms of political community and critical imagining—beyond the boundaries of race and nation—that became possible as a result.

ONE

Securing Asia for Asians

MAKING THE U.S. TRANSNATIONAL
SECURITY STATE

IT WAS FALL OF 1952, and Hsuan Wei was twenty-four years old when he entered the United States for the first time, determined to change his life one way or another. Wei was a first lieutenant of the Chinese Nationalist Marine Corps and had been given the opportunity to go to the United States to further his military training. The benefits of pursuing it far outweighed the uncertainty he may have felt about leaving home. In September, with few belongings, he arrived at the U.S. Marine Corps School in Quantico, Virginia. On the other side of the Pacific, the Korean War raged unabated, and tensions between the Republic of China and the Communist mainland increased to the threat of impending war. While global events were driving factors behind Wei's sojourn, they figured mostly in the back of his mind. As far as he was concerned, he was simply seizing an opportunity to advance his military education and career.[1]

Wei's transpacific journey hinted at an ordinary life soldiering through empire in the age of decolonization, a far more common story than historians have acknowledged. Wei, in fact, was one of an estimated 141,250 foreign nationals who made their way to the United States for military training in the 1950s. These visitors hailed from all over, from Taiwan, South Korea, South Vietnam, the Philippines, Iran, Indonesia, and many other countries, each undergoing the turbulent processes of nation building after colonial rule. Though they came from different parts of the world, these subjects shared striking similarities. Socioeconomically, they were not disenfranchised people desperate for work but were aspiring individuals who sought to elevate their positions in their national armed forces and, for some, in their governments. Many had served in colonial and imperial armies before their countries' liberation from colonial rule, and chose to continue a career they knew garnered respect. One Korean soldier, Yi Chiŏp, recalled his time serving in the Imperial Japanese Army during World War II: "I worked within the system to gain as much education and training as possible." This decision tainted him as a "collaborator" among other Koreans, but it allowed him to climb the ranks of the new Korean Constabulary after the war.[2]

The U.S. militarization that accelerated after World War II was the root of their transpacific journeys and military training. After the war, the United States confronted local insurgencies throughout the former Japanese empire, waged by ordinary people who refused the terms of the American liberation. Cross sections of the population including industrial workers, military base workers, peasants, labor organizers, and students in Korea, Japan, Okinawa, the Philippines, and elsewhere redoubled their efforts for national self-determination. They rekindled longstanding anti-Japanese sentiments and directed them at the United States. U.S. officials felt alarmed, convinced of a global communist movement afoot in Asia. The U.S. state responded by laying the groundwork to fortify indigenous forces, to assist "free nations" to defend themselves from "communists." In 1949, these efforts cohered in the Mutual Defense Assistance Program (MDAP), the first major U.S. military aid initiative that would funnel billions of U.S. dollars to train and equip the national armed forces of allied states over the next decade and beyond.

The making of this transnational security-state apparatus in Asia created massive disruptions on the ground and led to the proliferation of Asian soldiers across the Pacific. To be sure, Asian colonial conscripts had circulated in this region for some time, most recently during World War II when Koreans had been mobilized to far-flung places of the Japanese empire to serve in the imperial army and to labor in factories and mines.[3] In one sense, this chapter traces the lives of these martial subjects as they transitioned from the Japanese colonial empire to the U.S. liberal empire. In the context of the protracted global struggle against communism, particular Asians who were newly liberated from colonial rule became the functionaries of the United States's burgeoning transnational security state in Asia.

This chapter explains how overriding U.S. concerns about global decolonization led to the growing presence of Asian soldiers in the Pacific, and how they in turn provided the endless justifications for the U.S. empire. American military advisers spoke often of these Asian soldiers as "assets," prized as manpower and for their knowledge of the local terrain. During the heaviest fighting of the Korean War, their use as "buffer" troops purportedly saved "hundreds of thousands" of American lives.[4] U.S. state officials reasoned that they were not merely colonial mercenaries mobilized to do the gritty work of the U.S. military but were "free Asians," democratized subjects who could demonstrate the promise of U.S. liberal democracy to the rest of decolonizing Asia. Conscripted to build Japan's East Asia Co-Prosperity Sphere just a short time before, these subjects emerged as the vanguard of a new pan-Asianism—an "Asia for Asians"—that the United States pursued deliberately against charges of global white supremacy and imperialism. The militarization of Asia against communism and the liberation of Asians from colonialism, the twinned vexing projects of the United States in Asia after World War II, became embodied by these Asian soldiers.

While U.S. officials touted these soldiers as free Asians, they were also citizen-subjects with individual and collective aspirations and grievances that posed challenges for the U.S. state. At a time when these officials grew increasingly concerned about communism at home and abroad, they invariably cast these subjects as "subversives." The inclusion of free Asians into the U.S. transnational security state, this chapter contends, facilitated movements, encounters, and fleeting alliances among Asian peoples across the U.S. empire that magnified the very problem of subversion it aimed to contain. Not least, it brought people like Hsuan Wei into the United States over the course of the 1950s. The chapter ends by exploring how the projects to militarize and liberate Asia devolved into a national security problem at home, involving "immigrants," deserters, and asylum seekers. In the end, policing against subversive Asians, in the United States and across the Pacific, proved pivotal to preserving the security of the U.S. empire and the promise of "Asia for Asians" in the post–World War II era. The problem of subversion that came to confound U.S. state officials was a byproduct of the making of the transnational security state, an unintended consequence that became indispensable to its functions.

THE "RED" MENACE AFTER LIBERATION

This story begins in Korea, a country far from the minds of most Americans when the Japanese empire fell, but one that would matter greatly in due time. In September 1945, when Lt. Gen. John Reed Hodge and his XXIV Corps occupied the southern half of the Korean Peninsula, the United States had yet to articulate a coherent plan for what to do with the former Japanese colony. To Koreans, August 15 marked the abrupt and long-awaited end to colonial rule. But it seemed there were dark signs, for their liberators had bigger schemes. Save for a short and violent U.S. naval expedition to open up the "Hermit Kingdom" in 1871, a little-known war that precipitated the signing of a treaty of "peace, amity, commerce, and navigation" in 1882 and American expansion in the Pacific in the late nineteenth century, the United States had never taken direct interest in the peninsula.[5] In 1905, President Theodore Roosevelt had recognized Japan's "special interest" in Korea after Japan's victory in the Russo-Japanese War, and after World War II Korea's fate would appear to default to American interests in Japan yet again. In Japan, the goals of Gen. Douglas MacArthur's military occupation were clearer from the start: to effect a "complete" and "permanent" program of demilitarization and democratization, and to reform the enemy into "enlightened" subjects of democracy. Meanwhile, Hodge's task in Korea was to disarm the Japanese and send them back to Japan.[6]

Hodge's broader mission became clear soon enough, when his team encountered revolutionaries on the ground. Two days before Hodge's arrival, Yŏ Un-hyŏng, a moderate leftist with a long history of anti-Japanese activism, declared the founding of the Korean People's Republic, a de facto government driven above all to establish a unified independent Korean state. The People's Republic captured the aspirations of Koreans throughout the countryside, particularly of peasants who had borne the brunt of Japanese colonial policies. In the weeks and months after liberation, the work of building a new nation was animated through "people's committees" that proliferated in the rural south. These were locally administered, grassroots organizations that infused anticolonial patriotism with concrete goals such as land redistribution and the purging of colonial collaborators from the police and other government posts. Their radicalism alarmed U.S. authorities. After the People's Republic boldly called forth a national election to unify the country, Maj. Gen. Archibald Arnold, the military governor of Seoul, warned, "There is only one Government in Korea south of the 38 degrees. For any man or group to call an election as proposed is the most serious interference with the Military Government" and constitutes "an act of open opposition" to the United States that would not be taken lightly.[7]

This "open opposition" continued as the majority of Koreans realized that the United States had come not to liberate them—that is, to help them reconstruct society from the ground up—but to ensure the continuation of the established colonial order. Within a week of Hodge's arrival, the State Department had identified "several hundred conservatives" who officials believed could be entrusted to lead South Korea.[8] They were landowning elites who had profited on the backs of peasants during the colonial period, and exactly the kinds of "collaborators" and "feudalistic" legacies that the people's committees sought to purge. In addition, the Military Government revived the colonial National Police, a much-hated symbol of Japanese oppression, as its instrument for suppressing radical activities. Koreans who remained in Allied Occupied Japan also saw a return to business-as-usual. In a petition to General MacArthur in May 1946, three Koreans alleged that Japanese police violence against Koreans had escalated since the occupation. "We, Koreans, have welcomed [the] Allied Forces as the army of emancipation with maximum respect and affection," they prefaced their grievance, "[h]owever, to our great regret, the Japanese police has begun again to intervene, suppress and behave violently. . . . And we cannot understand that they do so by agreement with Allied Forces, as they propagate."[9]

According to Supreme Commander of the Allied Powers (SCAP) officials, the retention and expansion of the Japanese police force in the first year of the Allied Occupation of Japan was a matter of "necessity" due to the "adverse rate" of replacements and "acute shortage" of American troops.[10] Still, authorities could not ignore these allegations. They responded by digging into the political pasts of the petitioners. Upon investigation, agents of the U.S. Army Counter Intelligence Corps in Tokyo found that Chun Hai Kim, the "principle instigator" of the petition, was a member of the Japanese Communist Party and had a lengthy police record, including a homicide conviction. As for the claim of police abuse against Koreans, their closer look into some of these cases revealed "not cases of actual persecution" but of "Korean resistance to Japanese Police attempting to maintain order." Having fully discredited the petition, the agents took it one step further: "It is evident that the Allied Council and the Occupation Authorities are going to be bombarded with a series of such petitions, designed to create the impression that these statements are representative of popular opinion or expressions of bona fide groups of citizens." What they actually represented, however, was the "classical approach" of communists to "mislea[d] [and] exaggerat[e]" the facts, "and plainly designed to strengthen the Communist Party," in Japan and elsewhere "in the Orient."[11]

Officials' interpretation of local anticolonial grievances as strategies of a global communist crusade reflected more than paranoia; it indicated how the United States would come to criminalize recalcitrant colonial subjects. In the Philippines, for example, the Hukbalahaps, an anti-Japanese guerrilla force during the war, became an "internal security" threat promptly after liberation because it continued to rally peasants against corrupt landlords and colonial elites who maintained power.[12] In Okinawa, longstanding indigenous struggles against Japanese land policies were cast as the work of saboteurs to undermine the U.S. occupation and its plans to build military bases. "The pattern of the disturbance planned for the U.S. bases throughout Okinawa island," according to the 441st Counter Intelligence Corps Detachment in 1947, "will most probably take the form of a revolt by violence, following the line of strategy and tactics adopted in struggles in colonies throughout the world."[13] Throughout the post–World War II Pacific, anticolonial movements thus intensified in Central Luzon, Okinawa, Taegu, Cheju, and other locales, fueled by the re-entrenchment of colonial class relations and the violent suppression of worker and peasant revolts in the name of anticommunism.

The crisis of legitimacy that confronted U.S. officials in Asia would deepen as they revived the structures of the colonial state to make the region stable for capitalism. In Korea, Hodge understood the crisis and observed to the Secretary of State that, in the eyes of Koreans, "[t]he word pro-American is being added to pro-Jap, national traitor, and collaborator."[14] His solution for dealing with this "anti-Americanism," however, proved misguided entirely. "One of the principle factors adverse to Korean-American relationship in South Korea," he noted to the commanding generals of the U.S. Army Forces in Korea, "is a plain, unvarnished lack of courtesy" for Koreans by American soldiers. "I see evidences of this everyday," of Americans "mak[ing] fun of the Koreans, calling them 'gooks.'" Lest Americans be construed by Koreans as another colonizer with wanton disregard for their lives, the command should "effect spot checks on conduct and prompt handling of offenders."[15]

If Hodge thought that curbing the racial prejudices and "discourtesies" of American soldiers could placate Koreans and win their allegiance, he gravely misjudged the depth of their anticolonial aspirations, and failed to see how race played a far more important role in legitimating the U.S. occupation. From the start, Americans routinely characterized Koreans as a simple-minded people, with "few ideas" beyond a deep hatred for the Japanese and desire for immediate independence.[16] According to the State Department's political adviser, William Langdon, this was a main explanation for the Autumn Uprisings, a massive revolt in the fall of 1946 that shook the American occupied zone. He argued that the revolt exposed once and for all the Koreans' "latent savagery and incapacity for self-government." Langdon blamed the uprisings on the Koreans as well as the Japanese, whose authoritarianism taught Koreans "to only respect force," hence the reason why they "now submit meekly to a dictatorial alien controlled regime in North Korea."[17] What was once the Japanese empire's "Korean problem" (that of "uncivilized" colonial subjects within the body politic) had turned quickly into a communist problem for the U.S. Military Government. The task at hand, U.S. officials understood, entailed "teach[ing] the responsibilities [and] advantages of democracy" to Koreans and steering them clear away from communism.[18]

These dual projects—of civilizing Koreans and suppressing their radicalism—cohered in an experiment that Americans had tested long ago in a different colonial setting in the Philippines: to instill martial discipline in the population and to build up an indigenous security force. This process began with the arrival of Lt. Col. Russell D. Barros in September 1945 as part of the XXIV Corps. Barros was an officer in the Philippine Army who had mobilized a band of Filipino guerrillas as part of the liberation of Luzon in 1944, and who was prized for his experience working with Asian soldiers.[19] His travel from one U.S. colonial outpost to another, and the knowledge he acquired and implemented along the way, exemplified the kinds of transnational circuits that would shape the U.S. military empire in Asia over the next two decades. With Barros's guidance and with SCAP approval, Hodge directed the formation of a Korean Constabulary in January 1946, which served as an auxiliary to the National Police, with infantry units established at each province.[20] Similar to the one formed at the start of the U.S. colonial rule of the Philippines, the Korean Constabulary was tasked with maintaining "internal security" of the liberated colony in order "to get a start for the future" when a viable government was established.[21]

In the early months of 1946, young Korean men flocked to the recruiting stations, heeding the calls of newspaper ads and street recruiters, and eager for the chance to resume earning a steady wage. Many had been officers of the Imperial Japanese Army before liberation ended their careers abruptly. They tended to hail from middle-class backgrounds and had seen joining the Imperial Army as an opportunity to further their education and training, driven by the prospect of job security and an elevation of their class status. When the war ended, some envisioned an even greater purpose: they wanted to be the leaders of the new nation's army. To American officials, these men were exactly whom the Constabulary needed. They were ambitious and educated Koreans with the right blend of patriotic zeal, some English-language facility, and above all military experience. As recruitment progressed in the spring of 1946, U.S. advisers began making necessary changes: they replaced Japanese weapons and uniforms with American ones, translated U.S. military training manuals into Korean, and even added Korean history to the curriculum.[22] In short, the Constabulary was to become an American experiment in building a Korea for Koreans.

Faced with a population that seemed to grow increasingly resentful of the Military Government and its policies daily, Hodge pushed for an accelerated expansion of the Constabulary at the end of 1946, in preparation for potential future insurrections. To draw recruits, Military Government officials kept the entrance requirements to a minimum: a candidate had to be at least twenty-one years old, without a criminal record, and to hold the equivalent of an American eleventh-grade education to be admitted as an officer.[23] The lax requirements helped drive the numbers, but other forces were at work. As the National Police continued to crack down on political dissidents, those who bore the brunt of the repression came to see the Constabulary as an armed haven. "Many of the men the Americans recruited for our constabulary service," John Muccio, President Harry Truman's representative to Korea acknowledged later, "were self-styled refugees newly arrived from the north of the 38th parallel, who were accepted without proper investigation."[24] Within a year's time, between the spring of 1946 and 1947, the Constabulary had grown from a force of three thousand to ten thousand men.[25] Their loyalties could not be determined with certainty.

In October 1948, two months after Syngman Rhee declared the founding of the Republic of Korea (ROK), a massive rebellion rocked the southern peninsula and reverberated around the world. On October 19, upon receiving orders to deploy to Cheju Island to suppress a growing insurgency there, elements of the 14th Regiment of the Korean Constabulary pursued other plans: they mutinied. Forty soldiers stationed at Camp Anderson murdered their officers. They seized control of the city of Yŏsu within hours. The next morning, the number of rebels had swelled to two thousand, drawing disaffected soldiers and local people into the ranks. Officers told their men, "The thirty-eighth parallel has been done away with. Go get your guns and assemble."[26]

With this gathering force, the rebels quickly spread to the nearby city of Sunch'ŏn. They marched through the streets and waved red flags and sang communist slogans, announcing their victory. They established "people's courts" that tried and executed members of the police and their families as well as other government officials and landowners. The American adviser to the Korean Constabulary James Hausman recalled of what came to be called the Yŏsu-Sunch'ŏn rebellion, "All hell had broken loose and we had nothing to stop the onslaught."[27] Meanwhile, on that same day, the South Korean Labor Party called for a general strike in Taegu, rallying students and workers to demand the dissolution of Syngman Rhee's government and the withdrawal of American troops from Korea.[28]

The Yŏsu-Sunch'ŏn rebellion drew the attention of international observers and journalists; many who flocked to the area documented the bloodshed on the ground. "The city stank of death and was ill with the marks of horror," *Life* photographer Carl Mydans wrote in his notes to his editors.[29] In the eyes of the "free world," the mutinous soldiers and the violence they unleashed belied a precarious South Korean state that seemed to have lost its handle on the "Red menace" completely. Military officials appeared to have seen the signs coming. Earlier that summer, counterintelligence agents intercepted instructions from North Korea urging communists to "infiltrate into the South Korean Constabulary and begin political attacks aimed at causing dissension and disorder"; by late summer, agents had identified the 14th Regiment as the most dangerous and suspected it was close to mutiny.[30] A deeper look would have revealed that unheeded warnings stemmed back even earlier to the hasty recruitment drive of 1946–47. But there was no time to reflect on missed opportunities. Rhee struck back hard against the rebels. Led by American advisers and carried out by Korean colonels seasoned in Japanese antiguerrilla campaigns in Manchuria, the counteroffensive was swift and brutal. One week after the mutiny began, an estimated 821 rebels were killed and nearly 3,000 captured; 1,000 or more escaped and slipped into hiding. Peace was restored momentarily.[31]

The following weeks proved critical for Rhee in his drive to consolidate power in the budding South Korea. The conservative leader had been biding his time since his return from exile in 1945, and now he did exactly what he needed to demonstrate his legitimacy to his American backers. Soon after the pacification of Yŏsu and Sunch'ŏn, Rhee ordered the Constabulary to intensify investigation of all its units and to purge those with "communistic tendencies." All who had taken part in the rebellion were brought before courts-martial and charged with mutiny and sedition.[32] With the passage of the National Security Law in December 1948, the hunt for subversives grew more emboldened and led to the roundup and screening of more than two

FIGURE 2. Captured rebels of the Yŏsu-Sunch'ŏn rebellion, October 1948. (Photograph by Carl Mydans; The LIFE Picture Collection/Getty Images.)

thousand officers and the imprisonment of more than four hundred on charges of conspiracy, murder, and mutiny, among other crimes.[33] Such draconian measures reflected Rhee's shortsighted understanding of what had happened: the Yŏsu-Sunch'ŏn rebellion was only a problem of "Communist infiltration." As such, it required bureaucratic solutions, starting with the prompt purging of subversives. During the process, American military advisers resumed the buildup of the Korean Constabulary and implemented better screening of new recruits.

Rhee's crackdown facilitated the transition from the American occupation to the new Republic, ensuring no place existed for political dissent in his anticommunist state. The crackdown worked more broadly to secure South Korea's place in the newly reconfigured Pacific region, the contours of which were becoming clearer by this time. In October 1948, the National Security Council outlined the first U.S. policy strategy toward building a new Pacific regionalism, centered on Japan and its economic recovery. The "reverse course" of U.S. occupation objectives in Japan meant several things, most notably the return of previously "purged" conservative leaders to power and the promotion of unfettered capitalism. Both of these objectives had been pursued against the increasing militancy of organized labor and communist movements. But the reverse course also signaled a broader transnational calculus to revive Japan's industrial capacity and export markets in Asia, keeping the periphery firmly connected to the capitalist world.[34] The security of anticommunism in South Korea and the resumption of Japan's industrial economy emerged as integral projects to transform the Pacific region into a beacon of free trade and a part of the "free world."

Since the end of World War II, in the span of a few years, American policy had gone full circle, from dismantling the Japanese empire to resuscitating it. Common people throughout Asia revolted against what they saw as the revival of Japanese dominance in the region through the aid of "American imperialists."[35] But to U.S. officials, this was to be a more liberal and democratic pan-Asianism than the East Asia Co-Prosperity Sphere, one tempered by the U.S. commitment to support the independence of postcolonial nation-states. It was to be far removed from Japan's erstwhile militarist endeavors. Yet this was no mere ruse for empire. In fact, the promise of "Asia for Asians" demanded a differentiation between "good" and "bad" Asians, between those to be incorporated into the postcolonial state and those to be expelled from it, and American officials put their faith in the military to accomplish both. The Korean Constabulary, driven by the dual mandates of disciplining martial subjects and making war on those who refused the American liberation, functioned as the quintessential vehicle for postcolonial state building.

The Yŏsu-Sunch'ŏn Rebellion was not an aberration of an otherwise promising start toward the fulfillment of a national project. Instead, it was the result of the accumulated grievances of ordinary Koreans since the start of the U.S. occupation. It was their collective refusal of American designs for their postcolonial world. The failure of American officials to face this fact would haunt them not only in Korea but also in other contexts, wherever the U.S. military intervened.

MILITARY EXPANSION AND SUBVERSION

In November 1948, with the Yŏsu mutiny recently subdued, Secretary of the Army Kenneth Royall issued a directive to all U.S. Army commands that outlined the protocol for handling "subversive and disaffected personnel." The events in Korea made him nervous about the loyalty of his own American troops. The terms "subversive" and "disaffected" personnel described subjects who had engaged in any number of political activities or had "shown lack of loyalty to the Government and Constitution of the United States" by acts, writings, or speech.[36] Royall's directive breathed new life into these definitions by empowering commanders to "detect" and "investigate" such personnel. The directive tasked them with classifying and maintaining a detailed record of each individual, including name, rank, army serial number, and a statement indicating the basis for the subject's classification.[37] The suppression of the Yŏsu rebellion appeared to have contained one specter of communist subversion only to give rise to another within the U.S. military, one that gained increasing focus and clarity in the late 1940s yet would remain more elusive than ever.

In many ways, the problem of subversion in the U.S. armed forces was a product of popular front activism for racial equality in the early 1940s. In a memorandum dated February 1946 and titled "Communist Infiltration of and Agitation in the Armed Forces," the War Department's Director of Intelligence Lt. Gen. Hoyt S. Vandenberg made this connection clear. Admittedly, the problem had roots stemming back to 1920, he noted, when the Communist International first ordered communist parties around the world to "carry on a systematic agitation in its own Army against every kind of oppression of colonial population." By the start of World War II, this global movement had transformed into active pursuits against the Jim Crow military in the United States. As Communist Party members entered the services in an attempt to organize from within, they targeted "negro [sic] soldiers and enlisted personnel" in particular. The Communist Party, under the guise of "front" organizations such as the American Youth Congress and other civil rights groups, had unleashed a "whispering campaign" to indoctrinate soldiers and sailors, stirring up black servicemen especially.[38]

But it was after the war, as the United States continued to keep American troops overseas, that such activities posed an actual global threat to U.S. security. "At first," Vandenberg continued in his memo, "the apparent purpose of the Communists seemed to be propagandizing against this country's occupation of certain areas in the Pacific and the Far East." But by the end of 1945, "Communists" were actively agitating GIs wherever they were stationed abroad, fueling the growing sentiments of the American public that overseas servicemen ought to be returned home without delay.[39] Handwritten letters—hundreds and thousands of them—flooded the offices of elected officials in November and December, written by GIs in Hawaiʻi, Okinawa, Yokohama, Manila, Frankfurt, Nuremberg, Paris, and other places. In Manila, "Home by Christmas!" became a seditious slogan that seemed to appear everywhere; as Nelson Peery, a radicalized black GI at the time, recalled, the words were scratched onto road signs and painted on the latrines, on the doors of officers' quarters, in recreation rooms, and in mess halls.[40] Authorities watched these signs nervously, convinced of sedition stirring in the military.

Then on Christmas Day 1945, as though confirming these worst fears, four thousand American soldiers in Manila staged a demonstration. The soldiers marched to the 21ˢᵗ Replacement Depot in response to the cancellation of a scheduled transport home and carried banners that read, "We Want Ships!"[41] The Christmas Day protest was a sign of things to come, and they came more quickly and bigger than authorities could prepare for. The opening weeks of 1946, in fact, saw the largest wave of GI demonstrations ever to hit the U.S. military up to that time. It came on the heels of an announcement by the War Department on January 4 that there would be a further slowdown in troop demobilization; servicemen expecting to be released soon based on their number of years of service now remained uncertain of their future. The announcement touched off a chain reaction at U.S. bases around the world, beginning in the Philippines. On January 6 and 7, an estimated eight thousand to ten thousand GIs converged at City Hall in Manila and voiced dissatisfaction with the recent announcement, urging U.S. officials to scale back all overseas forces except those in Occupied Japan and Germany. On January 8, more than 3,500 enlisted men and officers at Andersen Air Base in Guam staged a hunger strike to express solidarity with those in the Philippines.[42] Over the next ten days, similar actions organized by "soldier committees" took place in Hawaiʻi, Le Havre, Paris, Rheims, Seoul, Shanghai, New Delhi, and elsewhere.[43]

The demobilization movement of January 1946 was the first concerted rebellion against the U.S. military and its growing worldwide presence. While few seemed to question the necessity of maintaining troops in Japan and Germany, in other parts of the world GIs asked probing questions about why they were needed. During Secretary of War Robert Patterson's tour of U.S. bases in the Pacific, one soldier confronted him directly by asking, "Did you bring the 86th Division to suppress the aspirations of the Philippine people?"[44] At a demonstration at Hickam Air Field in Hawai'i, a GI and labor organizer named David Livingston stated, "We are here because there seems to be a foreign policy developing which requires one hell of a big army. It's about time we joined with our buddies in the Philippines and said: 'Yes, let's occupy enemy countries, but not friendly countries.' It doesn't take a single soldier in the Philippines or on Oahu to wipe fascism off the earth."[45] Military officials sought to explain away the protests by attributing them to "confused and disheartened" GIs who simply wished to go home; but as the statements above indicate, GIs understood precisely what was at stake.[46]

More than a simple agitation to return home, the demobilization movement was part of a much wider and spontaneous anti-imperialist revolt that reverberated across the post–World War II world. During the same time, on January 24, one thousand Indian airmen of the British Royal Air Force staged a hunger strike in Cawnpore, India, against delays in demobilization and for equal pay, food, and housing conditions with British airmen. The strike lasted several days and incited a wave of similar "sit-down" strikes at British air bases in Ceylon, Egypt, and Palestine.[47] While these protests were under way, a far more violent mutiny struck the British empire. On February 21, lascars of the Royal Indian Navy seized control of nine vessels off the coast of Bombay. They engaged British forces in an armed confrontation that spilled into the streets of Bombay and soon to Calcutta and Karachi, and claimed the lives of more than two hundred people. What began as strikes over equal pay and living conditions quickly turned into bolder demands, which included the withdrawal of Indian troops from Indonesia where they had been sent to help the Dutch suppress an anticolonial movement.[48] These worldwide revolts told the same story: as empires scrambled to restrain the pulse of freedom in the decolonizing world, their soldiers and sailors, many of them dark-skinned colonial conscripts, refused.

Global decolonization and U.S. military expansion brought American servicemen into proximity with some of these radicalized Asian subjects, and it was the specter of their politicizing affinities that most alarmed U.S.

officials. The "eyes of the world, and particularly the Japanese people, are watching with interest," the Eighth Army's acting commander, Lt. Gen. Charles P. Hall, warned his troops during their rebellion in Yokohama: "Subversive forces, quick to sense dissension in your ranks, will take their cue for sabotage of plans for our future action."[49] Hoyt Vandenberg had the same concern in mind when he noted in his February 1946 memo that the GI demonstrations "were not instigated on Communist Party orders emanating from the United States," but by communists in Asia.[50] These were not unfounded concerns. A year later, one counterintelligence report from the Philippines-Ryukyus Command confirmed that "there were approximately 300 American GIs, white and Negro," who had joined ranks with the Huks in Bataan in 1946. The report went on to state that "an American GI, disguised by a long beard and dressed in old khakis, is traveling with a band of Huks" in the barrios of Tarlac Province.[51]

Such accounts of GI defection substantiated the worst fears of U.S. officials about the seductive dangers of international communism and illuminated a global alliance of color forged through the military. This racial menace, ironically, doubled as a military asset. During World War II, U.S. campaigns against fascism and white supremacy had demanded the inclusion of racially suspect populations into the armed services. Japanese Americans were tested for their loyalty in concentration camps to allow the "good" ones to showcase their patriotism through combat. Similarly, the Office of War Information targeted African Americans to support the war effort and to demonstrate their patriotic manhood by enlisting in the segregated military.[52] After the war, the utility of racial minorities in the military would continue and expand. In September 1946, the War Department ordered the army to assign "all inductees or enlistees of Japanese ancestry" to Japan for occupation duty, where they would serve as interpreters and translators for U.S. military and civilian agencies and continue their wartime function as "ambassadors of democracy."[53] Mobilizing "race for empire" in these ways left uncertain perils for the United States in the post–World War II Pacific.

The task of monitoring these racialized subjects in the military fell to the U.S. Army's Office of Intelligence (G-2). More than any other institution at the time, G-2 was at the forefront of producing racial knowledge about the decolonizing Pacific. Its case files of individuals, many of them rendered in great detail, hint at the complex lives of these subjects and, for some of them, even their desires to pursue a politics beyond U.S. objectives. At the same time, they also reveal the determination by U.S. military intelligence agents to diminish the very complexities of these individuals. These reports illustrate the impossible double bind in which these men and women found themselves. They were a military asset or a racial peril who invariably degenerated from one to the other.

The case of Misao Kuwaye is revealing in this sense. Kuwaye was of "Okinawan descent" from Honolulu, and had arrived in Tokyo in October 1945 as a Department of the Army Civilian Employee. She was assigned to the Press Section of the Civil Censorship Detachment (CCD), in which her primary duty was to censor Japanese mail. Kuwaye was one of fourteen "Nisei" women from Hawai'i recruited before the war to form the CCD, and they were the first Nisei linguists to arrive in Occupied Japan.[54] Kuwaye was part of this exemplary cohort and valued for her Japanese-language ability, but her employment record betrayed her talents. Soon after her arrival, the CCD discovered that Kuwaye "did not meet the qualifications as a linguist" and was, in the opinion of authorities, a "troublemaker."[55] At first, what this meant exactly was unknown, but it soon became clear.

In January 1947, military intelligence confirmed that Kuwaye had been an organizer and "a regular attendant" of the Honolulu Labor Canteen, a radical alternative to the United Service Organizations formed in August 1945 that brought together leftists in Hawai'i, including GIs, plantation workers, and labor organizers.[56] This initial discovery prompted an investigation that uncovered Kuwaye's mobility across multiple worlds of radicalism. Subsequent reports found that Kuwaye had been "closely associated" with communists and "Communist sympathizers" in Hawai'i, and that she had used her military assignment in Japan to build connections with radicals in Japan and Okinawa, which included members of the Japanese Communist Party and the League of Okinawans. In September, when she requested approval to transfer jobs from Japan to Okinawa, authorities found in her possession a letter from one of her associates in Honolulu urging her to obtain information about military installations on the island. On November 2, upon her return to Honolulu, customs agents confiscated "a number of documents, including press releases concerning communist activities and Japanese Women's Suffrage," loose pages of the Confidential Training Program for Censorship, and maps of "major cities in Japan, classified as Restricted."[57]

Despite all signs of Kuwaye's "leftist inclination," authorities did not pursue her case further due to a "lack of conclusive *proof* that subject was subversive," but her case had sufficiently alarmed officials.[58] Kuwaye's associations with leftists in Hawai'i, Japan, and Okinawa raised questions about the loyalty of Nisei subjects employed by the U.S. Army, and it illuminated the porous boundaries of the radicalizing Pacific. The agent assigned to her case had determined, "The damage inflicted by persons of this ilk upon the occupation effort is by no means limited to their activities while in this theater [the "Far East"]. As was recently demonstrated in another case, these people return to the United States as 'experts' on occupation policy and set about undermining Japanese policy to any group that will listen or read their leftist 'exposé.'" In short, the military had become a vehicle for individual and collective radicalization to undermine the U.S. empire. "The solution to this situation," the agent concluded, "appears to be more careful investigation prior to employment and more effective means for immediate removal of such persons from employment with the occupation."[59]

It was precisely this fear of subversion within the U.S. Pacific empire, even in the absence of "conclusive proof" of it, that drove G-2 to locate and determine the loyalty of Asian subjects in the military. The line between "good" and "bad" Asians never had been easy to decipher, but it nonetheless became more and more important to demarcate as the United States pursued its global war against communism. Another report on Calvin Kim, for example, revealed that the Korean American officer who was ordered to the Military Intelligence Service Language School in 1945 because of his Korean-language ability was later found to have engaged in questionable political activities, including signing two petitions in 1948 to have the Independent Progressive Party placed on the California State ballot and for an equal-housing initiative, both of which were "circulated by a known CP member." In 1952, the army conducted a polygraph on Kim to determine his political affiliations, and the agent concluded, "There is no information to indicate that Kim has ever embraced foreign ideologies or that his racial background makes him vulnerable to Communist propaganda." As for Kim's earlier political involvements, "[h]e was apparently duped by the IPP in 1948, as were many politically naïve people."[60]

From one report to the next, G-2 probed the political pasts of army personnel to determine their loyalty, especially those of a particular "racial background." Another report in 1953 sought to determine if a "Charles Kim" stationed in Pusan, Korea, was the son of Diamond Kimm, the Korean leftist from Los Angeles who was then facing deportation charges for his political activities.[61] Indeed, if the "foreign-born" had emerged as particular targets of the burgeoning anticommunist regime of the early 1950s, which sought to monitor and exclude "subversives" from the nation, then the army came under scrutiny for channeling in such large numbers of Asians and foreign nationals over the years. "The over-riding necessity to make maximum use of all available manpower" during World War II, a report stated in 1954, had led to "the liberalization of policy toward Communists in the Army." Accordingly, Senator Joseph McCarthy urged the Secretary of the Army to do everything to "wee[d] out . . . the misfits, the incompetents, the Communists and the fellow travelers who infiltrated the Army during the twenty years of Communist coddling."[62]

Determined to root out subversives hiding in plain sight, G-2 with its case files in fact accomplished something else entirely: it reinforced and reproduced the fear of racialized Asian subjects plotting against the U.S. empire. Although rare, when G-2 uncovered "conclusive proof" of actual subversion, it only confirmed the reality of this fear. The case of Yi Sa Min was one such case that elicited the intervention of the State Department in January 1950. According to the U.S. embassy in Seoul, Yi, an American citizen, traveled to Pyongyang in December as a representative of the Korean Democratic Front of North America and sought to secure the group's membership in the North Korean Democratic Front. At a press conference, Yi stated the following: "The American people and Koreans residing [in the United States] are supporting the unified independence of Korea and her democratic development. Because we live in America, we know very well what kind of country America is and what kind of fello[w] Rhee Syngman . . . [is]." He minced no words as he condemned the American "invasion" of "the southern half of our fatherland," and castigated Rhee and "his stooges" for "selling our country" to the Americans. "We will consolidate our efforts and fight for our Republic and for the unification of the North and South, and we will not permit American interference, whatever it may be."[63]

To state officials, the speech lent every indication that Yi was "an active agent of the Communist-controlled North Korean regime," and they became obsessed with his political past. As a telegram revealed, in 1919 Yi had taken part in the Korean underground independence movement in Shanghai, which led to his arrest and imprisonment for four years by Japanese authorities. Upon his release he founded the Korean Revolutionary Party and gained membership in the Korean Nationalist Association, a group "which had connections with the Chinese Communist Party." Like many others, Yi sensed an opportunity when the United States declared war on Japan; he enlisted in the U.S. Army, served in the India and China theaters, and acquired citizenship through his military service. Earning his citizenship did little to sway his political convictions. Disillusioned by the U.S. military occupation in Korea after the war, Yi maintained associations with Korean leftists in the United States and continued to agitate for Korean independence, all while working as a Korean-language instructor in Seattle and occasionally living in Los Angeles.[64] Looking back at Yi's thirty-plus years of "communist" activities, state officials wondered how such an outlaw ever managed to slip into the military, much less to obtain citizenship. In 1950, the State Department recommended that Yi's naturalization be deemed "fraudently [sic] obtained" and permanently revoked.[65]

The apparent ease by which Yi Sa Min led his dual lives as a domesticated U.S. citizen and a foreign agent confounded state officials beyond anything else. In ensuing years, it was precisely the indecipherability of these slippery categories that fueled the anticommunist persecution of Asian residents in the United States, resulting in the deportation of Filipino labor activists and the forced confessions of tens of thousands of "illegal" Chinese residents.[66] But Yi's expulsion also took place in the context of pressing geopolitical events, which renewed the question about the utility of Asians in the military. In the fall of 1949, the Chinese civil war between Communist and Nationalist forces came to a decisive end with the former declaring victory. The "loss" of China to communism stoked fears among some U.S. officials about the region's stability, especially if China should export its revolution to Southeast Asia and Korea. The imminence of Japan's economic collapse in 1949 compounded this scenario.[67] The specter of a sweeping revolution in Asia and the loss of Japan as a regional surrogate demanded a new U.S. strategy, one that would secure the region through communist containment and economic integration.

This strategy was provided by the Mutual Defense Assistance Act, approved by Congress on October 6, 1949. The act consolidated all U.S. foreign military aid projects up to that time under the Mutual Defense Assistance Program (MDAP), appropriating $1.5 billion in aid for the first year; and in August 1950, with the Korean War in full swing, President Truman requested an additional $4 billion. Beyond the scope and price tag, MDAP's more enduring significance rested on its conception of Pacific security. MDAP created essentially a "hub-and-spokes" security system in Asia, in which bilateral treaties between the United States and particular nation-states provided the basis for the security of the entire region. MDAP furnished new and old allied states with military equipment, economic aid, training, and technical assistance, granted with the firm assurance that an attack on one country was an attack on the United States and the "free world," and would be met with swift retaliation.[68]

From the beginning, this transnational security state in Asia drew on a language of "self-help" and "mutual aid" to underscore its legitimacy as a decidedly *anti*colonial arrangement. MDAP granted aid to those who requested it, to give "free nations which intend to remain free" the tools to defend themselves from communism.[69] On the ground, this discourse of helping Asians help themselves translated into the growing presence of U.S. military advisers that assisted with the buildup and training of national armed forces, a process that was under way in countries such as the Philippines and South Korea. In the fall of 1948, the first six Korean Constabulary officers arrived in the United States to receive training in U.S. military service schools, as part of a new training program initiated by the U.S. Military Advisory Group to the Republic of Korea (KMAG). This initial cohort was the precursor to the tens of thousands more from South Korea and other countries in Asia who did the same over the course of the 1950s through MDAP. After their training, these trainees were expected to return to their home countries, having acquired "first-hand knowledge of how Americans do things," and to help develop and modernize their own militaries.[70]

In the name of promoting freedom, MDAP thus set the foundation for the United States to extend its military empire in Asia. It was a process that led to the transit and circulation of "free" Asian soldiers across the Pacific, and their arrival in the United States occurred at the precise moment when U.S. officials faced growing concerns about the presence of "subversives" in the military. Their racialized presence reproduced and magnified the threat of communist subversion even as they were hailed as the solution to curbing its global spread.

STIMULATING A "GENUINE WILL TO FIGHT"

In September 1951, through MDAP, the first group of 263 Koreans arrived in the United States. A majority of them enrolled in a special twenty-week course at the U.S. Army Infantry School at Fort Benning, Georgia. The official records of G-2 identified each individual by first and last name, a headshot photograph, and scant biographical information. The file on Kang Chun Gill, for example, revealed that he was born on October 15, 1928, married with no children, and an educated man, having attended primary and secondary schools in Japan as well as two years each at Hanguk University in Seoul and Taegu Normal College. Kang was "fluent" in Japanese and "fair" in spoken English, but better in reading, writing, and translating. His religion was "Protestant," his politics, "none," and he occupied the rank of a second lieutenant. We know little else of Kang's life, or the lives of the other 262 trainees, for that matter.[71]

While G-2 divulged little, the historical record reveals that these individuals were the product of long and contentious debates among U.S. officials about the benefits of utilizing Asian soldiers. The debates began shortly after the Korean War started in June 1950. U.S. leaders knew already that the Korean War was the beginning of a much longer and wider war to secure the Asian periphery and link its economies to Japan, which in due time would embroil the United States in Vietnam. The seemingly boundless scope and geography of the war in Korea demanded flexibility and vigilance on the part of Americans. Secretary of Defense George C. Marshall told the Senate Armed Services Committee in January 1951, "We are confronted with a world situation of such gravity and such unpredictability that we must be prepared for effective action, whether the challenge comes with the speed of sound or is delayed for a lifetime."[72]

Marshall's statement echoed a broader concern among U.S. officials about the overstretched U.S. military and its state of combat readiness. With less than seven hundred thousand servicemen scattered around the globe, the prospects of waging a full-scale and effective war in Korea seemed a logistical impossibility.[73] Only days after the war began, the Senate Armed Services Committee initiated hearings on a bill to create a system of universal conscription to boost U.S. military manpower. As reports came in from the front lines about the ineffectiveness of South Korean soldiers, many who apparently had fled their posts and ceased to fight, the need to build up the U.S. Army grew acute.[74] "The balance of manpower is against us," the chairman of the Armed Services Committee Lyndon Johnson remarked during the hearings in January 1951, as the induction rate reached an all-time peak of eighty thousand a month. "The grim fact is that the United States is now engaged in a struggle for survival. . . . Unpleasant though the choices may be, we face the decision of asking temporary sacrifice from some of our citizens now, or of inviting the permanent extinction of freedom for all of our citizens."[75]

In June 1951, the Universal Military Training and Service Act passed and addressed the concern by lowering the draft age from nineteen to eighteen and extending the active-duty service commitment from twenty-one to twenty-four months, in total more than doubling the draft numbers between 1950 and 1951. The act also established the National Security Training Commission, which immediately took up the task of outlining a long-term U.S. military policy. "This solemn and far-reaching action of Congress and the President," the commission stated in its first report to Congress, "reflects a realization, even in the heat and tension of the present crisis, that the major problems we face in the world will be of long duration, that no tidy or decisive conclusion is to be expected soon." According to the report, the Korean War was but a phase of a global struggle that required a more or less permanent state of militarization. "The American people must be prepared, like their forebears who pushed the frontier westward, to meet a savage and deadly attack at any moment." The frontier mythology emphasized the current threat to "free society" in a language the American public widely recognized, and the similarities could not have been more transparent. The report concluded: "The return to frontier conditions demands a frontier response."[76]

In the first year of the Korean War, military and government officials experimented with this "frontier response," reconfiguring the American military for permanent war. Beyond increasing the draft numbers, the Universal Military Training and Service Act expanded the army reserves to create a more mobile and flexible force dispersed across the globe, "capable of instantly bearing arms" to meet conflicts anytime and anywhere they occurred. At the same time, another major reform was under way that encountered far more resistance in Congress, particularly among representatives of the white South: the desegregation of the armed forces. Slow to achieve in the years after President Truman issued Executive Order 9981, which had mandated "equality of treatment and opportunity" within the armed services, the integration of African Americans in the military became official policy in 1951 as part of the solution to the growing combat-troop shortage and morale problems. "It was my conviction," Gen. Matthew Ridgeway stated, that integration would "assure that sort of *esprit* a fighting army needs, where each soldier stands proudly on his own feet, knowing himself to be as good as the next fellow."[77]

The demand for more bodies on the front lines made racial integration a "high priority," and it resulted in another experiment of military integration that involved a different population.[78] On August 15, 1950, as U.S. casualties in Korea continued to mount, representatives of the Eighth Army, KMAG, and the ROK Army met to discuss the possibility of incorporating Koreans into the U.S. Army. The depleted ranks left nothing to question. Two days later, before a concrete plan for procurement and training was finalized, each of the four U.S. divisions in Korea received an initial increment of 250 soldiers under the Korean Augmentation to the U.S. Army (KATUSA) program. According to one report, they were "forcibly and indiscriminately recruited from the streets of Pusan and Taegu, who had received no military training whatsoever." Some of them received "a few weeks" of basic training, others were promptly assigned to units and trained just prior to being sent into combat. By November 1950, 22,000 Korean soldiers were integrated into the Eighth Army.[79]

The KATUSA program was part of a longstanding colonial practice of incorporating "native" troops into the imperial army. The Philippine Scouts, organized at the start of U.S. colonial rule as a separate organization of the U.S. Army, served as a direct blueprint. As with the Scouts, KATUSAs occupied a liminal position as "not technically a part of the U.S. Army," but who nonetheless filled the ranks as an intermediary who could gather intelligence and impart knowledge about the local terrain and population. Their language and cultural difference drew the ire of their American counterparts. "The ROK soldiers were unable to understand even the simplest command," according to one report. Their lack of "understanding of field sanitation and personal hygiene," and their general unfamiliarity with "U.S. conceptions of everyday living," including rations and clothing, turned them "from a welcome asset to an irksome burden."[80]

Military officials with no firsthand experience of these limitations sang praises for the KATUSA program, especially with their sights set on the future. In their view, the program gave Korean soldiers "sorely needed training in U.S. methods and techniques," and thus provided "a U.S.-trained cadre for the postwar Korean Army." The program proved useful even beyond the Korean context. As officials understood, KATUSA was an experiment in "military efficiency" that could inform how the United States conducted its future global conflicts. "The United States may well again be faced with the possibility or necessity of augmenting the U.S. Army with native troops," according to an operations research study conducted in 1953. As Asian nations became formally decolonized, the Pacific region emerged as a laboratory to experiment with various methods of incorporating "native" manpower into the U.S. military. "Future military operations in underdeveloped parts of the world," the 1953 study affirmed, would "unquestionably involve the use and support of native armies."[81] This idea, I show in later chapters, led to military experiments throughout the 1950s and 1960s.

Since the start of the Korean War, Secretary of the Army Frank Pace Jr. realized that a state of permanent war would require the mobilization of non-U.S. populations. In November 1950, as the integration of KATUSAs progressed at a peak rate, Pace requested Vice Chief of Staff of the Army Gen. Wade Haislip to conduct a study, as "a matter of urgency," of the possibility of using "foreign nationals to build up the strength of our forces in critical areas overseas" beyond Korea. In his request, Pace referenced the Lodge Act that had been enacted earlier in June, which allowed for the overseas recruitment of "aliens" into the U.S. armed forces. This act only applied to the countries of Western Europe, however, and recruited subjects who were "eligible to citizenship" (hence, racially "white"), thus rendering it ineffective and irrelevant in the "Pacific Area."[82] In light of the current war in the Asian rimlands, Pace advocated that the army increase the number of aliens in the armed forces "to a much greater figure," including the possibility of organizing Japanese nationals into separate combat units.[83]

Two weeks later, Haislip and his staff responded by publishing a study that outlined different methods of mobilizing foreign manpower, including the enlistment of "displaced persons, defectees and potential defectees from unfriendly countries" into the U.S. Army. The study also suggested the possibility of organizing alien service members into separate units for "unconventional" warfare.[84] Its range of ideas prompted further consideration by the National Security Council, which issued its policy paper on the subject in April 1951. NSC 108, as the policy was designated, spelled out the problem with a language similar to that used to justify Universal Military Training: "The United States should seek urgent improvement in the utilization of foreign manpower for military purposes in order to increase the flexibility of employment of our own military forces and to avoid a disproportionate contribution of the United States manpower to the over-all military posture of the free world." Taking a global view, the policy crunched some remarkable numbers: the availability of "physically fit" 15- to 49-year-old men from countries "favorably disposed toward the United States" stood at 130 million, roughly 17 million more than those in the "Soviet bloc." The mobilization of this vast pool of foreign manpower would bolster the overall military capability of the "free world" to act as an effective bulwark against "Soviet expansionism."[85]

By calculating the ways that foreign manpower could be mobilized, NSC 108 worked as a sort of addendum to the Universal Military Training and

Service Act that was enacted two months later. But beyond increasing manpower and improving "military efficiency," the utilization of foreign soldiers served a broader cultural function. The policy made clear that part of the goal of mobilizing these subjects was "to stimulate a genuine 'will to fight' by the winning of men's minds and the build-up of resistance to communist ideology and propaganda." The National Security Council insisted cultural diplomacy and military buildup were complementary projects, it was something that Soviet leaders had pursued for some time by recruiting soldiers from the "Soviet bloc," and Americans needed to catch up and do the same. "We have more to sell, but [the Soviets] have been the better salesmen to date."[86]

The dual imperatives of "selling" democracy and mobilizing foreign military labor, however, opened the United States to the charge of employing mercenaries, which threatened to undermine American credibility. As General Haislip and his personnel staff cautioned, the use of mercenaries by the United States would be "repugnant to the ideals of our people, would leave us open to the charge of 'imperialism,' and give substance to the charge of our enemies that we intend to hire others to fight for us." The French Foreign Legion, "composed mostly of aliens" and French colonial subjects, had drawn the indignation of world opinion precisely for this reason. Haislip and staff pointed out that even "our own Philippine Scouts," America's most recent experiment with a mercenary force, had responded to their "inferior pay and allowances" with a "minor mutiny" in 1924.[87] The times were no longer amenable to such practice. As both the National Security Council and the army personnel staff underscored, the United States must distance itself from "imperialism" and make a clear stance for "freedom."[88]

NSC 108 thus concluded the "most effective utilization of foreign manpower" rested on the development of the "armed forces of free nations," a process already under way through the MDAP. Specifically, this entailed a practice that the Department of Defense (DOD) termed "mirror imaging," in which U.S. training and doctrine, force structure, and supplies and equipment were exported and imposed on the organization of allied forces. Mirror imaging essentially was "modernization" theory applied through the military, in the sense that it approached the military as a vehicle for transforming "backward" countries into thriving nations oriented toward capitalism.[89] Lt. Gen. James Van Fleet, Commander of the Eighth Army who was credited with turning around the lackluster Korean army during the war, understood his role within this framework. In the spring of 1951, he arrived in Korea and found the ROK Army in a shambled state but also saw Koreans "anxious to fight for their freedom." The "Orientals apply themselves intensely," he commended, "tell them something once, and they have it," but all their individual motivation was squandered without the "competent leadership" of Syngman Rhee. In the end it was the leader of the republic, not the leader of the Eighth Army, who could command their allegiance. Once Rhee realized this fact and acted on it, the men of the ROK Army "suddenly were transformed into soldiers."[90]

In the end the processes of turning "boys" into soldiers and transforming a colony into a modern nation were one and the same. Both depended on the ability of Asians to defend themselves from communism, the threat to their newfound freedom. Van Fleet was convinced that "Asia can and should be saved by Asians," and it could be done precisely by teaching Asians how to embody martial citizenship through the mirror imaging of their national armed forces. Doing so would save American manpower and dollars as well as "strip the Communists of their powerful argument that ours is no real war for freedom but only a white man's 'imperialist' war to put Asia in chains."[91] MDAP was, in this sense, an imperial projection of anticolonial self-determination. It produced foot soldiers for the U.S. empire and provided an arsenal for the propaganda war with the Soviet Union.

In 1950, the DOD began to select and send foreign military trainees to U.S. service schools through MDAP, the cream of the crop of allied forces who would take the lead in America's "real war for freedom." In the first year, MDAP brought students from 14 countries, with each country committing between 22 and 627 students. Initially, most of the students came from so-called "Title I" countries, the nine European countries receiving the biggest portion of MDAP grants owing to their proximity to the "Iron Curtain." But by 1959, of the more than 140,000 foreign nationals who passed through the United States, 58,203 came from Asia. South Korea and Taiwan sent 14,445 and 15,552 students, respectively, the highest numbers among the total 54 countries. U.S. officials saw these students as military assets. In 1962, Secretary of Defense Robert McNamara reflected on the long-term benefits of MDAP: "In all probability the greater return on any portion of our military assistance investment—dollar for dollar—comes from the training of selected officers and key specialists in U.S. schools and installations."[92]

U.S. military officials saw these foreign trainees in instrumentalist ways and assessed their value through a cost-benefit analysis. As one KMAG officer put it, MDAP training program amounted to "a package plan to provide maximum instruction at the least possible expense in the least possible time."[93] But aside from serving purely military purposes, these trainees also embodied a story of progress that affirmed the modernizing potential of Asian soldiers and, in turn, the military's potential as a vehicle of modernization in Asia. Toward this end, in 1951, the State Department and the DOD collaborated on a series of projects highlighting the MDAP trainees as conduits of democracy. Aimed at audiences abroad, they developed "hometown type stories" presumably about the trainees' immersion in the local communities and produced a motion picture titled *Forces of Freedom*.[94] By the decade's end, their efforts would maximize the "collateral benefits" of training these foreign students, and hone their potential as "a multi-purpose cold war weapon" that served "political, economic, and social, as well as military" purposes.[95] Their efforts cohered in a cultural industry for the military.

Molding these trainees for U.S. cultural diplomacy was a two-way process that involved shaping their experiences in the United States as well. The DOD aimed to do this by producing a "guidebook" to acquaint the trainees with various aspects of American culture and society. The 1959 guidebook began with the preface: "We welcome you to the United States and we welcome the opportunity to share with you not only our professional military skills, but our hospitality and our way of life." What followed was a fifty-five–page distillation of the "American way of life," covering topics such as military customs, standard of living, diet, etiquette, and "the American Character" marked by freedoms of the press and religion, and by the "enterprising individual." The guidebook worked to preempt the visitors from forming their own negative understanding of U.S. "social problems." It explained that "prejudice against minority groups is a problem in the United States just as it may be in your own country. Although you have probably read or heard of incidents of discrimination against Negroes in certain sections of the United States, bear in mind that discrimination is not confined to Negro Americans. Wherever a minority racial, cultural, or religious group exists, it may be the object of discriminatory practice." The guidebook suggested "prejudice" was a universal phenomenon owing to "group" differences rather than an inherent defect of American society.[96]

The DOD guidebook's sanitized narrative of American life further translated into concrete experience for the trainees through social programs. The Command and General Staff College at Fort Leavenworth, for example, started an Allied Officer Sponsor Program in 1959 to "promote [the] cultural and social integration of Allied students" by pairing them with an American officer who would "act as personal friends" and guide them through their time at the college.[97] A "Hospitality Program" at the Great Lakes Naval Training Center attempted the same by encouraging local navy families to invite students into their homes "for visiting and informal dining." These programs, no matter their origins, characterized the task at hand as a "unique opportunity" to promote one-on-one relations, "to help acquaint these men with America and Americans [and] plan[t] the seeds of real friendship and understanding."[98] A *New York Times* editor confirmed these positive attributes of the training program by quoting the words of one Korean trainee in his letter to a friend back home: "Until I saw America and talked and associated with Americans I doubted if what I heard about America was true; I know that there can be, and we can have, the same freedom of religion, speech, and press in our own country and in this whole human world."[99]

Efforts to shape the perceptions of the military trainees invariably cracked at the seams. No number of guidebooks or sponsorship programs could keep the trainees from witnessing the blunt realities of the American color line, or from pursuing desires beyond the military lives imagined for them. For example, Pak Chŏngin, a division commander who studied at Fort Benning, recalled seeing "the discrimination against Negroes in the Southern region," which he found "terribly distasteful."[100] Given the value placed on these MDAP trainees as cultural diplomats, the inability of U.S. government and military officials to control their negative perceptions of life in the United States had the potential of backfiring irreparably. Although the historical record does not show these subjects returning to their home countries politicized by their experience abroad, it does reveal how they posed a problem of an entirely different kind, one that officials had not foreseen: their desertion and subversive mobility in the United States.

SEEKING ASYLUM IN THE TRANSNATIONAL
SECURITY STATE

No individual did more to confound the MDAP training program in the 1950s than Hsuan Wei, the subject who opened this chapter and who came to symbolize the unintended and undesirable consequences of U.S. militarization. By orders of the U.S. Navy for military training in September 1952, Wei arrived in the United States, and from 1952 to 1954 he attended a total of three courses at the Marine Corps School in Quantico and the Amphibious Base in Little Creek, Virginia. He completed his training with honors on

June 4, after which he received orders to fly to San Francisco. From there, he would report to the staff headquarters of the Twelfth Naval District and await transportation to Taiwan. On June 8, he proceeded as directed, and was cleared for departure three days later. When his plane departed, however, Hsuan was nowhere on board. An immediate investigation revealed that he had checked out of his hotel with all of his belongings. No foul play was suspected. Instead, naval authorities seemed to know without a question of doubt that Wei had gone AWOL. The investigation and endless confusions that followed were beyond anything that officials could have imagined at that moment.[101]

A national manhunt ensued over the next few weeks, coordinated among Chinese authorities and U.S. Navy and immigration officials. Wei, meanwhile, had sought temporary refuge in Evanston, Illinois, where he enlisted the legal aid of K. C. Wu, the ousted governor of Taiwan Province known for his staunch criticisms of the Chinese Nationalist government. Two months prior, Wei had made contact with Wu, expressing his growing disillusionment with Chiang Kai-shek's regime.[102] On Wu's advice, two weeks after his disappearance, Wei wrote a letter to the Immigration and Naturalization Service (INS) office in Washington, D.C. that revealed his whereabouts. This move was a shrewd political strategy. In the letter, Wei invoked section 243(h) of the Immigration and Nationality (McCarran-Walter) Act of 1952 and the Refugee Relief Act of 1953. He requested political asylum and expressed his wish to stay in the United States for fear of persecution back home. The letter announced his defiance against Chiang's government, at once removing his taint as a deserter by proclaiming himself an asylum seeker.[103]

On July 3 in Skokie, Illinois, U.S. naval authorities apprehended Wei and escorted him back to San Francisco, determined to return him to Taiwan immediately. But his request for asylum posed complications that the navy could not ignore. On July 7, while Wei remained in custody at the Twelfth Naval District, the State Department's Director for Chinese Affairs, Walter P. McConaughy, convened a meeting with other state and navy officials to discuss possible actions toward his deportation. The meeting generated a sea of confusion about whether Wei should be deported through immigration or military channels, and concluded with no agreement. According to the state legal advisers, the navy was not "legally empowered" to remove him from the country, "no matter how politically desirable such action might be." Joseph Chappell, the assistant director of the Visa Office, expressed the willingness of the INS to "look the other way" while the navy deported Wei. He admitted this had been done in past cases involving other attempted desertions by foreign trainees, but the state legal advisers could not verify this claim. They cited their own recollections that such cases "had been handled under regular deportation procedure."[104]

This discussion revealed the fundamental *newness* of the problem Wei's case presented. The uncertainty of whether Wei should be deported by the INS or the navy drove officials in endless circles. Hsuan Wei defied simple dichotomies—he was both a political problem and a military problem, yet there was no remedial means for handling both. The meeting ended with an agreement to consult more MDAP and INS officials.[105] That same day, the Chinese naval attaché drew a more definitive conclusion about Wei's case: "Hsuan's motivation was believed to be selfish rather than political," he stated, and "if he succeeded in his effort to abandon his post of duty and start an easier life in this country, other defections of Chinese military officers in similar circumstances could be anticipated, with serious prejudice to Chinese military discipline and to the Mutual Defense Assistance Program."[106]

Concerns about the possible ripple effects of Wei's "selfish" act were not misguided. In the following years, as Wei battled his way through lengthy court hearings and appeals to remain in the United States—in the process capturing the media spotlight and winning legions of supporters around Chicago where he continued to reside—the State Department confronted a handful more cases involving Chinese military deserters who filed for asylum and whose cases shared many other similarities.[107]

Wei's subversion defied easy categorization; he was neither a "Communist agent" like Yi Sa Min nor a subject who espoused "leftist inclinations" like Misao Kuwaye or Calvin Kim. Quite the contrary, Wei was an avowed "anti-Communist" who wanted nothing more than to see the communists driven out of his homeland. Nonetheless, he threatened the government because his decision to go AWOL and remain in the United States occurred at the precise junction of two overlapping forces: the U.S. militarization of Asia that depended on his labor as a military and cultural asset, and the anticommunist purge that deemed his "foreign" presence in the United States a threat to national security. That he was caught between these imperatives was not a coincidence. Instead, it revealed the contradiction at the heart of the U.S. empire in an age of decolonization: that the impulse to militarize and liberate Asia from communism reproduced and magnified the very problem of subversion it sought to contain.

This contradiction is further embodied in the McCarran-Walter Act, the law at the center of Wei's case that simultaneously empowered his claim to remain in the United States and served as the state's mechanism for his removal. Passed at the height of the U.S. anticommunist crusade, the McCarran-Walter Act rearticulated immigration reform as a cold war imperative, admitting "desirable" immigrant subjects through numerical quotas while administering new restrictions to exclude and expel "undesirable" aliens from U.S. borders. Although the act did not specify any provisions for admitting refugees, section 243(h) of the act stipulated that deportation might be withheld for any alien who faced physical persecution in his country of origin.[108] Reiterated in the Refugee Relief Act of 1953, the U.S. resolve to protect deportable aliens from persecution underscored the liberal anticommunist consensus that reaffirmed the United States's belief in itself as a beacon of democracy. Asian military assets like Hsuan Wei exploited this legal-cultural loophole, reconstituting themselves as "political refugees." In so doing, they not only deprived the Chinese government of "valuable human material ... likely to contribute to the development and the welfare of Formosa," as Francis E. Walter, the coauthor of the 1952 immigration law, put it, but they also subverted the boundary between "foreign" and "domestic" that was becoming increasingly important and difficult to pinpoint during this time.[109]

Wei had become an "illegal alien" at the end of his journey as a militarized subject, and this was not an anomaly. It was entirely logical within the broader U.S. project of policing the boundaries of "free Asia." His transformation from a military asset into an immigration problem revealed the severe restrictions undergirding the terms of Asian inclusion into the U.S. transnational security state. He could be one or the other and nothing else; any deviation demanded swift reprisal and containment. Against these legal subjections, Wei nonetheless and remarkably carved a life for himself beyond what U.S. and Taiwanese officials had envisioned for him. In 1967, after a six-year hiatus from the media spotlight, the *Chicago Tribune* resurrected Hsuan Wei to public attention in response to one reader's curiosity about his fate. A *Tribune* columnist discovered that Wei finally was granted permanent U.S. residence in the early 1960s, and at the time lived in Ithaca, New York, with his wife and son, and taught math at Ithaca College.[110] His long elusion of authorities and ultimate legal victory had once again transformed his status. Now, Wei was a "good immigrant," the kind who reaffirmed the domestic civil rights narrative of national inclusion and redemption.[111]

In the end, the failure of individuals like Hsuan Wei to live up to their promise did little to dislodge the racial logics that made Asians indispensable to the U.S. military in an age of decolonization. Against the anticolonial currents sweeping the decolonizing world, U.S. officials redoubled their claims of supporting postliberation freedom struggles in the name of supporting an Asia for Asians. Throughout Asia and the Pacific ordinary people had an immense role to play in bringing about this new reality, and the military was vital to the process. In 1954, the victory of Vietnamese nationalist forces over the French demanded renewed U.S. involvement in Southeast Asia. The project of securing Asia for Asians in the 1950s, the next chapter shows, unfolded along the expanding circuits of U.S. militarism that connected the Philippines and South Vietnam. Within this space of the decolonizing Pacific, the U.S. state mobilized its former colonial subjects in an endeavor to bring lasting changes to South Vietnamese society and to secure South Vietnam for the "free world."

TWO

———

Colonial Intimacies
and Counterinsurgency

THE PHILIPPINES, SOUTH VIETNAM,
AND THE UNITED STATES

SHORTLY AFTER THE UNITED STATES proclaimed Philippine independence in 1946, the liberating empire confronted a problem that threatened to unravel the legitimacy of its fifty-year-old colonial experiment. The
Huks, an independent guerrilla army that fought alongside American troops
during World War II, started to rally its forces after the war. The Huks galvanized peasants in Central Luzon and stirred rebellion against a peonage
system that government officials and corrupt landlords maintained. While
U.S. state officials hailed the Philippines as its "showcase of democracy" to
Europe and the decolonizing world, the Huk rebellion demonstrated that
the colony had subversive influences emerging in its midst. Secretary of State
Dean Acheson warned, "Victory of the Communist-led and dominated
Huks would place us in a highly embarrassing position vis-à-vis the British,
French and Dutch whom we have been persuading to recognize the realities
and legitimacy of Asiatic nationalism and self-determination."[1]

Much like what took place in Korea after World War II, the radicalization
of the peasantry in the postwar Philippines signaled a collective refusal
among the landless class to return to the colonial order. Efforts to suppress
the Huks by resorting to terror tactics invariably failed, similar to events that
transpired in South Korea under the U.S. occupation. JUSMAG, the U.S.
Military Advisory Group in the Philippines, decided to pursue a different
approach. In December 1950, JUSMAG aided the Philippine government to
launch the Economic Development Corps (EDCOR), a rehabilitation program aimed to incentivize surrender among the Huks that was carried on by
the Philippine Army. EDCOR adopted the popular communist slogan "land
for the landless," and proceeded to give former Huks and retired soldiers
government lands. Between 1950 and 1955, EDCOR continued offering

people "a new chance in life" by constructing four large-scale farm communities, including a vocational rehabilitation center, and relocating an entire barrio to "a more favorable area" beyond communist influence. In this five-year period, the Philippine Army reported that approximately nine thousand Huks out of an estimated rank of twenty-five thousand had surrendered. It seemed that EDCOR provided an effective solution to the subversive threats and potential radicalization in the Philippines.[2]

EDCOR was the brainchild of Edward Lansdale and Charles Bohannan, two American military men who had served in the Philippines during World War II. An advertising executive and an anthropologist-in-training before their military careers, respectively, Lansdale and Bohannan were aware that engineering social relations required appealing to the masses in creative ways. With their expert knowledge, they developed a unique entity through EDCOR and transformed the Philippine Army. "I have seen many armies," one foreign correspondent wrote, "but this one beats them all. This is an army with a social conscience."[3] The program marked the first attempt by the Philippine Army to conduct "civic activities," demonstrable actions that conveyed the meaning of democracy in ways that print propaganda did not. There was more to EDCOR's success, however. Lansdale later explained it succeeded because despite being a "U.S. plan, the Filipinos were led into thinking of it and developing it for themselves." EDCOR was a "foreign idea [that] became thoroughly nationalized—an important step" toward winning the support of the people.[4]

What Lansdale and Bohannan developed was a new approach to war and military conduct for the age of decolonization. In the early 1950s, military officials believed EDCOR was an exportable concept for countering guerrilla insurgencies. British officials flocked to Central Luzon to observe the EDCOR communities and drew up comparative lessons for their experiments of controlling the people in Malaya.[5] When events in Vietnam demanded heightened U.S. involvement in 1954, Lansdale and Bohannan saw the opportunity. They were among the first Americans on scene. The pair brought the tactics and agents of their counterinsurgency experiment in the Philippines to Vietnam.

Scholars have drawn the connections between U.S. counterinsurgency in the Philippines and Vietnam, but we still know little about what this transference of military knowledge and practices entailed.[6] The focus on Lansdale as a central figure obscures the role of lesser-known actors who played a key role. In 1954, months after the Geneva Accords divided Vietnam at the seventeenth parallel, Filipino doctors and nurses arrived in Saigon to begin their humanitarian mission of bringing medical relief to the hundreds of thousands of refugees migrating from the communist north to the south after the national partition. Later that year, retired Filipino army officers, many who had taken part in EDCOR, arrived to provide social services to Vietnamese veterans, and to teach the "lessons" of the Huk campaign to Vietnamese Army soldiers. These groups went by innocuous names, suggesting no American affiliation: the doctors and nurses were called Operation Brotherhood, and the veterans were called the Freedom Company of the Philippines. To the Vietnamese, these Filipinos were friends as opposed to colonizers; their acts were related to humanitarianism and nation building as opposed to war.

This chapter examines how these groups of Filipinos came to arrive in South Vietnam as well as the work that they accomplished on behalf of the U.S. and Philippine governments. It begins with the premise that the U.S. war in Vietnam emerged out of complex intercolonial dynamics in Southeast Asia after 1945, and that U.S. militarism in Vietnam was as much about waging the cold war in the former French colony as it was an ongoing part of the decades-long U.S. colonial project in the Philippines. As French control in the region waned and the United States stepped in to assume the French role, U.S. officials made their support of "Asia for Asians" loud and clear, challenged by the surge of anticolonial nationalisms in the Third World. Philippine state leaders, determined to shape regional geopolitics, lent support to the United States and performed their part as America's "show window of democracy." It was exactly this interplay between empire and decolonization that created the pathways for Filipinos' arrival in Vietnam in 1954. As "brothers," "neighbors," and "fellow Asians," these Filipinos, U.S. and Philippine officials hoped, would mobilize the lessons of American democracy and impart them to the Vietnamese.

Similar to the Chinese and Korean soldiers who traversed the Pacific for military training during this same period, these Filipino doctors, nurses, and veterans traveled on routes shaped by overlapping colonial histories and the imperatives of the U.S. military. They emerged as agents of U.S. psychological warfare, tasked to gain the trust of the population by performing different kinds of intimacies, such as caring for the body and other convivial encounters. While psychological warfare went by a host of other terms in this period—special operations, covert action, civic action—it reflected the growing collaboration between the military and the Central Intelligence

Agency (CIA) as they intervened in the processes of decolonization, by employing creative and deadly methods to suppress anticolonial movements and to redirect emergent state nationalisms toward the aims of the capitalist "free world." CIA operatives under military cover in Vietnam experimented with different tactics to befriend and win the trust of the Vietnamese. The CIA operatives thought the "Asiatic-to-Asiatic" approach of Operation Brotherhood and Freedom Company was a winning formula.

By mobilizing Filipinos to win the affection and loyalty of the Vietnamese, the CIA reanimated U.S. colonialism in the Philippines for the purpose of demarcating the boundaries of "free Asia." Adherents of such unconventional practices and doctrines insisted repeatedly that counterinsurgency signaled a new kind of war from the colonial wars of the past, one predicated on forging relations of intimacy between soldier and civilian, in which "the soldier [was] a brother of the people, as well as their protector," and in which racism no longer functioned to justify the tactics of colonial violence. The use of Filipinos in Vietnam reinforced and belied these claims simultaneously.

Most scholarly accounts of U.S.-Philippine colonial politics end in 1946, but the incorporation of Filipinos into the U.S. empire and their racialization as U.S. colonial subjects continued well past this point. These processes continued to unfold through the humanitarian and militarized labor of Filipinos across the South China Sea. In South Vietnam, at the interstices of multiple and competing visions of postcolonial nation building, the Filipinos made their mark on the Vietnamese people through psychological warfare. Their presence and impact at once concealed the violence of U.S. empire and made America's "Asia for Asians" seem possible.

COLONIAL INTIMACIES BETWEEN GENEVA AND BANDUNG

The French mistakenly thought it would be easy to crush the League for the Independence of Vietnam, or Viet Minh, led by Ho Chi Minh, but they had underestimated the strength and determination of their colonized subjects. In the spring of 1954, the Viet Minh dealt a stunning blow to French forces in the siege of Dien Bien Phu. The battle marked the end of the war, and news of the French defeat traveled quickly across the globe, soon inspiring revolutionaries in Algiers to call forth their own revolt against the French. The black American activist Paul Robeson, fighting white supremacy from the seat of U.S. empire, was moved to pen an essay hailing Ho Chi Minh as the "Toussaint L'Overture of Indochina." The Viet Minh's victory signified the beginning of the end of empire. However, the revolutionary meaning of the Viet Minh's victory evaporated rapidly.[7]

In the hopes of gaining advantage during negotiations, the Viet Minh had timed their victory perfectly to coincide with the Geneva Conference. The very day of victory, state leaders of the five major world powers (the Soviet Union, the People's Republic of China, the United States, France, and Great Britain) gathered at Geneva, prepared to settle the terms of the Indochina War. The Euro-American allies were most concerned with how French colonialism's end would redistribute global relations of power, instead of determining what an independent Vietnam should look like. In the end, the participants agreed to partition Vietnam at the seventeenth parallel, regrouping French forces to the south and the Viet Minh to the north, and to ban further military buildup and military alliances on both sides. The accords stipulated the reunification of the country by general elections in 1956. All world powers signed the agreement except the United States, because U.S. plans to subvert the Geneva Accords and to maneuver greater influence in Vietnam were already under way.[8]

During the Geneva Conference and even long before, U.S. leaders worried about the political implications of their ongoing association with France over Indochinese matters. In a policy statement, one State Department official, Charlton Ogburn, warned plainly that supporting the French was no longer tenable. He believed that backing France militarily would ensure "the loss of all Vietnam and all of Indochina" to the communists, and "cause a serious decline of American prestige in the Far East, widespread resentment and despair among the Asians over our short-sighted and bitter-end support of the French." Ogburn advised that the United States should seek a "common approach" with other Asian nations, which would pay dividends: "We [would] have put ourselves in the best possible light in non-Communist Asia, have given the Asians valuable experience in bearing responsibility and have prepared the basis for effective cooperation between the free Asian countries and ourselves in preventing the further expansion of Communism." Simply put: a stand for Asian unity was a stand against communism and colonialism.[9]

In an attempt to distance the United States from the French and from Euro-imperialism generally, U.S. officials found support in the Philippines to attest to America's exceptionalism. As early as 1946, Philippine Resident

Commissioner Carlos P. Romulo had hailed the U.S. independence legislation for the Philippines as "the beginning of the end for imperialism," saying that it "encouraged the dream of ultimate freedom among colonial peoples." Romulo embraced his part as a postcolonial middling elite, glowing about American democracy just as often as he presumed to interpret the desires of the "Asian masses" for U.S. leaders. In 1950, as the Truman Administration began to aid the French in the Indochina War, Romulo told Secretary of State Acheson, "In the eyes of the great mass of the people of Indochina and Asia, the French army . . . is a hostile army, an enemy of Viet Nam independence." The U.S. decision to support France in turn had resulted in "the virtual isolation of American policy from the sentiment of Asian countries." He made it clear that the challenge for the United States was to unburden itself "of the suspicion of pro-imperialism." He said, "I personally am convinced that this suspicion is unjustified, but how could it be otherwise in the untutored minds of Asia's discontented masses?"[10]

Shortly after the Geneva Conference, the U.S. pursuit of forging a collective "Asian front" to signal its commitment to anti-imperialism and anticommunism materialized at the founding meeting of the Southeast Asia Treaty Organization (SEATO) in Manila, which occurred from September 5 to 8, 1954. Representatives from the Philippines, Thailand, Pakistan, France, Britain, New Zealand, Australia, and the United States gathered at the Manila Conference to proclaim their anticommunist solidarity and collective resolve to safeguard Southeast Asia. They were keen on protecting Vietnam and its bordering states of Laos and Cambodia against the encroachments of Communist China and the Soviet Union. The conference resulted in the Manila Pact and articulated a broad, multinational responsibility to defend the region. Secretary of State John Foster Dulles emphasized that the Pact "is not directed against any people or any government," but "is directed against an evil, the evil of aggression." Lest the peoples of Southeast Asia suspect that the Manila Pact was a blueprint for some kind of neocolonial form of regional governance, the conference concluded with the signing of the Pacific Charter, which proclaimed the rights of peoples to self-determination, self-government, and independence.[11]

In contrast to the Geneva Accords, the Manila Pact provided justification for U.S. military intervention in Indochina in the name of countering communism. The Manila Pact also accomplished much more. Although the conference included delegates of "white" colonial powers with longstanding interests in the region, its ideological force derived from the idea that Asians were determining their political destiny in a democratic and postcolonial setting. The core of the agreement embodied an Asian regionalism that reflected the U.S. commitment to anticolonial self-determination.

The conference also signaled an emerging role in regional affairs for Philippine leaders. The Philippine Vice President and Secretary of Foreign Affairs Carlos P. Garcia affirmed that the formation of SEATO signified "the first big step" in facilitating closer ties between the Philippines and its neighboring countries, which previously had been foreclosed by "centuries of colonialism."[12] According to Garcia, "The measure of usefulness of the Asian participants to this conference will depend largely on the measure that we may win the confidence, the faith and the friendship of our neighbors and brothers of Southeast Asia."[13] The language of "friendship" and kinship that infused the conference proceedings solidified an imagined geography of "Southeast Asia," one that subsumed ethnic, linguistic, religious, and other forms of difference to project the image of a united region.[14] Philippine state leaders mobilized the language of kinship increasingly in the weeks and months after the Geneva Conference, particularly as they sought to formalize diplomatic relations with Vietnam.

The Junior Chamber of Commerce played an important part in this story. A civic organization founded during the U.S. Progressive Era, the Junior Chamber, or Jaycees, had transformed into a worldwide phenomenon with chapters in over fifty countries by the 1950s, represented by the international body Junior Chamber International (JCI). Organized around the tenets of "free enterprise" and "humanitarianism" that "transcends the sovereignty of nations," JCI served as a quintessential organization to facilitate what one scholar called a "global imaginary of integration."[15] As the Philippine Congress engaged in unresolved debates over the question of extending diplomatic recognition to Vietnam, JCI was already mobilizing the Philippine public to action. In July 1954, the Manila chapter of the Jaycees voted to extend its support by providing medical aid and volunteers to help Vietnamese refugees who were migrating south of the seventeenth parallel. The Geneva Accords and its mandate of a three-hundred-day period of unrestricted travel across the two zones had resulted in a massive movement of refugees. Nearly nine hundred thousand people, mostly Catholic civilians from the northern region of Tonkin, took advantage of the opportunity to escape the Viet Minh and to seek better life chances in the south. In the summer of 1954, the Jaycees brought the first group of Filipino friends to South Vietnam to care for these refugees.

A year later, at the University of the Philippines convocation in July 1955, Undersecretary of Foreign Affairs Raul Manglapus reaffirmed the stakes of recognizing the sovereignty of South Vietnam, and evoked the Filipinos already there. First, he alluded to the specter of communism: "Our policy of strengthening our freedom impels us to do all we can to strengthen freedom around us. . . . [I]t is our duty, *independent of altruistic considerations,* to seek the strengthening of free states around us for our own sake." Then he underscored that defending the Philippines from communist aggression demanded vigilance in the region, and emphasized that Vietnam and the Philippines shared a unique, natural bond. He continued, "The Philippines is not just any other State from the point of view of South Vietnam" but the "nearest overseas neighbors," and stated that the Vietnamese "have learned to look to us for guidance in their efforts at liberty." To substantiate this point, Manglapus recalled the "volunteer Filipinos" who, at that very moment, "are showing the Vietnamese the capacity of Asians for self-reliance." These Filipinos told a self-evident story: "We are not just any other country to the Vietnamese. We are a country of fellow Asians, friends, helpers and inspirers."[16]

On July 15, 1955, President Ramon Magsaysay formally extended diplomatic recognition to South Vietnam. While metaphors of racial and colonial intimacy had worked decidedly in favor of it, they also fueled the opposition. One week after, Senator Claro M. Recto assailed his colleagues on the Senate floor. Vietnam, Recto argued, did not have the "attributes of sovereignty" because it was "ruled by France and [the] United States." The Philippine commitment to SEATO, which the senator had opposed from the beginning, did not include obligations to extend diplomatic relations, contrary to the claim of Manglapus and others. With no justifiable basis, the Philippine recognition of South Vietnam amounted to nothing short of "interference" in the country's "internal affairs."[17] In voicing his opposition, Recto laid bare the colonial dynamics at the heart of the so-called "friendship" between the two countries.

Recto articulated a different kind of colonial intimacy, based not on anticommunist alliances and capitalist integration but on an emergent anticolonialism that was fanning across the region. He was inspired by the Afro-Asian Conference that had concluded recently in Bandung, Indonesia, where the leaders of twenty-nine newly independent nations in Asia and Africa met to proclaim their anticolonial solidarities and refusal to compromise their independence by submitting to the bipolar world order. This anticolonial spirit suffused his speech. He further lambasted the newly appointed

South Vietnamese Prime Minister Ngo Dinh Diem as "a puppet of Colonel Lansdale," doing the bidding of the United States. Recto declared, "Diem, although anti-French, is helping [to] implant in South Vietnam another form of Western colonialism." This form of colonialism might be "more profitable for the colonials . . . because of prospects of better standards of living, civil liberties and political rights, but for that very same reason more dangerous." He didn't believe the term "democracy" should fool anyone. He clarified, "Diem made his choice not between nationalism and colonialism but between two forms of colonialism." A few days before Recto spoke these words, Diem had announced South Vietnam would not participate in the 1956 election to unify Vietnam, a move that Recto feared would embroil Southeast Asia in future war. "Must our boys die on foreign soil and must our cities and countrysides by [sic] laid waste again, just because it occurred to Diem and his American backers to boycott the 1956 plebiscite?"[18] His words of caution proved prescient in time. But at the moment, he made his point clear: the recognition of South Vietnam had made the Philippines complicit in another U.S. colonial project in Asia.

In this sense, diplomatic recognition was little more than a formality, for all was already set. The Manila Pact had outlined the regional framework for U.S. circumvention of the Geneva Accords, and the Philippines was already implicated in any future U.S. military intervention in South Vietnam. The formalization of diplomatic relations between the Philippines and South Vietnam only further entrenched this complicity. Amidst these events, the tensions captured by Recto's trenchant remarks lingered unresolved. To the senator and other dissidents in his party, the events surrounding Indochina in 1954–55 were momentous not for what they purported to represent, but for what they concealed: that colonialism was being carried out in the name of democracy, and this meant dire consequences for the Philippines and its citizens.

THE DEPLOYMENT OF CARE

On October 14, 1954, three months after the Geneva Accords, Operation Brotherhood dispatched its first medical mission to Saigon. Headed by Antonio E. R. Velasco, a doctor and the Jaycee president of Southern Mindanao, the team of seven doctors and three nurses arrived to a spectacular welcome at Tan Sun Nhut Air Base. They arrived by way of Air America, a CIA-owned and -funded civilian airline that flew covert military missions throughout Southeast Asia in the 1950s; however, the U.S. orchestration of the entire affair was hidden at the moment. To the Vietnamese government officials and Jaycees who greeted them on the tarmac, they were "volunteer" medics and unofficial representatives of the Philippine government, contracted for three months to help relieve the emergency of the refugee influx.

Under different circumstances, the presence of Filipino workers in another country would have been unremarkable. Since the early twentieth century, Filipinos had engaged in cultures of transnational mobility, an effect and legacy of U.S. colonialism. In the first decade of the U.S. colonial period, the pensionado and nursing programs were established and brought Filipina/o students and nurses to the United States, opening new avenues for individual advancement and reproducing the gendered division of labor that were at the heart of the U.S. "civilizing" mission in the Philippines. Beginning in 1903, the U.S. Navy also recruited Filipinos, primarily as stewards and messboys. These patterns of labor migration intensified in the years after Philippine independence, as Filipina/os increasingly found work overseas and came to see themselves as participants in the export-driven economy of the postcolonial state. The doctors and nurses who traveled to Vietnam in 1954 were an integral part of this longstanding colonial diaspora.[19] Instead of going to the imperial metropole, they found opportunities closer to home, in a country where the United States was working to secure a new nation.

Lansdale, the U.S. intelligence officer who had spent the better part of a decade fomenting counterrevolution in the Philippines, was responsible for bringing the Filipinos to South Vietnam. Lansdale shunned conventional military tactics and opted to become close to the people and earn their trust. During the initial phase of EDCOR, Lansdale first met JCI Director Oscar Arellano who offered the services of his Manila Jaycees to collect basic medical supplies for Philippine Army soldiers to bring to the barrios. Lansdale believed the humanitarian work of the Jaycees could help soften the image of the army, which was a vital component to his EDCOR scheme. His psywar work in the Philippines, most notably his political manipulations that steered Secretary of National Defense Ramon Magsaysay into the presidency in 1953, impressed Secretary of State Dulles and his brother Allen Dulles, the CIA director. Operation Brotherhood was a distant outcome of those experiences. In January 1954, John Dulles instructed Lansdale to go to Vietnam "to do what you did in the Philippines." When Lansdale arrived in Saigon in June, Arellano was meeting with Vietnamese Jaycees to discuss ways to help with the refugee crisis. When Lansdale saw his old friend in Saigon, he thought it was "a touch of Philippine sunshine . . . [to the] gloomy Vietnamese scene."[20]

Lansdale's covert meddling in Manila and Saigon are legendary, and accrue greater lore with each recounting, specifically in novels, his memoir, antiwar exposés, and other secondary interpretations.[21] Indeed, Lansdale was a central figure, but not in the way that he described himself and that historians have then affirmed. According to these accounts, Lansdale invented the doctrines and tactics of U.S. counterinsurgency in the Philippines, and then he brought them to Vietnam. In Vietnam and the Philippines, he befriended leaders, won their affection, and convinced them to adopt his methods in order to secure their governments. These accounts gloss over the vast disagreements among U.S. officials at the time, and they obscure the role of the Vietnamese in their pursuits of nation building, which often countered U.S. objectives.[22] Focusing solely on Lansdale overlooks other nonstate actors who contributed to nation building in Vietnam. They had transnational itineraries facilitated by Lansdale, but their trajectories far exceeded his doing.

Illuminating other influential figures does more than fill a gap in the historical record; it helps broaden historical understandings of counterinsurgency within colonial history. American military advisers in the Philippines and Vietnam continually disavowed these colonial linkages. They focused on extracting "lessons learned" and applying them to different contexts. For example, in 1953, Bohannan, the American adviser to the Philippine Constabulary and Lansdale's partner in the field, reprinted the Philippine Constabulary Manual of 1915 for present-day use, after taking "fifteen years to find the only known copy in existence." Bohannan described the manual as "one of the basic works in the field of counter-insurgency, being a codification of the experiences and practices of one of the finest counter-insurgency forces ever developed." With the replacement of some antiquated wording, he believed it "applicable to virtually any organization operating in a tropical or subtropical theatre with indigenous personnel," including the Philippine Constabulary fighting the Huks. Bohannan's painstaking effort to make connections between the Constabulary of the colonial era and the present day materialized in a rulebook of codes and conduct. This artifact proved so valuable that in 1963 he produced a revised version for the U.S. Agency for International Development (USAID) in Vietnam.[23] Even as U.S. colonial violence in the Philippines provided the foundation for the development of U.S. counterinsurgency doctrine in the 1950s and 1960s, those historical connections were reduced to a set of ascribable codes that erased the specificity of the Philippine and Vietnamese colonial contexts both past and present.

The presence of Filipino doctors and nurses in Vietnam signaled more than just an export of counterinsurgency, but the reworking of colonial dynamics on the ground. The specific context that demanded their labor was the refugee emergency after the Geneva agreements. Diem saw great propaganda value in the high number of refugees, and enlisted his American backers to assist with the evacuation and resettlement.[24] In July 1954, the U.S. Operations Mission (USOM) unveiled a four-point community-development program, geared toward instilling economic self-sufficiency and governmental support among the refugees. The USOM report emphasized that people should "be made to feel they belong, that they have a 'stake' in the present and future" of their country. What the mission proposed was a bottom-up approach to nation building, in which the cultivation of healthy bodies, individual productivity, and happiness were vital to the ultimate goal of securing a "strong economy" in Vietnam.[25] Operation Brotherhood went in with medical aid to make these bodies work.

Early on the morning of October 15, less than a full day after they landed in Saigon, the Filipinos were shuttled to Bien Hoa Province, where approximately 52,000 refugees awaited resettlement. According to Antonio Velasco, about half of the population required some form of medical treatment, and "thirty percent needed immediate medical attention." He compared the scene to a concentration camp and observed that the "sanitation facilities were the worst" he had seen.[26] Within the first hour of his arrival, Velasco tended to his first patient and confronted the language barrier. He proceeded to diagnose ailments through "sign language." According to an Operation Brotherhood statement, medicine was a "universal sign language," one that transcended linguistic, religious, and national differences to alleviate the "common ties of suffering" that bound "all Asians for centuries."[27] One Filipino journalist who observed Operation Brotherhood at work wrote, "The unselfish efforts of Filipino doctors and nurses have pushed to new heights respect for and faith in the *Phil-Luat-Tan* ["Filipino"]."[28] The first Operation Brotherhood mission seemed to be paying off.

Operation Brotherhood's success encouraged American nation builders in Saigon. As William McKeldin, the Far East Regional Inspector for USOM, stated, "The common knowledge by the people of Vietnam that the Free World (i.e. the Filipinos) is willing to assist the common people will do more to inspire them to help themselves than any propaganda campaign conducted

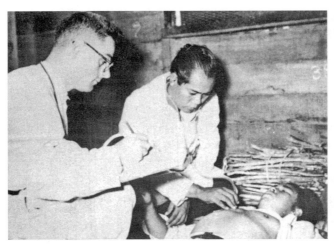

FIGURE 3. Dr. Antonio Velasco of Operation Brotherhood tending to a patient in Bien Hoa, October 1954. (From Miguel A. Bernad, *Adventures in Viet-Nam* [Operation Brotherhood International, 1971].)

by agencies can accomplish." With an eye toward the coming election to unify the country, USOM decided to make Operation Brotherhood a permanent part of its pacification program. In January 1955, at the end of Operation Brotherhood's three-month contract, USOM coordinated plans to bring thirty new medical teams from the Philippines—each consisting of two doctors, one nurse, and one social worker—to the central provinces of Vietnam, where "they could move from village to village as rapidly as possible." Arellano already had done his part by conducting a recruitment drive in Manila to secure new graduates who were "outstanding in their profession in the Philippines." Lastly, they needed financial support from the Foreign Operations Administration (FOA), the U.S. foreign economic-aid program and predecessor of USAID. They needed exactly $300,000 in pesos and piastres to cover the costs of allowances for family dependents, transportation, and medical supplies for six months. "If the program is to operate successfully," McKeldin reminded the FOA assistant director, "the assistance given should not appear to come from FOA but should appear as that coming from the other nations of the Far East." For obvious reasons, any associations with the United States would damage Operation Brotherhood's reputation as a "sincere" volunteer effort.[29]

After FOA approved funding, the continuation of Operation Brotherhood moved quickly. By February 1955, the first new medical team was set to travel to Ca Mau, the southernmost province of Vietnam and a Viet Minh strong-hold. Unlike the project in Bien Hoa, the one in Ca Mau was no ordinary relief mission because the Filipinos were deployed as part of a military opera-tion of the Vietnamese Army. Over the past several months, the Vietnamese Army had undergone accelerated training in civic action, a concept intro-duced by Lansdale and his contacts in the Philippines. In October 1954, Lansdale sent a small group of Vietnamese Army officers to the Philippines to observe the Philippine Army's civic-action tactics against the Huks; he also brought Major Jose M. A. Guerrero, a seasoned army officer of the Huk campaign, to Vietnam to lead a training program in psychological warfare.[30] Coming just months after the Geneva Accords, these circuits of military training between South Vietnam and the Philippines exposed how the United States circumvented the international ban on remilitarization. They also marked the transnational beginnings of a military civic-action program in Vietnam, one that would enable the doctors and nurses of Operation Brotherhood to carry on their work.

The Geneva Accords mandated one clear goal: to evacuate the Viet Minh and to establish the South Vietnamese government's authority. Dubbed "Operation Liberty," the operation at Ca Mau proceeded with this mandate. In the first week of February 1955, Operation Liberty commenced when leaf-lets that explained "the peaceful mission of the Army" were dropped from the sky in the villages. On February 7, ten doctors and nurses of Operation Brotherhood arrived in Ca Mau, and on February 8, the Vietnamese Army entered the villages and proceeded to win the people's trust and confidence. The soldiers greeted civilians warmly, shared cigarettes, and talked openly about "the aims of the Free Vietnamese Government." Stopping by each hut, they offered to swap out old posters of Ho Chi Minh for new colorful ones of Diem. They staged folk-song concerts and nationalist dramas; they drew crowds with films and audio recordings of Diem's speeches. The U.S. Information Service had produced the films and recordings, but to preempt the villagers' perception that all this was "a foreign-sponsored enterprise," the Vietnamese Army limited the American presence to one officer. Rufus Phillips was the lone CIA operative present, dressed in civilian clothes with a handgun concealed on his back. He presented himself as a member of the foreign press, but in actuality he observed and ensured the safety of the Filipino medics.[31]

A few of them had landed in Saigon only a few hours before. When the doctors and nurses arrived, they realized resources in Ca Mau were limited and began to improvise. They turned packing crates on the side of the road into their dispensary, and converted an abandoned building into a makeshift hospital, by placing hand-painted signs in front that read, "Doctor" and "Free Medical Clinic, All Are Welcome," in Vietnamese. According to Phillips, "mainly mothers with sick children" started lining up "wordlessly," and soon more and more people "with every conceivable affliction" visited the hospital. By the third day, the hospital operated around the clock and treated more than three hundred patients in one day.[32] As the demand increased, the Filipinos began training Vietnamese nurses to help, and some drove jeeps to nearby villages and distributed soap and mosquito netting and taught about malaria control and nutrition. They seemed to have won the Vietnamese's affection even off-duty. Lansdale recorded later that they "made up their own songs, held parties in off-duty hours, and were a real tonic to the dispirited." He also added that the "presence of pretty Filipino girl doctors" alone was enough to encourage "many a male Vietnamese" to start "learning English so he could talk to them."[33]

Americans believed the pacification of Ca Mau proceeded splendidly because of Operation Brotherhood's work. Reports enthusiastically praised Filipinos and their "unique" ability to make rapport with the Vietnamese. USOM's Public Health deputy chief remarked, "The Asiatic-to-Asiatic approach seemed successful and popular," and noted that the Filipinos were "very effective and well received by the populace."[34] Lansdale played a key role in affirming the success of a program he considered his own. In a memo for the Pentagon in 1958, he wrote that in Ca Mau, "the esprit de corps of the Filipino volunteers was a major factor in overcoming Communist political work." He added, "These were Free Asians, who cheerfully and energetically helped their fellow men."[35] In his reports, Lansdale included details of intimate sociality such as the songs, festivities, and conversations, because friendship, kinship, and even lust were techniques for winning trust. These intimacies between Asians demonstrated counterinsurgency at work. In a letter, USOM Regional Director McKeldin revealed that nurses and doctors' winning trust was more valuable than their direct medical aid, and that counterinsurgency was what Americans valued most.[36]

Personal anecdotes from the Operation Brotherhood medics appeared to confirm the counterinsurgency imperative. Josefina Pablo, a twenty-five-year-old nurse who went to Dac Nong Province in early 1955, recalled her experiences fondly: "They trusted us and accepted us very well," which made it possible for her to teach the villagers about public health and sanitation. Her language indicated the extent to which the discourse of trust framed her understanding of her actions, but it also revealed her deeper motivations. She was a fresh graduate from the U.S. colonial institution St. Luke's Hospital School of Nursing that instilled the desire to help and uplift others. Josefina Pablo felt drawn to Vietnam through a mixed sense of idealism and adventure. She wanted to "travel and see other countries." She considered teaching to be her most lasting and crucial accomplishment, as opposed to any notion of saving South Vietnam from communism. Her dreams and sense of purpose, inspired by broader forces of nation and empire building, were channeled into the work of counterinsurgency.[37]

American imaginings and manipulation of a racial affinity between Filipinos and the Vietnamese were less convincing to Vietnamese officials who sought to build a nation on their terms. Vietnamese resistance characterized the challenges of Operation Brotherhood from the beginning. The commander of Operation Liberty, Lt. Col. Hoang Van Duc, was adamant against sending Filipinos and Americans to Ca Mau. He felt determined to show villagers of the Diem government acting without "foreigners." By Phillips's account, Colonel Duc acquiesced only after Lansdale explained the dire medical needs of the villagers and then sat "the prettiest and most vivacious of the Filipino nurses" next to Colonel Duc during a lunch meeting.[38] Soon more serious complaints emerged. In November 1956, Commissioner General for Refugees Bui Van Long "complained bitterly" about the "professional behavior of OB team members" and their refusal to accept orders from Vietnamese Ministry of Health officials. One notable mishap involved Filipinos' "stopp[ing] public buses on the road and request[ing] the passengers to accept cholera shots" without clearance from Vietnamese officials.[39]

Complaints about Operation Brotherhood were symptomatic of a deeper discord between Vietnamese and American officials in their pursuits of nation building in South Vietnam. Americans saw Vietnam as a vital part of an overall scheme to revitalize Japan's economy to facilitate the spread of U.S. capitalism. The U.S. capitalist empire required the transformation of Vietnamese society from the ground up, to impact "the very way of living of the people."[40] In the eyes of American nation builders, Operation Brotherhood created this transformation and fulfilled their manifold desires of a "free" Asia for Asians. To Vietnamese officials, the acceptance of U.S. aid was never meant as an acquiescence to U.S. liberal democracy. Rather, Operation Brotherhood was nothing more than temporary assistance granted to the Vietnamese government to alleviate the refugee crisis. In 1956, as the U.S.

Mission and Diem pursued increasingly divergent and butting paths toward an anticommunist South Vietnam, Vietnamese complaints amplified.[41]

The spectrum of public opinion in South Vietnam revealed an entirely different perception of Operation Brotherhood's effectiveness and intents. Complaints from Ministry of Health officials continued and at one point referred to the Filipino medics as the "lowest quality personnel" who have "caused unnecessary deaths" of Vietnamese. Other nonstate Vietnamese representatives charged Operation Brotherhood with political motives. In early 1956, for instance, Vietnamese students conveyed to some Filipino student visitors that the program existed "to establish Vietnam as a capitalist South East Asia stronghold," and that the Filipinos' presence "replace[d] French control with the United States."[42] Their comments reflected the anticolonial sentiments circulating within the decolonizing world and exposed American imperial designs. USOM officials, however, quickly cast aside these comments as nothing more than "a communist influence . . . operating to the detriment of [Operation Brotherhood] in Vietnam."[43]

Yet American officials and Operation Brotherhood personnel described the program as nothing short of a success. After the inaugural campaign in Ca Mau, Operation Brotherhood expanded considerably. From February to June, 51 Operation Brotherhood personnel were added to the roster, 170,468 medical cases were treated in 5 provinces, and by the end of June, the number of Filipino personnel doubled.[44] In August 1955, USOM Director Leland Barrows believed so much in Operation Brotherhood's success that he directly funded the South Vietnamese government to "intensify and expand" the program.[45] Beginning the following year, Operation Brotherhood appeared to have shaken away "the skepticism of the people" and taught them "that they [were] capable of improving their own lot through their own efforts" by providing them with medical services and public-health education. Apparently, these accomplishments of Operation Brotherhood had a powerful and lasting impact. According to the U.S. Mission, Operation Brotherhood had "reach[ed] up to make [the] community economy stable, raise[d] the standard of living of the people and, above all, ma[d]e communities . . . economically productive."[46] Such a glowing assessment reflected not so much the reality as it unfolded, but an idealization of what Americans hoped to create.

In December 1956, Operation Brotherhood ended in Vietnam. In contrast to the jubilation that marked their arrival two years prior, the last Operation Brotherhood team members departed without ceremony. For Diem and his government, Operation Brotherhood had been a costly experiment, a bureaucratic hurdle, and its publicity left South Vietnamese officials open to charges of enabling foreign intrusion. For Americans and their government, Operation Brotherhood was a blueprint for successful counterinsurgency. In the 1960s, during the height of the U.S. war in Vietnam, American officials alluded to its achievements repeatedly. In the meantime, U.S. officials wasted no time putting it to work in a different place. In January 1957, Operation Brotherhood medics arrived in Vientiane, Laos, to execute the program in the neighboring country. As this was under way, a different group of Filipinos was already present in Saigon, acting as the new go-betweens for the U.S. empire.

PARAMILITARY ENTANGLEMENTS

In 1946, a group of Filipino World War II veterans formed the Philippine Veterans Legion (PVL) and emerged as one of the first humanitarian organizations in the post-independence Philippines. The emergency at the end of the Indochina War in 1954 drew the veterans' attention to South Vietnam, and PVL members collected donations and medicine. On December 6, 1954, PVL's national commander, Col. Frisco San Juan, departed Manila for Saigon to help Operation Brotherhood distribute the collected donations.[47] However, his task was more complicated than simply distributing supplies on behalf of the PVL, because he was also acting as a member of the Freedom Company.

The Freedom Company was formed in November 1954 with the help of Lansdale and Bohannan. Although far less known about than the PVL, the Freedom Company was similar because it was made up of former guerrilla fighters and retired soldiers of the Philippine Army, Philippine Scouts, and the U.S. Armed Forces of the Far East (USAFFE). During the Japanese occupation of the Philippines, many of the veterans had fought alongside Bohannan, so he knew intimately of their skills in guerrilla warfare and trusted their politics. In the early 1950s during the Huk campaign, Bohannan was called to advise the Philippine Constabulary, and he enlisted the veterans' help in developing the Constabulary's training program. By 1954, the U.S. intervention in South Vietnam inspired the Freedom Company to package and market their services and make them available to the CIA. The beginning of Freedom Company's involvement in South Vietnam was marked by

San Juan's humanitarian tour in Saigon. This beginning activated a circuit of militarization that connected the two countries into the next decade.

The Freedom Company was a paramilitary organization that functioned through the CIA, and that emerged at the juncture of decolonization and U.S. militarization in Southeast Asia. In the archival records, fragments of the Freedom Company's existence remain scattered, demonstrating its covert nature and deliberate concealment.[48] The fragments also reveal the complicated origins of the Vietnam War. In its articles of incorporation, the company asserted its purpose "to promote, assist, train, and employ Filipino citizens and citizens of legitimate freedom-loving countries in the techniques of preserving their freedom."[49] Its mission statement phrased it slightly differently: to turn Filipinos and the Philippines from "Asia's Show-Window of Democracy" to a "down-to-earth, workaday exponent of Asiatic freedom."[50] Activated in 1954, the Freedom Company specifically enabled the U.S. government to circumvent the Geneva Accords's prohibition of remilitarization in Vietnam, revealing how veterans mobilized colonial legacies to action.

San Juan's first task with the Freedom Company in December 1954 was to survey the condition of Vietnamese veterans who were demobilized after the Franco–Viet Minh war. Upon completion of Operation Brotherhood's tasks, he traveled to nearby provinces to visit the veterans and relayed discouraging signs. In January, he cabled the secretary general of the World Veterans Federation that "[o]ver a hundred thousand vets" were "being discharged [with] no govt or private planning [for] their welfare."[51] He feared they would fall prey to communist recruitment and join the dissident forces unless the Diem government initiated plans toward their rehabilitation and reintegration into society. Instead of waiting for Diem to take action, San Juan and other Freedom Company members drew up plans to establish a national veterans organization similar to the Philippines Legion. "These Filipinos are experts at handling just such a situation," Lansdale reassured Gen. J. Lawton Collins, President Dwight D. Eisenhower's personal envoy in South Vietnam. He added, they "will have the ability to so organize the vets that they will be a good hard-core group of anti-Communists out through the provinces."[52]

Lansdale had EDCOR in mind when he praised the Freedom Company's abilities to reform the Vietnamese veterans and make them staunch anticommunists. The problem facing South Vietnam in 1954 was practically the same that beset the Philippines after World War II, when demobilized Huks became a security threat to the new nation. In Vietnam, a similar threat emerged in the form of three powerful noncommunist nationalist groups, the Cao Dai, Hoa Hao, and Binh Xuyen. Born in the heyday of French colonial rule, these groups would mount persistent challenges to Diem's authority after 1954 as they vied for power in the postcolonial state. In 1955, for example, some demobilized soldiers of the Cao Dai military, who "refused to join or were not accepted by the National Army," raided a refugee center in Tay Ninh Province as a "purely political" act.[53] Their potential danger to the stability of Diem's government demanded preemptive action. In January, San Juan and his associates enlisted the help of the Vietnamese clergy to contact these veterans. Able to secure sixty representatives of the National Army, the Cao Dai, Binh Xuyen, and other demobilized veterans, the Filipinos proposed their plan to help create a national veterans organization. They assured that the organization would serve as a productive outlet for the veterans to voice their grievances to the government.[54]

As the Freedom Company meddled in South Vietnamese politics, acting as a mediator of longstanding disputes between nationalist factions, American officials faced another pressing problem: military demobilization. On January 1, 1955, Americans assumed command of the Vietnamese National Army (VNA) from the French and scaled down the force, from 187,000 personnel to 100,000 in a year's time. U.S. officials believed demobilization was vital to the VNA's effectiveness in maintaining internal security but would simultaneously lead to a growing population of veterans that could fuel the communist insurgency. According to Lansdale, who had assumed the role of chief of the National Security Division in charge of training the VNA, "Conditions within Vietnam remain sufficiently unstable, so that armed groups which are outside the government forces continue to exist and to offer recruitment possibilities to former soldiers."[55] To Americans, these veterans represented a relic of French colonialism that needed to be "settled" and made "stable." Americans believed the government had to embrace these veterans in order to prevent them from becoming "an additional threat to the social order."[56] Americans needed a plan to put these soldiers to work, and they needed to implement it quickly. The Freedom Company provided the crucial link by helping to establish a veterans organization.

In the spring of 1955, political upheavals involving the Binh Xuyen and an attempted coup of the Diem government had forestalled the Freedom Company's efforts to form the veterans group; but in May, shortly after Diem crushed the Binh Xuyen and fortified his regime, the Freedom Company succeeded in creating the Vietnamese Veterans Legion (VVL). The VVL mirrored its Philippines counterpart, the PVL, and played a crucial role in South Vietnamese state-building initiatives. Almost instantaneously, VVL posts emerged across the countryside, charged to spread Diem's new propaganda campaign. The VVL worked closely with the U.S. Information Service and took over the distribution of all newspapers and magazines, including the *Cach Mang Quoc Gia,* the official organ of the presidential palace.[57] Formed at the same time that Diem was consolidating power under the banner of the "National Revolution," the VVL became instrumental in spreading the gospel of Diem's official state nationalism throughout the country.[58]

The Filipinos' hand in bolstering the Diem government is seldom acknowledged in historical accounts of South Vietnam during these years; yet the colonial intimacies were widely shared and celebrated among Philippine and South Vietnamese officials at the time. On June 9, the PVL invited members of the VVL as honored guests at their annual convention in Cebu City. The occasion marked a rare time of celebration amidst the political turmoil in the two countries. Philippine Vice President Carlos Garcia opened the convention by congratulating the Vietnamese delegates on their milestone achievement. The VVL, he assured, "will become a source of great strength for your war-torn country." The Philippine Congress had yet to settle the question of recognizing South Vietnam, but Garcia and the convention participants took the moment to reaffirm the stakes. With "unanimous approval," they passed a resolution for the Philippine government to extend recognition to South Vietnam. Senator Macario Peralta Jr., a past national commander of the PVL, felt moved by this support, and also filed a similar resolution in the Senate. In the intervening weeks before the legislation's passage, the Freedom Company attempted to sway Congress's decision by alluding continually to the VVL. On June 13, Alfonzo Enriquez, a Freedom Company officer credited with organizing the VVL, penned a joint letter with two senators to Peralta and reminded him of the colonial ties between Vietnam and the Philippines. He wrote, "The Vietnamese . . . look up to us as their elder brothers and have considered us as a fountain of inspiration in their efforts at nation building."[59]

It was toward this elusive goal of securing the South Vietnamese nation from communism that the Freedom Company pursued additional tasks. On June 7, the U.S. embassies in Saigon and Manila exchanged cables about sending ten Vietnamese officers to the Philippine Constabulary School at Camp Crame. Although "no formal course" was yet developed, the U.S. mission in Manila requested that they depart Saigon "without delay."[60] On July 15, ten officers of Diem's provincial militia force, the Garde Civile, arrived at Nichols Air Force Base to the personal reception of Bohannan. From there, the trainees proceeded to Camp Crame, located near the Freedom Company headquarters, and began their six-week training in guerrilla warfare.[61] The course objectives were to teach trainees "the organization and functions" of the Constabulary, to give them "a perspective of our police techniques and procedures," and to prepare them to carry out a training program in Vietnam.[62] Before the first cycle concluded, fifteen more Vietnamese officers arrived at Camp Murphy for a psychological-warfare course conducted by the Philippines Army.[63]

Vietnamese training in the Philippines reactivated Philippine colonial history. The Freedom Company fashioned itself precisely on the notion that Filipino veterans embodied a set of extractable military knowledge and skills that could be mobilized and applied in other settings. It attempted to codify and export the lessons of the Huk campaign to Vietnam. In August 1955, for example, the Military Assistance Advisory Group in Saigon requested the assistance of Lt. Col. Fredrico Calma to help the Vietnamese Army establish a course in combat intelligence, similar to the "original Philippine course" that Calma had established for the Philippine Army in 1951–52. "If Lt. Col. Calma [is] not available," then a "similarly qualified adviser" should take his place.[64] In the mid-1950s, military experts of the Huk campaign were prized as assets and in high demand for U.S. counterinsurgency experiments in Vietnam, and increasingly in Laos and Indonesia. Such intercolonial exchanges at times exceeded imperial boundaries. In September 1957, the British embassy invited the Armed Forces of the Philippines (AFP) to send ten Filipino officers to its jungle-warfare course in Singapore, to "promote friendship and British prestige in [the] area." U.S. military officials deemed the invitation a positive gesture, if nothing else to develop a greater awareness of the "problems" of neighboring countries and to strengthen "area alliances."[65]

The training allowed U.S. officials flexibility in developing the Vietnamese forces, and it kept "U.S. support within reasonable limits" as set by the Geneva Accords.[66] Unlike the work with the VVL, the training of Vietnamese police and military officers mostly eluded public scrutiny. When it was acknowledged openly, it was framed by the familiar sentiment of "Asians helping Asians." For instance, three weeks into their training in the Philippines, the

Vietnamese officers penned a letter to President Ramon Magsaysay, expressing their gratitude. They wrote,

> It is really an honor for us as the first citizens of Vietnam to be received here in this Palace after the recognition of our country by the government of the Philippines. Since we came here three weeks ago, we have visited many regions of the Philippines and everywhere we met a warm welcome from the people. From up in San Luis to down in Cotabato, from a humble peasant working in the paddy field to an officer of the General Staff and the Philippine Constabulary, and specially our instructors, we realized their endeavors . . . to make us feel at home from the very start.

They assured the president that colonial hospitality and education would "always guide us in our present struggle against the Communist-led Vietminh."[67]

Intra-Asian aid indeed sparked the imagination of U.S. officials like Lansdale who were always keen on seeing the bigger picture. In his notes on the prospects of Philippines training, Lansdale scribbled that "overall," the goal was to "change aspect or world picture of war, from that of colonial whites (French) fighting oppressed native Asians (Vietminh) to civil war between newly independent Asian nationals (Vietnam) and natives dominated by Soviet-Chinese imperialists." Along with other Americans, Lansdale believed involving "free Asians" in Vietnam would help convince the entire decolonizing world that the war Americans inherited from the French was no simple race war.[68]

Senator Recto saw right through the deceit. He knew the kind of racial and colonial intimacy espoused by Philippine and U.S. state leaders was nothing more than a ruse to enable U.S. militarism by other means. In a Senate speech in 1955, he charged, "We were pressed into recognizing Diem's government in order to legalize and continue the training which has been secretly going on at Camp Murphy."[69] As he feared, JUSMAG proceeded to institutionalize third-country training in the Philippines after securing Philippine recognition of South Vietnam. In August 1955, the commander in chief of the U.S. Pacific Command requested JUSMAG to "make maximum feasible use [of] Philippines Army Training facilities" for the following fiscal year by allotting space for 329 students from other countries in Southeast Asia. At the start of January 1956, John Watchtel, Freedom Company's general manager, reported that the Freedom Company already had sponsored five military classes for Vietnamese officers. Additionally, the schedule for 1956 included the resumption of the Garde Civile Training Program at Camp

Crame, a new psywar training program for Indonesian police officers, and a thirty-day visit of five Indonesian police commissioners to observe the Philippine Constabulary's methods.[70]

By the late 1950s, Philippine state leaders were actively promoting the AFP as a storehouse of applicable knowledge and skills to support U.S. counterinsurgencies in the region. In one sense, exporting Filipino military experts and knowledge reinforced the Philippines's economic dependency on the United States. This dependency has been ongoing since 1946, notably enshrined in the Bell Trade Act (1946) and Military Bases Agreement (1947) that gave the United States preferential access to Philippine markets and bases.[71] It continued after the SEATO meeting in 1954. In late 1955, for example, Ambassador Romulo communicated to the U.S. State Department a proposal to establish a Psychological Warfare Training Center in the Philippines. He stated, "It is believed that one of the most effective counter measures against communist subversion is psychological warfare. However, to insure its success and to render most effective psychological warfare in Southeast Asia, it is felt that the Asians themselves should direct the project." In a follow-up conversation with State Department officials one month later, Romulo criticized SEATO as a "paper façade" that had "fail[ed] to capture the imagination of Asians." As a solution, Romulo suggested that the United States support activities "in the treaty area" related to psywar and countersubversion training, in particular the proposed training center. Such a school would not only instill the trainees with practical knowledge from experienced officers of the AFP, but would further "encourage the concept of Asian Help Asian."[72]

While the Psychological Warfare Center did not materialize at the time, Philippine leaders pursued other proposals in subsequent years. They invariably invoked SEATO and its failed promise of creating an Asia for Asians. In May 1957, Philippine officials forwarded a proposed "counter-subversion school," under the Philippine National Intelligence Coordinating Agency, that would train Southeast Asian police officers in counterinsurgency methods. This time, the proposal garnered the critical support of several U.S. agencies, including the DOD, the State Department, and the CIA. The CIA believed it a "worthwhile project" provided "the school [could] be operated in such a way as to give the appearance of being completely a Philippine effort." In August 1958, the State Department agreed to establish the Security Training Center, a countersubversion school that proceeded under SEATO auspices.[73] The institutionalization of the Security Training Center was one part of this broader postcolonial alignment that, over the next decade and beyond, would suture America's "showcase of democracy" to America's war in Vietnam.

Time and again, Recto warned against these "dangerous and provocative entanglements" with the U.S. empire. He warned that the Philippines's complicity with U.S. militarism in the region would "distract our attention away" from the country's "local problems" that had been left unaddressed for too long, specifically reconstructing the state economy free from "alien domination." It also threatened to expose the Filipino people to another war "on Asian soil."[74] The institutionalization of the Security Training Center and the Philippines's involvement in the Vietnam War were precisely the nightmare that Recto predicted in 1955.

BLOWBACK

Recto's words came back to haunt Philippine and U.S. officials sooner than expected. Both President Magsaysay's death in 1957 and rising nationalism in the Philippines generated an onslaught of public questions about the role of the United States in Philippine affairs. An early casualty of this scrutiny was the Freedom Company. In January 1958, Freedom Company members decided to terminate the company officially as "its close relationship and identification with the Americans operating in Vietnam became more and more of public knowledge," and in order "to obviate unfounded criticism and accusations of 'intervention' or 'meddling'" in South Vietnam. However, the members laid the groundwork for a new entity, a private commercial firm called the Eastern Construction Company, Incorporated (ECCOI). According to its mission statement, the ECCOI would conduct the same tasks as the Freedom Company had, "to acquire, apply, and impart technical knowledge and ability to the people of newly developing nations of the Free World."[75] By reconstituting itself in a different form, the organization continued to survive.

The scrutiny of the Freedom Company was a result of surging anticolonial nationalism in the Philippines, which Recto called "an awakening."[76] In August 1958, the National Economic Council passed a resolution calling for "substantial participation of Filipinos in commerce and industry."[77] This was the centerpiece of President Carlos Garcia's "Filipino First" Policy, which aimed to concentrate economic and political power in the hands of Filipino citizens rather than "foreign" American interests. Although newly packaged by the Garcia Administration to signal a break in national policy, "Filipino First" was rooted in an anticolonial sentiment that was years in the making, which Recto had consistently espoused since 1954. The institutionalization of this form of nationalism alarmed U.S. officials. Seemingly nothing was spared from criticism, even among trusted allies. "There are fragmentary indications that the U.S. military in the Philippines are due for a rather nasty attack, possibly from an old friend," Lansdale alerted the Secretary of Defense in late 1959. Lansdale suspected that longtime American ally Ambassador Romulo felt motivated to embrace "Filipino First" to retain his ambassadorship. He observed that Romulo might soon join the chorus of criticism of U.S. military bases, especially targeting American GIs and their "criminal" and "immoral" behavior toward local women.[78]

Concerns about the Philippines's ability to perform as America's showcase of democracy converged with other alarming trends in South Vietnam. Revolutionary activities against the Diem government had escalated sharply by the fall of 1959, a result of organized resistance led by Vietnamese Communist Party cadres in the South and Diem's increasingly brutal tactics against dissidents. In January 1960, southern revolutionaries launched a "concerted uprising," marking the start of a year of rebellion and military attacks that capped off with a failed coup in November.[79] Diem and U.S. military officials hoped the presidential election of John F. Kennedy that year was a promising sign that the United States would renew its support for the counterinsurgency in the south. On May 25, 1961, President Kennedy's first speech to Congress painted a dark picture of this new "type of warfare" and enemy: "[T]heir aggression is more often concealed than open. They have fired no missiles; and their troops are seldom seen. . . . But where fighting is required, it is usually done by others, by guerrillas striking at night, by assassins striking alone . . . by subversives and saboteurs and insurrectionists, who in some cases control whole areas inside independent nations."[80] His call for "a wholly new kind of strategy" to combat this world menace set off a "counterinsurgency ferment" in Washington, D.C. in the early 1960s.[81] In military circles, "lessons learned" from past insurgencies were discussed and debated vigorously, and a new military strategy was in development.

This renewed commitment to developing a counterinsurgency strategy in South Vietnam, however, rested on shaky grounds at best. In 1955–56, the success in Vietnamese pacification had hinged upon the colonial intimacies between the United States, the Philippines, and South Vietnam that

Lansdale and his team had cultivated. But these intimacies could not survive the tides of nationalism sweeping the Philippines and the wider region. In fact, Lansdale experienced it firsthand. In January 1961, Secretary of Defense McNamara sent Lansdale to survey the political situation in South Vietnam for the new administration, and he wanted to make his typical stopover in Manila. The U.S. embassy soundly warned against it, predicting the visit "at this time would raise questions," especially in light of the "conviction here that he played [an] important role in [the] election of Magsaysay" in 1953. They anticipated that his presence would be "interpreted by many as evidence of our direct involvement [in] their present political campaign."[82] Instead of heeding their caution, Lansdale proceeded brazenly and made the visit. On January 3, the *Manila Bulletin,* a widely circulated daily, headlined that he had "slipped into town" the day before on a "secret mission," adding that his appearance in Manila "set off speculations." According to the source, a number of "close friends" met him at the airport, including the director of the National Bureau of Investigation and the coordinator of Operation Brotherhood.[83]

The political times had changed since 1954, but Lansdale still doled out the same advice to Secretary McNamara upon returning from his Vietnam trip. In his report, he acknowledged that the anticommunist struggle in the south had entered a critical phase. "[T]he wise thing to do is to pick the best people you have, . . . a hard core of experienced Americans who know and really like Asia and the Asians," and who could "guide the Vietnamese towards U.S. policy objectives with warm friendships and affection which our close alliance deserves."[84] His suggestion of putting racial liberalism to work in order to win the affection of Asians revealed that he was disconnected from the present revolutionary times. The swath of public opinion in the Philippines roundly rejected any further affiliation with the United States, yet Lansdale continued to put his faith in employing Filipinos in Vietnam. In 1962, Jose Banzon, a longtime associate of Lansdale's and the first Philippine diplomat to arrive in Saigon in 1954, wrote Lansdale, searching for "the chance, once more . . . to work in any of the troubled spots" in Southeast Asia, and Lansdale was cautiously optimistic. He acknowledged Banzon's rich experience in Vietnam and responded, "Why don't you see if the Philippines couldn't make a real contribution to the struggle in Southeast Asia and send you over to Diem as a 'secret weapon' in Vietnam?"[85]

Neither Lansdale nor Banzon had to wait long for the opportunity to put more Filipinos to use in Vietnam. By 1964, the "counterinsurgency ferment" in Washington, D.C. had evolved into a push for a full-scale ground war in South Vietnam. The war was a continuation of the war that began in 1954 and a continuation of the longer colonial war for independence that had begun decades before that. The war would generate new demands for Filipinos to answer the call of "freedom" across the seas. It reverberated all across the decolonizing Pacific, in South Korea, Hawai'i, the Philippines, and elsewhere, mobilizing citizens from "liberated" nations and territories to demonstrate their gratitude to the U.S. empire.

THREE

Race War in Paradise

HAWAI'I'S VIETNAM WAR

ON MARCH 5, 1965, twenty-two paratroopers of the 24th Special Forces Group, U.S. Army, descended by helicopter in Kahuku, the northernmost point of O'ahu Island in Hawai'i. This marked the start of Exercise Black Night, an elaborate war game that spared nothing from the imagination. Over the next fifteen days, soldiers played the part of guerrillas in the Ko'olau Mountains. Their target was the village of "Catu," the capital of Kurlandia, a hypothetical Southeast Asian country. Many of the dark-skinned Native Hawaiians of the 1st Battalion 8th Field Artillery Regiment impersonated the villagers. At first, the villagers distrusted the American "friendly forces," but the soldiers' affection won them over quickly. The Americans distributed gifts, initiated public-health campaigns, and demonstrated concern for the villagers' well-being. The Kurlandians accepted the soldiers and even welcomed them into their "homes." Meanwhile, along the perimeter of the village, American forces closed in on the guerrillas and eventually forced them to surrender. After fifteen days, the commanding general of the 25th Infantry Division, Fred C. Weyand, assessed that Exercise Black Night was the "most comprehensive, extensive, and well organized training exercise that has already made a better fighting outfit of this Division." He stated, "There is no mission you could not accomplish."[1]

Exercise Black Night took place at the Jungle and Guerrilla Warfare Training Center of Schofield Barracks, an expansive army complex on O'ahu. In 1965, the year President Johnson intensified the U.S. war in South Vietnam, the Jungle Training Center processed tens of thousands of American GIs for rotation and turned into one of the most active yet obscure destinations in Hawai'i. In October of that year, two army officials at the School of the Americas in Fort Gulick flew to Schofield Barracks to coordinate with the jungle-training program in Panama. On their observational tour, they noted the instruction programs were nearly identical at both places, except for "one important difference" being the added "instruction in village clearing, a phase of training conducted in a mock Vietnamese village." Upon their recommendation, army engineers at the School of the Americas began constructing a "Vietnamese village."[2] It was a novel concept that was promptly implemented at army bases across the United States.

In the 1960s, the simulation of "native" territory for military-training purposes certainly was not an unusual practice for the U.S. Army, but in Hawaiʻi it represented a colonial violence that had never fully ended. In the early nineteenth century, the Euro-American incursions led to the dispossession of Native Hawaiians of their lands. This process was formalized with the U.S. annexation in 1898, and continued after World War II as U.S. military expansion across the Pacific became imprinted firmly in Hawaiʻi's landscape and political economy. In post–World War II Hawaiʻi, as in other Pacific territories such as Okinawa, Guam, the Northern Marianas, and the Marshall Islands, military-training exercises and weapons testing generated a growing arsenal for U.S. wars in Asia. At the same time, the military justified its presence on these islands by restaging memories of Japanese militarism and American "liberation" during World War II. These convergent forces of U.S. militarization and martial patriotism have hindered other demilitarized and anticolonial forms of sovereignty from taking root.

This chapter traces an imagined geography connecting Hawaiʻi to Vietnam as twin sites of war in the 1960s. This spatial formation is a part of the decolonizing Pacific that I call Hawaiʻi's Vietnam War, and it makes visible the processes of militarization "hidden in plain sight" on the islands that include army war games, civic celebrations, the built environment, and other manifestations.[3] Central to Hawaiʻi's Vietnam War was the racial liberalism that coalesced around Hawaiʻi statehood. Hawaiʻi statehood, I contend, was a formal mandate of national inclusion that silenced struggles for decolonization, and obscured the ongoing effects of U.S. colonial violence in Hawaiʻi. It also enabled that violence to extend across the Pacific. In 1965, American soldiers deployed from Schofield Barracks channeled their "aloha spirit" to the Vietnamese through humanitarian civic-action projects. And just as quickly, American soldiers used the tactics of colonial violence practiced at the Jungle Center. I argue the atrocities they committed underscored the intrinsic violence of Hawaiʻi's liberal inclusion into the U.S. nation-state, a promise of freedom that reproduced and intensified state violence across the U.S. empire.

By the late 1960s, struggles for decolonization in Hawai'i resurfaced in full force, invigorated by the opposition to the Vietnam War. The energies of student activists, antiwar GIs, clergy, and sovereignty activists coalesced and gave form to a decolonization movement that broadly connected issues of war, militarization, development, and settler colonialism. In its sheer expansiveness and creativity, the movement for decolonization in Hawai'i revealed the deep entanglements of racial liberalism and state violence in U.S. culture.

MILITARIZATION, RACIAL LIBERALISM, AND STATEHOOD

The idea that Hawai'i formed a gateway to the wider Pacific world was a nineteenth-century idea connected to commercial trade routes, but by the onset of the Pacific War, the gateway was linked to a military imperative. In 1890, the naval strategist Alfred Thayer Mahan penned his imperialist tract about the necessities of American "sea power" to secure the growing U.S. empire. This confirmed that the fortunes of commercialism depended on a strong military presence on and around the Hawaiian Islands, which American sugar planters and mercantilists in Hawai'i already knew. In 1898, the annexation of Hawai'i hastened the construction of military bases throughout O'ahu and fortified an island "ring of steel," securing the supply of sugar production for the coming decades.[4]

The defense of Hawai'i during and after World War II became important to the Pacific's security as a region of U.S. national interest. In November 1945, Gen. Douglas MacArthur revealed his plans for a postwar "Pacific Basin," in which Hawai'i occupied the site of central command for a defensive line connecting the Marianas, the Philippines, the Ryukyus, and the Aleutians. MacArthur believed that Hawai'i was well situated for the deployment of "long-range, land-based airpower, emphasizing initial readiness, flexibility, rapid concentration and expansion."[5] Hawai'i's business leaders jumped at the opportunity to promote the territory in the name of defense. In 1952, Chamber of Commerce President Farrant Turner wrote to the U.S. Senate Preparedness Committee, "We are very close to Asia and have good intelligence from the countries of the Far East as well as Southeast Asia, and we are certain that preparedness to meet the grave situation in Asia is becoming urgent rapidly."[6]

Territorial leaders and military officials shared a common vision for a permanent military presence in Hawaiʻi that would secure U.S. geostrategic interests and the territory's economy simultaneously. In March 1951, the U.S. Army announced plans to establish the Hawaiian Infantry Training Center at Schofield Barracks to train inductees from the United States and the territories of Guam, Samoa, and Hawaiʻi for the Korean War. Territorial leaders quickly supported the move and, with foresight, argued that the training center would, in the long term, promote Hawaiʻi's economic growth as well as prospects for statehood after the Korean War. According to Territorial Governor Ingram Stainback, "The overall boost to the economy of the Territory [derived from the training center] could easily amount to six or seven million dollars annually." Those training at Schofield Barracks would be an asset to the military, and "a potential Statehood booster and a future tourist."[7] The army began to describe the trainees as "tourists in uniform," and civic boosters called them "ambassadors of good will" who would return to the mainland and tell other Americans "about these wonderful islands of ours." Hawaiʻi's draw to the military was unmistakable. The Chamber of Commerce reasoned, "our climate, our plains, our mountains and jungles, our beaches, our archipelago" created "the ideal place for year-round and intensive draft training of troops," which made up for Hawaiʻi's lack of war manufacturing.[8] The argument was clear: a new militarized Hawaiʻi promised to transform young American men at once into exemplary soldiers and tourists.

The discussions surrounding the Hawaiian Infantry Training Center revealed the extent that militarization became intrinsic to Hawaiʻi's economic growth after the Korean War. In 1958, the Territorial Planning Director received an urban-planning firm's report that detailed the military and civilian land use on Oʻahu. By its calculations, the military had generated over $300 million in revenue the previous year, far surpassing the combined revenue brought by the sugar, pineapple, and tourism industries. The military had cemented itself as "the major contributor to the Island's economy." Additionally, the military presence on the most densely populated island of Hawaiʻi also created other concerns, namely an impediment to urban development. Analyzing U.S. geological survey maps, the report found that Oʻahu's topography of mountainous terrain left only 43 percent of the land "reasonably economical to develop," of which one-third already was occupied by the military. The report concluded, the "best solution would result from a collaborative effort [from which] both the military establishment and the civilian community can profit."[9] Over the next two decades, this "collaborative" effort between the military and civilian communities would accelerate massive construction projects on Oʻahu, especially around Waikīkī Beach, which served as a prime destination for soldiers and their families during R&R after 1965.

The mutual partnership between military and civilian communities had been under way for some time. In 1954, a new generation of political leaders, comprised of some World War II veterans and descendants of Japanese plantation workers, swept the Democratic Party to power by promising far-reaching economic reforms. They embraced military spending as a welcome path to Hawaiʻi's development, as a way to transform the unequal patterns of land ownership that had long foreclosed the economic mobility of Hawaiʻi's Japanese communities. "The time had come for us to step forward," Daniel Inouye, a decorated veteran and Hawaiʻi senator, reflected after the war. "We had fought for that right with all the furious patriotism in our bodies and now we didn't want to go back to the plantation." After fighting in the war, few Nisei veterans returned to the plantations where their parents toiled; instead, they secured positions of political leadership in an effort to shape Hawaiʻi's political and economic future.[10]

By the 1950s, for the Hawaiʻi-born and -raised Japanese and Chinese, statehood had become the primary vehicle for political ascendency.[11] Increasingly, they were called upon to marshal evidence of their patriotism and, by extension, of Hawaiʻi's rightful place in the nation and the world. In 1957, proclaiming himself a "Hawaiian" and an "Army Veteran," David Namaka appealed to President Eisenhower: "A nation is only as strong as its component parts, and I feel strongly that Hawaiʻi is not only an integral but an essential component of our great American Nation." In 1957, the governor's press secretary, Lawrence Nakatsuka, told the White House, "Many Asians look upon Hawaii as a 'colony,' a status from which they assume all colonial peoples want to be freed in order that they can become independent." He assured the president the people of Hawaiʻi didn't want "independence." Instead, they wanted *equality,* and statehood was the answer. At a time when the United States sought to secure the "free world" from communism, granting statehood to Hawaiʻi affirmed the United States as a champion of racial equality and freedom.[12] In this light, Hawaiʻi statehood was imperative. It also meant that the violence of the U.S. liberal empire was under way.

In proclaiming statehood a civil rights achievement, statehood proponents silenced Native voices for decolonization by rendering them illegitimate and, in some cases, criminal.[13] Statehood was framed as the only logical step forward in realizing America as a multiracial democracy. It equated decolonization with the inclusion of Hawai'i's Native and Asian population into the nation, which derailed and disavowed the pressing demands for Native sovereignty. Although Native Hawaiians organized a grassroots opposition against statehood, they could not overcome the liberal political establishment's power, and the Hawai'i territorial legislature voted and passed the statehood bill in January 1959.[14] In fact, the plebiscite had violated a 1953 United Nations resolution that mandated the ballot include other choices besides territorial status or statehood, namely "independence" and "separate systems of self-government." Voters had neither of these options available, and they overwhelmingly chose statehood.[15] Widely hailed by the press as a victory for Hawai'i's Asian population, statehood cemented Hawai'i as an "international melting pot" that would shape the course of freedom in the Pacific world. Against the violation of international trust obligations and the ongoing repression of Native Hawaiian struggles for decolonization, the stage was set for the United States to expand its "liberation" projects in Asia.

In the end, statehood was more than just an event. It was an ideological project of the U.S. government to preserve empire in the name of freedom, a "freedom with violence" that rippled and intensified across the Pacific in the next decade.[16] Statehood reaffirmed that a commitment to liberalism was a commitment to war, a reality that manifested in the ongoing suppression of Native sovereignty and in the steady militarization of the islands under the demands of economic growth and national security. By the start of the 1960s, the military presence in Hawai'i was an unquestioned necessity. In April 1961, before the first state legislature, Governor William Quinn spoke in uncompromising terms: "The Federal government should and must remain one of the major users of land in Hawaii." By "Federal government," he meant "primarily the Armed Forces," and he reasoned the benefits were mutual: the military needed Hawai'i for its location, and Hawai'i needed the military for revenue and nationalist cohesion.[17] Such neat rationalizations concealed underlying tensions. Despite statehood, the tensions between militarism and liberalism in Hawai'i remained unresolved.

ALOHA, VIETNAM

On August 3, 1964, U.S. news headlines reported that North Vietnamese patrol boats had seized the U.S. naval destroyer *Maddox* in the Gulf of

Tonkin. Within the week, this news prompted a resolution in Congress that amounted to a declaration of war. Overnight, the debate about the military's presence in Hawai'i had transformed into one about impending war. Hawai'i's leaders were hopeful about the war's impact on the military community and state economy. As one economist summarized, the "long-term U.S. military commitment to the Pacific and to Hawaii will make government spending a continuing important element in the Hawaii economy for a decade or more ahead." In July 1965, Governor John Burns announced confidently, "I think all of Hawaii is 100 percent behind the President's position [on the war]." His statement glossed over the dissent within the Hawai'i legislature and the public that erupted in due time. On the surface, the Vietnam War reaffirmed Hawai'i's national purpose as a bastion of U.S. military power in the Pacific.[18]

The military urgently mobilized the same discourses of racial liberalism that helped secure statehood. As war became a reality, people in Hawai'i focused on the 25th Infantry Division. Its record in the Pacific was legendary. Since the end of the Korean War in 1953, the 25th Division had been stationed at Schofield Barracks as the army's Pacific reserve force. During World War II, the 25th Division had conducted famed campaigns in Guadalcanal and Luzon, and its successes since then had become an intrinsic part of Hawai'i's political culture. The division was even called "Hawai'i's own," even though its soldiers were mostly white Americans from the U.S. mainland, but that did not seem to matter. By the 1960s, the 25th Division had secured a reputation in the army as "the only counter-guerrilla trained division" skilled in navigating "native" terrains and cultures, as well as several Asian languages. The 25th Division's cultural fluencies and military experiences ensured its part in the initial buildup of U.S. ground forces in South Vietnam. With a four-thousand-man task force deployed to the Central Highlands of Pleiku Province, and a local recruitment drive and reserve training program in high gear, Hawai'i's protracted engagement in the Vietnam War began in December 1965.[19]

Although the war officially started in 1965, its inception occurred a decade prior, when military advisers engineered counterinsurgencies to steer South Vietnam toward liberal democracy. Years after these initial efforts, Americans encountered the same military problems that had mired their predecessors. In February 1965, U.S. Ambassador to South Vietnam Maxwell Taylor warned the State Department against deploying U.S. troops. He cautioned, the "[w]hite-faced soldier armed, equipped and trained as he is [is] not [a] suitable guerrilla fighter for Asian forests and jungles." The "French tried . . . and failed; I doubt that U.S. forces could do much better." Cast as a conflict waged in unconventional territory and against a population suspicious of "white-faced" soldiers, the Vietnam War proved entirely incompatible for the U.S. military, whose superior firepower was all but useless in a guerrilla situation. "Finally," Taylor continued, "there would be [the] ever present question of how [a] foreign soldier would distinguish between a VC [Viet Cong] and [a] friendly Vietnamese farmer. When I view this array of difficulties, I am convinced that we should adhere to our past policy of keeping ground forces out of [a] direct counterinsurgency role."[20] Such concerns foreboded all too precisely the kind of race war that would ensue in the coming years. But nonetheless, American soldiers went forth, determined to change hearts and minds.

The soldiers of the 25th Division sought to overcome their racial difference with the Vietnamese by engaging in humanitarian projects, which enacted Hawai'i exceptionalism from the start. In January 1966, the division's 2nd Brigade arrived in Cu Chi District of Hau Nghia Province, a historical stronghold of the National Liberation Front (NLF). In recent years the area had transformed into a laboratory of military governance, beginning with the creation of South Vietnam's first strategic hamlet in January 1962 and the demarcation of the province's administrative boundaries two years later. Despite these ongoing experiments in social engineering, the population remained intransigent. One year before the 25th Division moved in, a conservative estimate of Hau Nghia's population found 35 percent in open support of the NLF and only 15 percent in favor of the government, with the rest swayed by neither. Against such unfavorable circumstances, the brigade moved forward with its civic-action campaign. The soldiers' tasks included building schools, roads, and clinics and initiating training programs on public health and vocational skills. Military and state officials believed these projects were crucial to transforming South Vietnam into a modern nation, a process similar to Hawai'i's transition to statehood not long before. Weyand, the 25th's commanding general, believed civic action was at the heart of the 25th's mission. He stated often, "My Tropic Lightning m[e]n must be good neighbors to the Vietnamese people." He also remarked in a press release to Hawai'i's citizens, "We are proud of the fact that the 25th Infantry Division, 'Hawaii's Own,' is serving as an important element of the United States' effort in support of the struggle by the people of Viet Nam to retain their independence and freedom. However, to win in Viet Nam, it will take more than bullets, guns and soldiers. Unless we can also assist the Vietnamese in their efforts to improve their way of life, the winning of battles may well be in vain."[21]

General Weyand's press statement framed the 25th's military activities through a language of liberal inclusion that the people of Hawai'i understood well. If statehood had secured Hawai'i's freedom for the age of decolonization by incorporating its subjects into the nation, then the soldiers of the 25th could help do the same for the Vietnamese. Shortly after his press announcement, Weyand clarified his intentions to Governor Burns: "We believe a major victory in the civic action battle to win the Vietnamese people can be won *in Hawaii*." He believed Hawai'i's citizens had a role to play. Weyand had devised a campaign called "Operation Helping Hand," which would be an integral part of the 25th's civic action. This campaign would collect donated items from O'ahu's civilian community, and his soldiers would distribute the items in Hau Nghia.[22] Governor Burns fully supported the operation and announced to the public, "The people of Hawaii today have an opportunity to become directly involved in this most important phase of our country's overall efforts in Vietnam."[23] The stakes of the people's participation were high. Weyand emphasized, "Man lending a helping hand to his fellow man is what the 'Tropic Lightning' soldier will use to secure the friendship so necessary in a country where suspicion and distrust are commonplace." Operation Helping Hand, which Weyand called "an extension of our aloha" to the Vietnamese, at once instrumentalized Hawai'i's liberalism and mobilized its population for war.[24]

The public's response to the drive was overwhelming. In the weeks following, citizens donated a wide assortment of goods, including soap, toothbrushes, tools, books, clothing, and foodstuffs, and civic groups such as the Boy Scouts set up stations at schools and markets to assemble the donations. By the drive's end, over $800,000 worth of goods were tallied and shipped. The result was everything Governor Burns hoped for, and more. He declared, "The depth and breadth of support which came to Operation Helping Hand is a measure of Hawaii's inherent greatness." He added, "Our people can deliver when it counts." This "greatness" had much to do with the people's generosity and consumer wealth. As Chinn Ho, the civilian aid to the army and appointed coordinator of Operation Helping Hand, stated at the outset, "What is plentiful for Hawaii's citizens is frequently either a great luxury for the Vietnamese people or simply not available. In Viet Nam, where medical know-how is frequently many years behind that of western practice, toothpaste and toothbrushes become vital dental preventatives." Tools like "knives, screwdrivers, saws, shovels, and picks will help the villagers improve their standard of living." He assured the list was "virtually endless," and that whatever objects the people of Hawai'i offered, "the Vietnamese will find a good use for your contribution."[25]

The scenes of Hawai'i's humanitarianism continued to unfold when the soldiers reached Vietnam. On February 24, as the first truckloads of goods entered the villages of Hau Nghia, an army photojournalist was on hand to document the scene. The reporter glowed, "The hostility of villagers ... melted into smiles."[26] Photographs captured images of barefoot schoolchildren who stood in line and received gifts from the soldiers; one photograph depicted children in a crowd awaiting "their very first shower" with the soap and shampoo donated through Helping Hand. Ngo Xuan Truong, a representative of Tan An Hoi village, remarked in a letter to Weyand, "A happy scene has returned to our village." He wrote that before the arrival of the American soldiers, "Cu Chi District was desolate and like a desert," the result of the Viet Cong's years of neglect. But "since the 25th Infantry Division has been stationed in this local area ... my people's standard of living has returned to normal." It seemed the Americans had brought about a small-scale revolution in the village. As Truong affirmed, they "have helped us to triumph over communist aggression, poverty and disease," not only by the actions of the soldiers but also "by the gifts from Hawaii donated to our people."[27] Through Operation Helping Hand, Hawai'i's citizens saw that their humanitarian efforts had a positive impact.

The photographs of Vietnamese children produced a gendered gaze on the Vietnamese that depicted them as helpless victims of communist aggression and that naturalized the presence of American soldiers, obscuring the U.S. military violence.[28] Hawai'i provided the critical narrative frame to these anticonquest images. While the images restaged the familiar paternalism of the U.S. military, they focused on Hawai'i's "gifts" as the instruments of pacification, literally passing from the hands of benevolent white soldiers to the Vietnamese children. Hawai'i's gifts sustained the colonial fantasy that the United States always has been an inclusionary empire. In this instance, the U.S. empire brought "native" Vietnamese into the fold of Hawai'i's newly constituted multiracial family, even as that domestic vision was contingent on Native Hawaiians' exclusion and dispossession.

In the end, these scenes proved all too illusory. Two months after the 25th Division completed its mission in Cu Chi, a report by the RAND Corporation

FIGURE 4. A 25th Infantry Division soldier delivers "Helping Hand" gift to a Vietnamese child. (*The 25th Infantry Division in Vietnam: 1966–1967*, Tropic Lightning Association, 1967.)

found that the villagers' opinion of the South Vietnamese government "appeared, in general, to be worse than it was before pacification began."[29] The counterinsurgency's failure was shut out from public discourse, and in some ways proved inconsequential. From its start, Operation Helping Hand—and the civic action of the 25th Division in general—exemplified U.S. liberal inclusion through the benevolence of the military and Hawai'i's humanitarianism, the two inextricably entwined. The ultimate aim of Operation Helping Hand was to capture a moment, however fleeting. Military officials hoped the moment would etch a lasting impression on the Vietnamese and the American public, and both would understand the benefits and necessity of the U.S. military's presence in Vietnam.

Ideologically, Operation Helping Hand distinguished itself from the military's escalating violence. By the end of 1965, there were 184,000 U.S. military personnel in South Vietnam, and one year later that number doubled to 362,000.[30] The military was unleashing disproportionate violence, and the range of American firepower required to carry out a war of this scale—bombs, mortars, napalm, M-16s, claymore mines, and other weapons—wrought unspeakable destruction in the countryside. It also demanded a concise method to gauge the war's success: the body count. According to Assistant Secretary of Defense Alain Enthoven, the body count of confirmed Vietnamese kills was "*the* measure of success," and this incentivized American combat troops and low-level officers to produce more dead Vietnamese bodies.[31] Military officials seemed generally unconcerned about the contradiction between the war's systemic violence and the image of benevolence they sought to cultivate through civic-action campaigns. For its part, the 25th Division sought to contain this contradiction with a different gift, a "Helping Hand solatium box" that was given to dependents of civilians and U.S. personnel who were "accidentally killed or injured" by U.S. forces.[32]

In short, Operation Helping Hand made a racial war against the Vietnamese seem an impossible reality for Hawai'i's citizens. It was a kind of war wholly incompatible with Hawai'i's multiracial democracy. The 25th Division stood for inclusion and progress, its soldiers deemed incapable of committing racial violence. Supposedly, only the unstable environment of the Southeast Asian jungles could cause any deviation from their course. When soldiers returned to Hawai'i for R&R in 1966, they rejoiced in their respite and reunion with families, and local business leaders enjoyed the boost to the economy. In Hawai'i, the scenes of R&R reaffirmed the military as vital to Hawai'i's economic growth, and reinforced the vast distance and difference between the islands and the raging war far away. On the beach-front paradise of O'ahu, the violence of racialized war seemed a distant reality. Little did the Hawai'i public know that some twenty miles inland from these sites of rejuvenation, the U.S. Army had cultivated Hawai'i's own "jungles" to prepare soldiers for their unruly encounters in Vietnam.

COLONIAL VIOLENCE UNLEASHED

By 1965, the dominant image of Hawai'i as a metaphorical bridge to Asia had taken on a more literal meaning. With the escalation of the Vietnam War, Hawai'i's militarization continued, fueling the dispossession of Native Hawaiians from their lands. It also entailed the engineering of landscapes to mimic the "native" conditions of Southeast Asia for military-training purposes. This imagined geography took place largely on Schofield Barracks.

Located in the island's interior, Schofield Barracks sat on rugged terrain that urban planners in the 1950s had deemed unsuitable for development.

What land developers had no use for, however, the army increasingly prized. In January 1960, the DOD reported that the fifty thousand acres of federally leased land on Oʻahu consisting largely of "forest reserve, lava fields and mountainous areas, which have little revenue potential" for developers, should be exploited for training purposes. It was during this time that "jungle warfare" training emerged as the specialized mission of the U.S. Army Command in Hawaiʻi.[33] As the U.S. military focused on waging counter-guerrilla operations worldwide, Schofield Barracks became the place for conducting novel military-training exercises for these operations. By 1965, the Jungle and Guerrilla Warfare Training Center at Schofield Barracks was processing one thousand men per month for rotation to Vietnam.[34]

The soldiers of the 25th Division owed much of their initial success in 1966 to the "realistic" conditions of training at Schofield Barracks. According to Gen. William Westmoreland and Gen. Stanley Larsen, the top U.S. military commanders in Vietnam, the 25th had "some of the best trained and certainly best acclimated troops." "The Wolfhounds have never found terrain [in Vietnam] as difficult as that they found in the Koolaus," Weyand opined. "The conditioning they got ... has enabled them to come here and fight in this heat and at this place without dropping."[35] The "realism" did not stop with the terrain and climate. To enhance the simulated environments of the war, the army constructed "Kara Village," which was comprised of twelve "Southeast Asian type villages" outfitted with thatched huts and "native" inhabitants.[36]

The mock village was a technology of race war, a simulacrum that conjured the racialized enemy through spatial enactments. It taught soldiers to approach their surroundings as a target of violence. Its elaborate design, complete with rice paddies, secret tunnels, and false walls and fireplaces, reinforced the entire "village" as a site of hostility. The absence of the enemy functioned to confirm their always-lurking presence. Weyand explained, "My people go into this area [Hau Nghia], sweep through and try to round them up and kill them. Maybe we only get 10 at a time but we are like vacuum sweepers. Eventually, the rug comes out clean."[37] By 1966, mock villages appeared at army bases all throughout the United States and the Pacific, including Takae, Okinawa, and Fort Gulick in Panama. At each site, soldiers prepared for "search and destroy" operations that had become the war's trademark.[38]

The imagined geography of Kara Village stood in sharp contrast with the "progress" cultivated elsewhere in Oʻahu and represented the colonial violence at the heart of Hawai'i's liberal modernity. Through enactments against "natives," played by the soldiers, Kara Village reenacted the displacements of Native Hawaiians and the disavowal of their sovereignty through statehood. Typically hidden from the rest of the island, the violence of Kara Village made a spectacular appearance before the public in the summer of 1967. At that year's annual state fair, tourists and residents converged in downtown Honolulu to celebrate the ninth year of statehood, and the presence of Vietnamese "natives" in Hawai'i suddenly became glaring at the army's display. Alongside its showcase of modern military technologies, the army also displayed a "Vietnamese" showcase, featuring an assortment of "Viet Cong" weapons, and even "Viet Cong" themselves. Wearing black pajamas, straw hats, and rubber sandals, these subjects embodied the Vietnamese enemy in the flesh. The staging of the Vietnamese as "primitive natives" in their natural warring habitat simultaneously justified the war abroad and reinforced Hawai'i's progress.[39]

But these "native" men were not shipped across the Pacific from Vietnam—they were actually from Hawai'i. They were members of Hawai'i's National Guard, which consisted mostly of Native Hawaiians and Asians from Hawai'i. In the 1950s and 1960s, "local" youths joined the Hawai'i Army Reserve and National Guard as part of their indoctrination into the islands' political culture. Army commanders consistently prized their exceptional training and patriotic vigor. At the conclusion of its summer basic training at Fort Ord in 1966, one commander remarked of the All-Hawaiian Company, "This unit has the best esprit and morale of any on post." Alluding to the legacy of the famed 100th Battalion, a platoon sergeant added: "Of course, there's a built-in spirit which makes the men want to do a good job. And they are doing it."[40] Although the guardsmen were praised for their high morale, part of their value stemmed from their perceived racial difference. Unit commanders often singled out Asians and Hawaiians from the ranks as part of their training exercises and adorned them with "native" garb to play the role of villagers and Viet Cong interchangeably. In the mock village, their racialized presence lent another dimension of realism that the army most cherished. After August 1965, when the army designated units of the Hawai'i National Guard as part of the Selected Reserve Force for potential deployment to Vietnam, these war enactments acquired more urgency.[41]

On June 15, 1967, the 1st Battalion, 20th Infantry of the 11th Infantry Brigade commenced training at Kara Village. Activated one year earlier, the brigade was

One of many huts housing "villagers" during their stay in the Koolaus.

Chaplain (Capt.) William R. Hollis, 3rd Bde., removes his boots before entering temple at Clanu.

FIGURE 5. Soldiers "going native" in Kara Village. (Images and original caption appeared in *Hawaii Tropic Lightning News,* May 26, 1965.)

preparing for deployment. First, Sgt. Manuel Alverado instructed soldiers impersonating "Viet Cong" to proceed to their "hiding places" —under a set of stairs, on top of a temple, inside a well. Then he gave a lecture to trainees, acquainting them with the characteristics of Kara Village. Finally, training began when he sent the trainees in squads to scout for hidden weapons, tunnels, and booby traps and to clear out "Viet Cong" suspects. From start to finish, the exercise mimicked a search-and-destroy operation, recreated in minute detail.[42]

On December 5, 1967, the brigade shipped out to Vietnam. While the first month passed by unremarkably, the following month the Tet Offensive changed everything. With military intelligence that one battalion of the NLF had dispersed into Son My village for refuge, Col. Oran K. Henderson, the brigade's commander, urged his troops to be vigilant. "Go in there aggressively," he ordered. "Close with the enemy and wipe them out for good." On March 15, Capt. Ernest Medina rounded up his platoon of Charlie Company and told them, "There are no innocent civilians in this area." On March 16, the platoon entered the hamlets of My Lai. They prepared to root out the "Viet Cong and Viet Cong sympathizers," just as they had practiced at Schofield Barracks. Yet from Medina's instructions, the operation seemed very different from their training. One soldier understood of his task, "We were supposed to wipe out the whole area—waste it." Another had demanded clarification the night before and asked, "Who is my enemy?" Medina replied, "Anybody that was running away from us, hiding from us, or appeared to be the enemy." On the morning of March 16, 1968, Charlie Company laid waste to the hamlets, killing anybody and anything in sight. Men, women, children, and livestock were not spared, and before the morning's end, an estimated three hundred to five hundred civilians were murdered.[43]

News of the My Lai massacre did not surface for more than a year, but when it did, the reports shocked the nation and galvanized the antiwar movement. Protesters nationwide decried its "senseless" violence; elected officials and the White House declared the episode "abhorrent to the conscience of all the American people." The White House also prompted the Senate and House Armed Services Committees to launch a full investigation. On November 26, 1969, the committees showed colored slides depicting gruesome images of dead Vietnamese "before shocked and sickened members of Congress." In horror, one senator condemned this as "an act of brutality that cannot have been exceeded in Hitler's time."[44] Senator Inouye joined in the chorus of criticism and exhorted, "If there is to be any way out of this national disgrace, it is to be found only through the prompt, complete and public investigation of what has occurred, the proper punishment of those responsible and through every effort to determine why My Lai happened." To the Hawai'i senator, the massacre implicated officials at every echelon of the military command, and he went so far as to question the foundation of U.S. military training, "which permits common reference to the Vietnamese as 'gooks,' 'dinks' or 'slopes.'" He asked, "Are there racist overtones at work here?"[45] For a brief and rare moment, the My Lai massacre reports cast light on the racial dimensions of U.S. military violence and created the space for public officials to condemn U.S. policy. Little did these public officials realize that this violence was honed and refined at Schofield Barracks. The violence at My Lai had deep entanglements with Hawai'i's liberalism, but this was a contradiction that remained unspeakable, expressed only by utterances of "surprise" and "horror."

And just as quickly as it emerged, the protest of racial violence in the mainstream press was contained. In the end, the prosecution for the war crimes focused neither on ideological constructs nor on the policies that maintained them but on lone perpetrators. In particular the media fixated on 1st Lt. William L. Calley, the army platoon leader charged with premeditated murder for ordering the shootings of civilians. In a lengthy exposé on December 4, 1969, the *Honolulu Star-Bulletin* mused that Calley was "an average guy"—"the same old Rusty," as one friend recalled—which made his ability to commit mass murder all the more incomprehensible.[46] Except for one *Star-Bulletin* headline in early reports of My Lai that mentioned Schofield Barracks as the troops' training site, Hawai'i's role in the incident was obscured entirely in public discourse.[47] The erasure of Hawai'i from narratives of My Lai was intentional and predictable. In fact, the erasure spoke to Hawai'i's exceptionalism. It was a militarized paradise that stood for racial progress and modernity, and it was not a place for imperial violence. This was the same false divide that enabled the push for Hawai'i statehood in the 1950s and in turn justified Hawai'i's role in the Vietnam War. Hawai'i's activists wasted no time in exposing these false claims.

RESISTING WAR, RESISTING "PARADISE"

The blood of My Lai still soaked the ground when Hawai'i's residents, official representatives, guardsmen, and reservists awoke to unexpected news. On April 11, 1968, President Johnson announced the activation of Army Reserve and National Guard units for levy to Vietnam. The call-up involved 3,288 National Guardsmen and 782 Reservists from the state of Hawai'i, which comprised elements of the 29th Infantry Brigade and the 100th Battalion, 442nd Infantry, the latter to be attached with the former. The brigade was slated to activate on May 13. The announcement came as a shock to the public. It was the first reactivation for the 100th Battalion since World War II and the first altogether for the 29th Brigade. It was the largest mobilization in Hawai'i since the 25th Division had deployed from Schofield Barracks more than two years ago.[48]

The news of the mobilization galvanized the Hawai'i public once more, but not with the fanfare that had occurred in 1966. Promptly after the announcement, Hawai'i's congressional representatives fired off telegrams to Secretary of Defense Clark Clifford and President Johnson and expressed concern that Hawai'i bore a disproportionate burden in the call-up. Representative Spark Matsunaga pleaded to Clifford, "The people of Hawaii have always responded strongly and patriotically to the Nation's call to arms," but that "17 percent of the troops affected by the call-up should come from such a small state like Hawaii is difficult to justify."[49] Citizens also voiced their protest. In a *Star-Bulletin* editorial, Robert Aitken framed the issue broadly. He charged that the disproportionate call-up was part of "the history of exploiting men from Hawaii as colonial troops." He drew a comparison to the Nisei soldiers of World War II: "Our men in the 442nd Infantry Regiment and other predominately Hawaiian outfits were used during World War II in much the same way that England used her colonials.... That is to say, they were given disproportionately dangerous missions." He argued, "Now, Hawaii is again being asked to sacrifice far out of proportion to the size of its population." Others shied away from such trenchant criticisms, but still conveyed the same underlying message. In a letter to Senator Hiram Fong, one "worried parent" pleaded, "Save THE BOYS OF HAWAII being shipped to Vietnam for this NONSENSE."[50] Unlike the jubilation surrounding the departure of the 25th Division in 1966, the call-up of the 29th Brigade catalyzed Hawai'i's antiwar movement.

This certainly was not the first time that people in Hawai'i voiced their dissent against American militarism. In the wake of World War II, the Honolulu Labor Canteen formed and brought together labor organizers, stevedores, plantation workers, and GIs to protest the demobilization slowdown of 1945–46.[51] The Vietnam War drove many of these same activists back to the frontlines. In an unprecedented move in April 1967, the Senate Military and Civil Defense Committee of the Hawai'i Legislature held a hearing that brought an older generation of left activists, including members of the International Longshore and Warehouse Union and the United Public Workers, to testify against the war. The hearings signaled an historic moment when Hawai'i's liberal establishment and the old left aligned in solidarity to call on President Johnson to end the war.[52]

In addition to mobilizing an older generation of activists, the activation of the 29th also politicized many young people, including students and in particular students of color who were inspired by the Third World and Black Power movements. On April 11, 1968, members of Students for a Democratic Society at the University of Hawai'i gathered to address the urban rebellions that erupted across the country in the wake of Dr. Martin Luther King Jr.'s assassination. Their meeting quickly turned into an antiwar demonstration. Richard Tanimura stood and spoke, "The time has come for me personally to take a stand as a member of the National Guard." "I find myself compelled to oppose any participation of any units of the Armed Forces of the United States in either Vietnam or in quelling racial disorder on the mainland. If I am asked to suppress any people of any color, I cannot in good conscience reply, 'I will.'" The crowd gave a standing ovation, prompting one student to ask: "What are you going to do? . . . Are you going to let Richard be dragged off to jail or are we going to fight?" The response was unequivocal. One by one, twelve students went up to the front of the crowd and lit their draft cards on fire.[53] This spontaneous antiwar demonstration gave rise to The Resistance, a loosely organized group of draft resisters that gained the support of lawyers, professors, clergy, and other community leaders in Hawai'i. A few weeks after the demonstration, student activist Wayne Hayashi summarized, "What happened on April 11 is a revolution born amidst storms of dissent and protest against the war in Vietnam, the racism of our country and the inequities of the draft system."[54]

One of The Resistance's founding members, Stanford Masui, recalled that the impetus for both the April 11 demonstration and the founding of The Resistance "was actually anti-racism, not anti-war." The week before April 11, a storm of protests took place across the country in response to King's assassination. There was speculation in Hawai'i that the National Guard would be deployed to subdue the rebellion on the mainland. On April 9, a group of two hundred University of Hawai'i students and faculty marched to Iolani Palace and demanded that Governor Burns keep the National Guard from being sent "to suppress the blacks in the ghettoes." Two days later, when the president announced the activation of the 29th Brigade, there seemed to be no doubt about its motivation. Masui emphasized, "Dr. King was making anti-war statements," and the "Black Power movement was starting to educate against the war."[55]

People in Hawai'i understood that mobilizing Hawai'i's servicemen meant waging counterinsurgency against the Vietnamese and black Americans.[56] On May 13, mobilization day, the Hawai'i National Guard assembled at Fort DeRussy to become federalized into the army. The event, according to the army, heralded a "day of aloha throughout the Islands." Governor Burns praised the guardsmen for their "quiet devotion to the country." Nearby, people had gathered to protest the ceremony. When the National Guard proceeded down Kalia Road to Schofield Barracks, ten people from the crowd broke through the barricade. They sat down in the middle of the road and blocked the troops from moving forward. The "Kalia Road sit-in" was the first major demonstration organized by The Resistance. While bystanders hurled racist verbal assaults, the protesters sat "peacefully," for about an hour. Masui recalled feeling most concerned with communicating solidarity with the soldiers rather than actually stopping the trucks from

FIGURE 6. Stanford Masui arrested at the Kahlia Road Sit-In,
May 13, 1968. (Photograph by Ian Lind.)

their destination. The police moved in to disperse the crowd and arrested and
charged ten individuals with trespassing. According to official reports, the
protests made little impact on the day's procession. The army reported, "There
was a brief interruption of the troop movement when local dissidents halted
the convoy," and that it had caused "no appreciable delay." The guardsmen
showed no visible or emotional reaction to the protesters. With the exception
of a few reservists who did not show up for the induction, the members of the
29th Brigade seemed to "present a proud image of Hawaii" and appeared "quietly devoted."[57] But the men of the 29th did not stay quiet for long.

On July 13, "some concerned members of the 29th Brigade" made their voices heard in an open letter. They began the letter by using the familiar language of obligation, as fathers and citizens, to appeal for equality: "Haven't the men of the 29th, most of whom have already fulfilled the mandatory requirement of six years of service to their country and who now have families, served this nation in accordance with the oath they took upon entering the National Guard?" They quickly took their indictment much further. "There is only one part of the world where over 500 men (mostly Infantrymen) are WEEKLY losing their lives, and that place is Vietnam." They stated, "More troops will only result in more deaths and soon Hawaii will leave its National Guard to rest forever in the jungles of Southeast Asia."[58] Three months later they wrote another open letter, this time condemning the troop activation as a "misleading political ploy." Employing statistical analysis, the guardsmen concluded that their activation actually enabled lower draft numbers for the rest of the United States. This projected "a false sign" that the war was ending. They urged, "The time has come for Hawaiians to wake up to reality."[59] Finally, the men of the 29th took legal action, and on September 6, 257 members of the brigade (out of a total of 3,288) filed proceedings in U.S. District Court to challenge the legality of their mobilization. By November, 1,300 officers and enlisted men had signed a petition calling for the immediate demobilization of the brigade.[60]

The large number of dissenters and their public outrage and legal action caught officials by surprise. Senator Fong admitted to Congress, "We did not expect them to riot when we called them up." When one senator asked for clarification, Fong responded: "They did it because they felt Hawaii was a docile State, because it was a law-abiding state, that was why they picked on my State." His statement drew laughter in Congress even though the situation in Hawai'i was severe.[61] Immediately after the 29th Brigade publicized their petition, the commanding general, Frederick A. Schaefer, issued a response, which was read to units at Schofield Barracks and reprinted in the *Star-Bulletin*. He scolded his men by declaring, "It is most disappointing to me to think there is a group within this fine organization . . . that feels they want to be a party to a document as flamboyant and misleading as is this petition." He proceeded, "Do you want to see us disintegrate into a group of discontents without the resolve or character that has always distinguished any unit from Hawaii?"[62]

General Schaefer's paternalistic tone and his point of view resonated with other critics, particularly among Nisei veterans. At an event commemorating the service of the 100th Battalion, Sam Sakamoto, president of Club 100, the battalion's veterans' organization, asserted: "Despite the political, economical and social injustices and indignities suffered by you and your parents prior to and during WWII, you did not protest by sit-ins, sleep-ins, violent demonstrations . . . or other abusive public displays. You protested constructively and well, in contrast to the vocal, violent and abusive minority who protest everything from college administration to the war in Vietnam today."[63] Charles Miyamoto, an army specialist serving in Vietnam, railed against the protesters and also drew a historical comparison: "This disgraceful, undignified conduct has brought shame to the people of Hawaii who are very proud of their military past. Rather than serve with pride and honor our reservists have acted as rash, immature, ungrateful orphans."[64] The legacy of Nisei military service in World War II surfaced as a symbolic reminder about the fulfilled promise of U.S. liberal inclusion. Military and civic leaders mobilized the narrative of martial patriotism to counter the antiwar movement. It was the same narrative that territorial leaders had mobilized to legitimize statehood and to delegitimize Hawaiian sovereignty.

The petition failed to sway the judge in court, and soon the protest of the Hawai'i National Guard lost momentum. In January 1969, eager to erase the incident from public memory, General Schaefer praised his troops: "Yes, some of them would like to be back as civilians, but as long as they're here . . . they are doing a good job." [65] Ultimately, his attempts to downplay the GIs' activism did not contain the movement. As members of the brigade were levied for duty in Vietnam, and by the time the brigade was demobilized in December 1969, the antiwar movement had already transformed into something else. In July 1969, the *Hawaii Free Press,* a Marxist alternative to the mainstream press, clarified the connections between the war in Vietnam and the racial-colonial violence in Hawai'i. The editors beckoned, "Brothers and Sisters, people of Hawaii, is it not time to admit that our islands, our homes, are being taken from us, that our lives are being directed by powers that we cannot control?" They argued that the forces of urban development and tourism that have displaced "locals" are made worse "by our irrational patriotism" and support for the war. They continued, "The future here under existing conditions looks very grim so we enlist in the service. . . . We go over to Vietnam and kill people who have done us no harm because the haoles told us we should and wait." Over the past two decades, land development, tourism, and the war functioned together to fuel the dislocation and impoverishment of Native Hawaiians and the working poor.[66] The people of Hawai'i were caught in a cycle of devastation.

At the end of the 1960s, the eruption of antiwar politics gave activists a new language to make sense of the structural violence of U.S. colonialism in Hawaiʻi, which they understood as an inseparable part of U.S. militarism in Asia. By 1970, global connections that linked Hawaiʻi's "development" to the U.S. war in Vietnam inspired a grassroots struggle in Kalama Valley on Oʻahu that, by most accounts, marked the beginnings of the modern Hawaiʻi sovereignty movement.[67] At Kalama Valley, the same activists who had opposed the war on the principle of Vietnamese self-determination now rallied to support local residents and indigenous peoples as they resisted against their forced eviction by the Bishop Estate, the largest private landowner in Hawaiʻi. "Land for local people, not tourists" was the slogan of the anti-eviction struggle. The activists were making it clear that tourism and militarism caused the violent displacement of local residents, and their message resonated far beyond Kalama Valley. The war in Vietnam that was expanding into Laos and Cambodia provided a transpacific anti-imperialist framework for activists to recognize and to address issues that Hawaiʻi's peoples faced. Through their engagement with local and indigenous struggles for land rights, these diverse activists sowed the seeds for a protracted sovereignty movement that emerged in full force by the mid-1970s.[68]

Activists deployed creative tactics to connect antiwar activism to a deeper critique of the historical conjuncture of liberalism and colonialism in Hawaiʻi. In February 1972, for example, *Liberated Barracks,* an "underground" newspaper of the local GI movement, published a map of Oʻahu. The map recalled the myriad other maps published over the past two decades, specifically maps that depicted military installations for official use or maps that pinpointed tourist attractions. Previous maps had depicted either military sites or tourist sites, but the one published in *Liberated Barracks* illustrated both. The map's disjunctive title, "Enjoy Hawaii: Home Staging-Ground for the Vietnam War in Indochina," introduced readers to an unorthodox interpretation of Oʻahu's geography. By using recognizable language found in standard tourist brochures, the map rendered the unknown familiar. It guided readers, "Be sure to visit all U.S. Military-occupied lands indicated by blacked-out areas," followed by a description of four such highlighted areas. Under the highlighted area labeled "My Lai Jungle Training Center," the caption read "Hawaii's Little Vietnam," revealing the genesis of the My Lai massacre and pointing the readers' gaze to the center of Oʻahu. In the top right corner, the map listed other facts about Hawaiʻi's role in the Vietnam War, disclosing the sheer extent of its militarization: "Did you know ... that Hawaii is the most heavily militarized group of Islands in the world?" The point of the map was simple: to make clear the connection between Hawai'i's militarization and its transformation into "paradise." The final words sprawled below the map suggested that the two processes occurred in lockstep. They read: "Paradise in the Pacific for Genocide in Indochina."[69]

Against the ongoing erasure of histories of violence from narratives of Hawai'i's liberal progress, the map illustrated the two as inescapably entwined. The map was created by Liberated Barracks and Catholic Action, a religious left group formed in late 1970 to raise public awareness about Hawai'i's role in U.S. militarism in Asia. According to Jim Albertini of Catholic Action, it had functioned as a "key organizing tool." The organization distributed the map widely in Hawai'i and even to Japanese Prime Minister Kakeui Tanaka during his visit with President Richard M. Nixon in Honolulu in August 1972. But in their organizing efforts, the activists wanted more than to disclose the "blacked-out areas" of Hawai'i's geography; they wanted to disrupt its entire existence. On Christmas Eve 1971, a silent vigil against the war took place at the Wahiawa United Methodist Church, just a few miles east of Schofield Barracks. After the vigil, the protesters walked to Schofield Barracks in a continuation of their demonstration. By journeying to the base, they traversed physical and imagined distances. These distances had defined Hawai'i's obscured centrality to the U.S. empire. The group's destination was the Jungle Training Center, the location tainted with the blood and memories of the My Lai massacre. There, they planned to memorialize a Vietnamese woman who had immolated herself in protest earlier in the year. The demonstrators walked through Kara Village and were taken aback by the sights of pagodas, huts, and straw figures mimicking the Vietnamese. "It was bizarre, surreal, to come across a Vietnamese village ... right on your island," Albertini recalled. "This is where you would train to do My Lai." As they walked silently through the training center, they were surprised that military authorities, who observed from afar, did not react to their presence and that the media paid no attention to them. The protests at Schofield Barracks on Christmas Eve 1971 passed by simply as a nonevent, forcibly suppressed in public memory, just like the history of Kara Village and its deep connection to the My Lai massacre.[70]

Within the frame of the decolonizing Pacific, these protests were the accumulation of a long, protracted struggle for demilitarized sovereignty. The protests in Hawai'i were connected to those occurring in the Philippines,

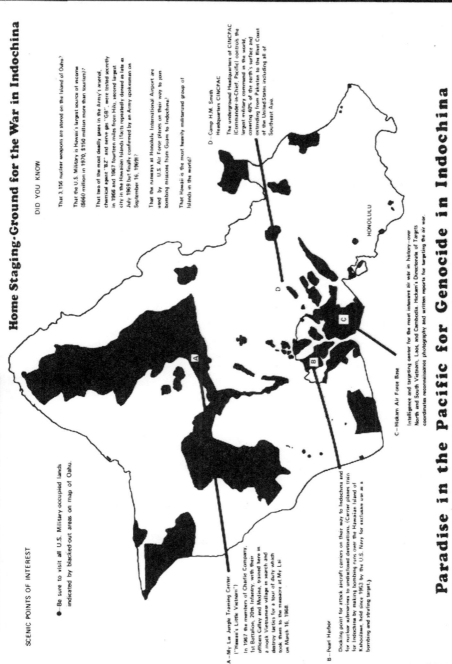

FIGURE 7. Map reprinted in *Liberated Barracks*, February 1972. (Courtesy of Jim Albertini.)

Okinawa, Guam, and other locales. In these places, anti-imperialist movements emphasized the destructive force of the military on everyday people's lives; and in Hawai'i this took the form of foregrounding the contradictions of race and empire. Activists argued Hawai'i was not a paradise, but a military garrison; it was not a model of development for decolonizing Asia but a colonized territory. But in making these distinctions, activists also understood that it was not simply one or the other, because they knew that empire functioned far more insidiously. They dwelled on the disjuncture, to make meaning of their "weird coexistence," in Albertini's words.[71]

The politicization of these strange affinities—of liberalism and war, "paradise" and "genocide"—radicalized the antiwar and anti-eviction struggles of the early 1970s and transformed them into a broader movement for Native Hawaiian sovereignty. If the post–World War II U.S. empire proposed the military as a vehicle for modernization in the Pacific islands, sidestepping the question of demilitarization and political independence altogether, then the antiwar, anti-eviction, and sovereignty movements shaped a different interpretation of the decolonizing Pacific, specifically through their transborder solidarities and collective insistence on self-determination.

FOUR

Working the Subempire

PHILIPPINE AND SOUTH KOREAN MILITARY
LABOR IN VIETNAM

IN 1985, THE SOUTH KOREAN writer Hwang Sŏkyŏng published *The Shadow of Arms,* the first Korean literary work about the Vietnam War. Unlike much contemporaneous U.S. cultural production that sought to recast the war as a "good war," fought by heroic (and victimized) American soldiers, *The Shadow of Arms* was a searing critique. The novel revolves around Ahn Yong-gyu, a young Korean sergeant pulled from the front lines and assigned to investigate the black-market transactions at the PX (post exchange), "a place where an exhausted soldier with a few bloodstained military dollars can buy and possess dreams mass-produced by industrial enterprises," such as television sets and Coca Cola (65). In the novel the PX comes to represent the war itself, which Hwang calls a war of "commodity imperialism." Taking readers through the war's systemic violence, racism, and structuring role in the Asian-rim economies, Hwang sought to expose the underside of South Korea's modernity. Hwang wrote the novel in the 1970s and early 1980s as a veteran of Korea's Vietnam War and a dissident of South Korea's authoritarian regime; to his mind, both were the twin effects of U.S. imperialism in Asia after World War II.[1]

This chapter traces the lineaments of the imperial history captured in *The Shadow of Arms* by explaining how postcolonial nations in the throes of nation building and economic development in the 1960s, particularly South Korea and the Philippines, came to play a part in the war in Vietnam. It begins with Hwang's conception of the PX to highlight the imperial economic relations that sustained and animated this other Vietnam War in Asia. Indeed, what does it mean for a South Korean soldier to be sold "mass produced dreams" through the U.S. military at the price of his own blood? Or that a particular kind of modernity, defined by a nation's economic growth and incorporation into the capitalist world system, could be achieved for South Korea and the Philippines, paid for with Korean, Filipino, and Vietnamese lives? The incorporation of South Korea and the Philippines into the U.S.-led global capitalist economy, often told as a story of unequal relations between the former colonized and colonizer, was a far more complex one involving soldiers and workers traversing the militarized expanse of the decolonizing Pacific.

By 1966, when the U.S. war in Vietnam was in full swing with 362,000 American troops on the ground, nearly 45,000 South Korean soldiers and marines were also there fighting alongside Americans, in addition to 2,000 Filipino army medics and engineers. By war's end in 1973, more than 340,000 South Korean troops had fought in South Vietnam, representing the largest third-country force to contribute to the American war.[2] To U.S. officials, these forces were part of a collective international response to President Johnson's "More Flags" initiative announced in April 1964, to showcase "free world" solidarity for the U.S. war effort. But in South Korea and the Philippines, they represented that and much more. To South Korean President Park Chung-hee (1963–79), the war presented an opportunity to achieve his dream of industrializing the nation through the securing of U.S. military aid, offshore contracts, and revenue from soldiers' labor, all to set the nation on a path to greater economic prosperity and influence in the region. To Philippine President Diosdado Macapagal (1961–65) and his successor, Ferdinand Marcos (1965–86), the war spelled opportunities to do the same albeit on a smaller level. At the same time, American leaders also understood these countries' participation in the war as a route toward achieving greater regional cooperation and interdependence in the maintenance and expansion of U.S. capitalism. In the mid-1960s, nationalist ambitions in these former colonies thus entwined and collided with the U.S. imperial desire of securing an "Asia for Asians."

If U.S. leaders promoted "Asia for Asians" as a liberal strategy of decolonization in the 1950s, by the following decade, popular nationalisms in the Philippines and South Korea, among other places, had wrest that language from U.S. control and imbued it with greater meaning. Beyond an elite discourse, "Asia for Asians" materialized in the 1960s most clearly as a labor formation, animated by the social experiences of workers and soldiers as they pursued jobs and economic security through the war in Vietnam. For men and women in South Korea and the Philippines who faced diminished life chances under the export-led industrialization drives of their governments, war meant work, first and foremost, and tens of thousands clamored for higher wages and other social incentives across the seas. Scholars have noted the contradictions of liberal citizenship that simultaneously incorporates citizens into the nation and subjects them to increasing state violence.[3] For South Korea and the Philippines in the 1960s, this contradiction was transposed onto and animated through the Vietnam War, as Koreans and Filipinos demonstrated their worth as citizens by engaging in, or at the very least being complicit in, the production of organized violence for the U.S. empire.

As these soldiers fought and died in the war, imperial dynamics in Asia and the Pacific were being reworked fundamentally. Their military labor, couched in terms of economic opportunity and anticommunist nationalism by the government, worked to reinforce, and to obscure, the ongoing colonial dependence of South Korea and the Philippines on U.S. economic aid and Japan's capitalist revitalization. Jin-kyung Lee and other scholars have underscored South Korea's war mobilization as a vital process in the making of South Korea as a "subempire."[4] In general terms, a subempire names a semiperipheral nation-state that functions on behalf of a core hegemonic power. A subempire, or subimperial state, tends to reinforce the goal of regional capitalist integration in its drive to expand its markets beyond its national borders. This imperial ordering in Asia was part and parcel of the making of the decolonizing Pacific. As a cultural process, the subimperial describes the post–World War II condition and geopolitical configuration in Asia in which decolonization was not yet achieved, and an imperialist desire came to fill the space of the unfinished liberation among the former colonies.[5]

For South Korea and the Philippines in the 1960s, the Vietnam War emerged as an engine of subempire. Exporting citizen-workers to the hinterlands of South Vietnam secured great financial capital for these countries that propelled their economic development, and enhanced their prestige among nations. For the United States, the war facilitated the transnational circulation of people that promoted the spread of capitalism in Asia in the age of decolonization. The militarization of the Vietnam War and the development of Asian-rim economies occurred in lockstep, intimately connected through the labor and violence of South Koreans and Filipinos in Vietnam.

The subempire, however, rested on shaky grounds from the start. It depended on workers who could presumably separate their desire for economic gains from their more worldly desires shaped by histories of colonial subjection. The subempire, in short, could not contain the full depth of their aspirations. As Philippine and South Korean officials enlisted their citizens for their respective nation-building projects, counterpublics began to take shape. Beginning in 1964, the same social conditions that drove working-class young men to war also pulled activists and ordinary citizens into the streets of Manila and Seoul, to protest the war in Vietnam and the narrow conceptions of citizenship and economic development that were championed by their governments. Against government officials' willful denial of the links between the war in Vietnam and the resurgence of Japanese and U.S. imperialisms in the region, activists boldly drew the connection by highlighting South Korea's and the Philippines's ongoing colonial dependency and complicity in U.S. imperial violence.

THE PHILIPPINE SOLUTION

In April 1963, Ricardo Galang, a Filipino national and a U.S. Army reservist from Manila, wrote to Edward Lansdale in search of work. He was hoping to get involved in a civic-action project that could take him to Vietnam or elsewhere in Asia. He confided, "I am all steamed up for this new type of operation because of its applicability to areas like the Philippines and neighboring countries." Galang demonstrated his knowledge of what this work entailed, explaining, "The challenge of pioneering work requiring the laying of a foundation of community development to deter the growth of communism has had always a strong appeal to me." And he wanted to learn more. His pursuit led to correspondences in the summer of 1963 with Lansdale and the Director of Civil Affairs and Civil Defense, Col. John Duffy, who suggested that Galang enroll in a six-week counterinsurgency-training course at Fort Gordon, Georgia. The course interested Galang but was beyond his reach due to a lack of funding. In November, he wrote to Lansdale again, this time inquiring specifically about the Chieu Hoi, or "Open Arms," program recently started in South Vietnam by the Agency for International Development, the State Department's newly renamed aid agency. "I have feeble attempts here in Manila to establish some contacts with some AID officials" to see about getting involved, "but I have found it somewhat difficult."[6]

Galang was as savvy as he was persistent in his endeavor to take part in the labor circuits of the U.S. military. He conveyed his enterprising spirit, something he must have known would spark Lansdale's attention, and he knew the bureaucracy and networks. For Lansdale, Galang's appeal could not have been timelier. In February 1963, Lansdale received some old friends at his Washington, D.C. office who wanted to talk about bringing more Filipinos to South Vietnam. One of them was Nguyen Thai, a former press officer for President Diem, who was among the group of South Vietnamese officials who traveled to the Philippines to observe President Magsaysay's civic-action program in 1955. Nguyen knew the Philippine political landscape. He told Lansdale that Filipino leaders under the current Macapagal Administration had an "exciting but constructive impact" on young Vietnamese people by infusing them with ideas about liberal democracy. Some of them, Nguyen advised, should be sent to Saigon to rejuvenate Diem's leadership. One week before Nguyen's visit, Lansdale had a similar conversation with two Philippine leaders, Secretary of National Defense Macario Peralta and Ambassador Amelito Mutuc. The two had expressed to Lansdale that the Philippines "is willing, ready, and able to help" in Vietnam with proper U.S. support. Mutuc, who was president of the Philippine Jaycees in 1955, even suggested remounting Operation Brotherhood, "perhaps on a smaller scale."[7]

Lansdale's talks with old friends rekindled his imagination. On February 13, Lansdale fired off a letter to the head of the U.S. Army Concept Team for Counterinsurgency Operations, Edward Rowny, to discuss his past experiences in the Philippines and their relevance for the ongoing pacification in Vietnam. In his view, the Chieu Hoi program that just started a few months before to induce Vietnamese communists to lay down their arms and "return" to the South Vietnamese government was showing limited effect. Lansdale suggested that it should be revamped along the lines of the Economic Development Corps (EDCOR). What made EDCOR successful in the Philippines, Lansdale told Rowny, was that it made good on the communist slogan, "land for the landless." If giving land to the people could turn the radicalized peasantry into "die-hard capitalists" in the Philippines, "are there opportunities ... to exploit the fabulous natural resources of Vietnam?" Whatever provisions Americans chose to capitalize on, the project must appear an entirely Vietnamese initiative, with Americans receding far into the background.[8]

Talks of reviving the counterinsurgency experiments from the early 1950s soon brought some of the same people back into the field. One of them was Rufus Phillips, the CIA officer who had directed Operation Brotherhood's campaign in Ca Mau in 1955. In 1962, the U.S. Agency for International

Development tapped Phillips to help devise a counterinsurgency program for South Vietnam. He was tasked specifically with directing U.S. support for the Strategic Hamlet Program that Diem and his brother Nhu had recently initiated. Phillips took the job with hesitation, knowing that South Vietnam was not the same country he had helped steer in 1955, and that "much of the earlier spirit of civic action had been lost."[9] In September 1962, he returned to Saigon to head the Office of Rural Affairs, a new division of the U.S. Operations Mission (USOM) whose primary aim was to secure the hamlet populations and to win them over to the side of the government. Phillips needed motivated people on his staff, "people with enthusiasm, energy, imagination and initiative," and who showed "a manifest capacity to understand and work with Asians."[10] He knew just the right people.

In November 1962, Phillips offered Charles Bohannan a job as a consultant for the Chieu Hoi program. He knew that Bohannan had firsthand knowledge of EDCOR as well as personal contacts with Filipinos who were eager to put their skills to use abroad. Through his guidance, the Chieu Hoi program could reactivate the networks that had brought Filipinos to South Vietnam in the 1950s. Frisco San Juan, the president of the Eastern Construction Company, Incorporated (ECCOI), formerly the Freedom Company, wasted no time in reaching out to Bohannan. On November 27, San Juan wrote to Bohannan and asked him to help market ECCOI's "counter-insurgency specialists" to South Vietnamese officials. He was confident that the Filipinos "will catch the interest of our friends" in Vietnam who "may soon ask me for an elaboration of this type of service ECCOI offers."[11]

Ricardo Galang eventually made his way to South Vietnam through the Eastern Construction Company sometime after 1963. The company employed Galang and a handful of other Filipinos to participate in USOM's expanding race war in the provinces. In January 1964, "three very savvy Filipino friends" circulating in the Mekong Delta area wrote to Bohannan to report their observations about the progress of the psychological warfare that was under way. In short, it was not going well. They noted that some Vietnamese officials seemed to have bought into the communist propaganda that the Americans had replaced the French as a colonial power. To offset this perception, the Filipinos recommended a "considerably enlarged use of Asians in the provinces, to explain, as one brownskin to another, what the real purpose of American assistance is."[12] One of these savvy friends named Rizalino Del Prado elaborated the point on a later occasion: "The Vietnamese officials are more receptive and are more sincere and frank in their dealings with the Filipinos. The Vietnamese extols the fact that the Filipinos are fellow-Asians and understands their sentiments as an 'Oriental.'" Del Prado emphasized that unlike white Americans, Filipinos "are inconspicuous in their performance of their missions, because they can pass for Vietnamese" and "can go about the hamlets without arousing much attraction to the children and curious people."[13]

From this assessment, little seemed to have changed in the ten years since the deployment of Operation Brotherhood. As before, Filipinos' seemingly innate ability to perform racial intimacy spelled the strategy to winning the Vietnamese over from the communists. And as before, this blind faith obscured the deeper resentments that some Vietnamese officials held toward Filipinos. Lansdale acknowledged these resentments but dismissed them as expressions of petty "jealousy" among certain midlevel officials. "The Philippines was a warmly favored nation at the birth of Vietnam's independence, and it is nonsense to let a few Vietnamese bureaucrats spoil this," he had said to Mutuc and Peralta.[14] Such idealizations did not align with the political reality in the Philippines and South Vietnam. By the fall of 1963, U.S. support for the Diem project had waned considerably. In addition, the American decision to escalate the war in 1964 and to request military assistance from the "free world" placed the Vietnam question at the center of long, contentious, and highly public debates about the legacies of colonialism in the Philippines and South Korea.

COLONIAL DEBT, NATIONALISM, AND WAR

Park Chung-hee seized power by military coup in May 1961 during revolutionary times in South Korea. One year earlier, on April 19, 1960, students had staged a massive nationwide uprising demanding a radical restructuring of Korean society. They called for the reunification of Korea based on "antifeudal, antiforeign, and anticomprador capital," and Park's promise to chart an autonomous path to national economic development won their cautious support. Some even compared him to Egypt's Gamal Abdel Nasser.[15] His plan for South Korea's economic modernization, which was not publicly known at the time, became clearer during his first state visit to the White House. At the White House in November 1961, he made an unsolicited offer to President Kennedy to send Republic of Korea (ROK) combat troops to

Vietnam, in exchange for increased U.S. economic aid the following year.[16] In his pursuit of export-led growth of the South Korean economy, Park had set his sights on Vietnam as the nation's frontier; and the military was an essential part of the plan. Park thought that South Korea's military involvement in Vietnam would redirect the excess of the democracy movement of April 1960 in part by framing military service as economic opportunity for individual young men. It would also bring South Korea firmly into the circuits of East Asian capitalism. According to Kim Sŏng-ŭn, the ROK Minister of National Defense, "The Vietnam War was the one and only golden market for the Korean government to export its unemployed men and manufactures."[17] Even before the war officially started, the South Korean leadership was already eyeing its promise.

The decision to send American combat troops remained contentious among U.S. officials in 1964, but there seemed to be far less disagreement on one point: if the United States were to commit troops, it should not do so alone. In June 1964, Ambassador Henry Cabot Lodge framed the issue for President Johnson as one of strategic necessity: "It is apparently not planned to bring in Chinese Nationalists, even though this would definitely be an action against Chinese Communists in which their presence would be appropriate. Nor is it planned to use ROK troops." Earlier in May, Lodge put it more bluntly: "I understand that the ROK has well qualified personnel for the type of work where our men are getting killed and wounded. Why not use a few of them here?" American power must be applied deliberately, and allied soldiers presented an untapped opportunity to "share in the really dangerous work" in Vietnam.[18]

The president agreed. In May 1964, Johnson had requested "more nations of the free world to show their flags in Vietnam." With an initial lackluster response from the international community, he called on U.S. embassies to apply pressure. "What the U.S. is now doing in Viet Nam is exactly the sort of thing we have done on earlier occasions," particularly in Korea and the Philippines. "We did not on those earlier occasions act out of exclusive U.S. interest or for selfish purposes associated with U.S. ambitions. On the contrary what we have done in the past and what we are now doing in Viet Nam represent *disinterested sacrifices* by the people of the U.S. on a scale never before known in history." According to Johnson, this history lesson about American altruism bore repeating. The war in Vietnam was not an act of aggression, but a phase of an ongoing anticommunist liberation struggle to secure the "free world."[19]

Johnson's simplified rendering of postcolonial history through a discourse of sacrifice reaffirmed American exceptionalism and justified the participation of allied countries as a matter of course. The U.S. involvement in the Korean War and support in the various anti-insurgent campaigns ("what we have done in the past") appeared in this way a done deal, when in fact these wars remained a defining, if not permanent, feature of daily life within postcolonial nations. More fundamentally, U.S. military and economic aid from the late 1940s onward represented not the "disinterested sacrifice" of the United States but a calculated strategy to create and mechanize the U.S. transnational security state to facilitate the spread of capitalism. Contained within Johnson's history lesson, then, was an explicit iteration of a colonial debt: the U.S.-led economic incorporation of these postcolonial nations into the "free world" exacted a price, to be paid by "sharing the burden" in the exercise of U.S. imperial violence in Vietnam.

President Park was not only willing but eager to share the burden. On July 31, 1964, the ROK National Assembly unanimously ratified a bill to dispatch the first contingent of noncombat troops, including 124 medical officers, 6 nurses, and 10 Tae Kwon Do instructors. Park presented the offer publicly as repayment of the debt for the American intervention in the Korean War; but his contemporaneous negotiations with Japan revealed deeper motives. In March 1964, revelations surrounding Park's negotiations on a treaty to "normalize" relations with Japan sparked public outcry in South Korea about the perceived resurgence of Japanese imperialism. Since restoring Japan's sovereignty in 1952, the United States had pressured Japan and South Korea to forge diplomatic ties as a step toward creating a self-functioning, U.S.-oriented "Asia for Asians." Toward this end, in 1964, the United States scaled back economic aid to South Korea and pushed Japan "to assume a greater share of the burden in subsidizing South Korea" through reparations and granting access to Japanese export markets.[20]

Park pursued normalization with Japan despite popular opposition, recognizing reparations as a vital source to jump-start South Korea's manufacturing industries. At the same time, he also sought to maximize U.S. concessions for the ROK troop contribution to Vietnam. Park's scheme to modernize the South Korean economy thus rested on two unpopular decisions in 1964 that fundamentally reshaped colonial dynamics in East Asia. These decisions—to normalize relations with Japan and to pursue war in Vietnam—gave rise to a new subimperial formation that connected South Korea to Vietnam through the revitalization of Japanese economic dominance in the region.[21]

If South Koreans remained relatively quiet about their country's entry into the Vietnam War in 1964, they were far less silent about the other aspect of the South Korean subempire: its renewed relations with its former colonizer. From March 1964 to September 1965, approximately 3.5 million citizens took to the streets in South Korea to protest the normalization treaty.[22] Signed in June 1965, the treaty paved the way for the reintegration of South Korea's economy with Japan's, and secured $800 million in grants and preferential loans as reparations to fund Park's export-led industrialization ventures. Park justified normalization as redress of colonial legacies, a step toward making South Korea economically autonomous and prosperous. Putting aside anti-Japanese feelings, he secured foreign capital and markets.[23] Normalization with Japan also provided further justification for the ROK's participation in the Vietnam War, which by the summer of 1965 involved more than two thousand noncombat troops. As one ROK foreign minister told Park, "Vietnam was a battlefield but it was also a market" to be exploited.[24] The normalization treaty, in short, solidified the ROK subempire by integrating South Korea into the East Asian capitalist economy and facilitating South Korean militarism in Vietnam, all in the name of national economic development.

The normalization of ROK–Japanese relations mirrored trends in the Philippines, where Macapagal's "New Era" reform policies paved the way for the liberalization of the Philippine economy. Through a five-year socioeconomic development plan, Macapagal lifted U.S. import controls and removed barriers to free trade to stimulate economic growth. The "special relationship" with the United States remained as crucial as before, despite mounting anti-American sentiments in the Philippines stemming from a series of incidents in 1962 involving an American business tycoon's corrupt meddling in Philippine politics and the U.S. rejection of World War II damage payments. Macapagal treaded carefully, seeking continued U.S. military and economic aid while charting an independent path to foreign policy, especially toward neighboring countries that shared a common "Malay" race. "The powerful affinities of race, culture, and geography," observed the State Department Bureau of Intelligence and Research in 1964, "as well as Filipino views of their own regional security and their own long-range interests as an Asian nation will operate as increasingly important aspects in reshaping Philippine foreign policy."[25]

The assertion of Philippine regionalism aligned with the U.S. aim to internationalize the war in Vietnam. In May 1964, following President Johnson's call for more flags, the State Department solicited the Philippines's contribution to the war. In October, shortly after the Philippine Congress approved the Vietnam Aid Bill to dispatch seventeen civic-action personnel, Macapagal urged a greater commitment from the United States—not for more U.S. troops but for Asian allies. The military situation in Vietnam was approaching "desperation," he told Defense Secretary McNamara, in part because American soldiers, being "Westerners and white men" who reminded the Vietnamese too much of the French, had failed to "convey a sense of common purpose to them." He suggested that the sixteen thousand American soldiers currently in Vietnam be replaced by an equal number of Asians. "We can live with the natives," he offered, "but it will be difficult for Filipinos to do it alone. Perhaps a sprinkling of Thais is needed." Dean Rusk welcomed the gesture but understood exactly what he was asking. "We expect that, in addition to requesting us to finance Philippine activities in South Viet-Nam, Macapagal will use his proposal as a point of departure for further requests for significant increases in our MAP [Military Assistance Program] aid."[26]

Macapagal used the language of racial intimacy to push for a greater role in the Vietnam War, but the Philippine public was not easily swayed. On December 27, 1964, thousands of Filipino protesters rallied outside Clark Air Base against "U.S. Imperialism" and "Yankee Violence," carrying placards that read, "Send Your Trigger-Happy APs (air police) to Viet Nam." The demonstration was in response to the recent shooting deaths of two Filipinos on American bases. On November 25, Airman Larry D. Cole shot and killed fourteen-year-old Rogelio Balagtas, who had trespassed onto Clark Field, followed three weeks later by the slaying of fisherman Gonzalo Villedo by U.S. Marine guards at Subic Naval Base for entering restricted waters. Public outrage over the killings amplified with the subsequent failed efforts to convict the U.S. servicemen in Philippine courts. All involved were tried under U.S. courts-martial, with Larry Cole found guilty of unpremeditated murder and sentenced to three years of hard labor. The two Marines involved in the Villedo shooting were acquitted of all charges.[27] The killings and failure to convict the Americans under Philippine jurisdiction served as potent reminders of the limits of Philippine sovereignty under existing U.S. military and economic arrangements, and it sparked anti-American protests throughout the country.

As the protests mounted, U.S. and Philippine state leaders agreed to hold off on all further discussions about a Philippine contribution to Vietnam, at least temporarily. Secretary of National Defense Peralta urged the U.S.

ambassador to help "quiet the agitation" before Macapagal could approach Congress about sending more troops.[28] But the storm never quieted. With anti-Americanism still riding high in the summer of 1965, Macapagal failed to sway a divided Senate to dispatch a two thousand–man Filipino engineer battalion. He reassured U.S. officials that he would get the job done after his reelection in November, but the opportunity never came. Instead, Filipinos overwhelmingly stood behind Ferdinand Marcos, an uncompromising nationalist who, they believed, would put Filipinos above American interests, and who galvanized the nation on an antiwar platform.

The Filipino people learned soon enough that Philippine nationalism and U.S. neocolonialism made logical bedfellows, when President Marcos made an about-face and announced his plan to send troops to Vietnam. What he desired all along, Marcos told a Philippine military official soon after his election, was to display a gesture of "real and sincere Philippine assistance" by sending a contingent that was "100% financed by the Philippine government," without U.S. aid.[29] Marcos's game of illusion resulted in tumultuous debates in Congress in the early months of 1966. Proponents of the new Vietnam Aid Bill conjured the specter of falling dominoes and the Philippines's obligation under SEATO to aid neighboring countries. In this context, nothing less than Filipino manhood was on the line. Filipinos have always been "in the thick of any war or fight," the Liberal congressman Ali Dimaporo reminded the House, such that to now shirk from "a battlefield so close to its shores could be construed by other nations as cowardice."[30]

Dimaporo's remarks drew ringing applause from the galleries, but outside the capitol building, demonstrators carried a different message. "We have not been attacked by an enemy nation; we have not been invaded by foreign troops," a University of the Philippines student council leader, E. Voltaire Garcia, told reporters. "By the sacred words of our constitution, we renounce war as an instrument of national policy." On February 21, thousands of protesters representing different factions of the Philippine left, including students, unionized workers, and peasants, gathered outside the U.S. embassy and Malacañang Palace to protest their government's complicity with U.S. imperialism. On March 25, days after the House approved a Vietnam aid package valued at P35 million (about US$836,000), with concessions permitting only "volunteers" to engage in "civic action," thousands stormed the capitol and the U.S. embassy as part of the International Days of Protest against American Military Intervention. Originally called forth by American antiwar activists, the protests in the Philippines broadened the antiwar message to a more far-reaching critique of U.S. imperialism and refusal to accept war as an engine of economic development.[31]

The anticolonial politics that were criminalized and largely suppressed in the Philippines and South Korea after World War II reemerged in full force in the mid-1960s around the buildup of the Vietnam War. On August 13, 1965, one day after 62 opposition party members walked out of the Korean National Assembly in protest against the normalization treaty, and as Korean citizens continued to demonstrate in the streets, the Assembly voted 101–1 with 2 abstentions to send a combat division to Vietnam.[32] By October 1965, twenty thousand soldiers and marines of the "Tiger" Capital Army Division and the "Blue Dragon" Second Marine Corps were deployed to Qui Nhon and Cam Ranh Bay. One year later, Park dispatched an additional division, bringing the total number of South Korean troops in Vietnam to 45,605. These numbers, together with the two thousand Filipinos of the Philippine Civic Action Group (PHILCAG) deployed in September 1966, had far exceeded the token gesture initially requested by the United States. And they reaped extraordinary payouts for their governments. The Philippine government earned $9.13 million a year for its deployment, combining overseas allowances for troops and increased U.S. military and economic aid.[33] Park's regime secured far greater rewards, including U.S. payments for all deployments, overseas allowances, and benefits, and increased U.S. military aid, as well as a pledge to hire Korean civilians and procure military supplies from South Korean contractors when possible. Between 1965 and 1973, the ROK government earned over $1 billion from the United States for its role in the Vietnam War.[34]

The war, in short, transformed parts of Asia and the Pacific into a military-industrial complex for the United States. As postcolonial nation-states reaped economic benefits, the dreams of economic mobility among ordinary citizens were channeled into military labor overseas.

THE WORK OF SOLDIERING

In April 1966, a Vietnamese delegation from the Ministry of Information and Chieu Hoi visited the Philippines to recruit more workers for the Chieu Hoi program. In recent months, the program had a successful run inducing National Liberation Front (NLF) defectors, and there was an "urgent" need for more Filipino advisers. "Demands are increasing," Foreign Service Officer

Douglas Pike told Bohannan, "just don't know whether or not our ECCOI Manila can supply the right quality. Quantity is not a problem." News about the job prospects spread quickly in Manila. On May 14, Damaso Cabacungan penned a letter to James L. Smith, a USAID officer who traveled with the delegation and to whom Cabacungan gave his "verbal application" to work in Vietnam. "I was the one who briefed your party at the National Headquarters and Training Center of the Philippine Rural Reconstruction Movement (PRRM)," Cabacungan reminded Smith. Besides having spent eight years working in the PRRM, a government-sponsored counterinsurgency initiative to improve village life, he had helped train various organizations in civic action, including the Special Forces of the Philippine Army, Rural Reconstruction Teams in Guatemala and Colombia, and U.S. Peace Corps volunteers. When Smith authorized Bohannan to begin screening for applicants the following month, he attached Cabacungan's letter and explained that this was "the type of man that would be nice to have in the program."[35]

That summer, Bohannan organized a Chieu Hoi orientation in Manila, drawing hundreds of hopeful applicants to fill forty-five slots. Bohannan thought the ideal applicant should possess some paramilitary background, including experience working in agricultural- and community-development projects, and should be highly motivated. Handwritten letters from aspirants quickly filled Bohannan's mailbox. "My wide experience in agricultural projects [and] cottage industries are, I believe, suffice to land me a job in Civic Action or Chieu Hoi program for Saigon, S. Vietnam," wrote one applicant named Charles. "I have the knowledge and ability, but who will provide the materials and tools?" Even those who did not attend the orientation caught rumors about the man who brought Filipinos to Vietnam. "I have heard that you have a hand in the recruitment of Filipinos for Vietnam work," Teofilo Gulla solicited Bohannan in September. "Because of lucrative jobs being offered in that country thru the U.S. and in view of the meager salary I am now receiving [in the Philippines], which is not even enough to make both ends meet, I am KNOCKING at your door for entrance."[36]

These letters capture the aspirations of Filipinos as they scrambled to take part in the labor circuits of the U.S. military in the 1960s. Like countless unemployed or underemployed workers in the Philippines at the time, these Chieu Hoi applicants were mostly educated and highly skilled in their trades, yet constituted an unsustainable labor force within the export-driven economy of the emerging antidevelopment state under Marcos.[37] The shift from import-substitution industrialization to export-oriented industrialization that began during the Macapagal Administration accelerated after Marcos took office in 1965. Marcos's economic and land policies, together with the devaluation of the peso aimed to incentivize foreign investment, furthered the decline in real income for the middle and working classes. Under such precarious conditions, marginalized citizens searched for opportunities overseas, where they hoped to put their experience in various land-reform and counterinsurgency projects to work. The Chieu Hoi program, and the growing U.S. military involvement in South Vietnam generally, provided those opportunities.[38]

These letters reflected the economic calculations of individuals but were also expressions of a deeper desire to overcome colonial legacies by utilizing their skilled labor to help others. "I have weighed the dangers as well as the good services to be offered towards mankind," Gulla continued in his letter to Bohannan.[39] A sense of humanitarianism suffused their pleas for work, and this should not be seen as a ploy that belied their economic motivations. Those who sought opportunities in Vietnam understood their experience in counterinsurgency in the Philippines as preparing them for the work of improving the lives of others in the global community. It was the same kind of desire that had motivated Operation Brotherhood doctors and nurses to channel their knowledge and skills toward helping Vietnamese refugees a decade earlier. Celestino Panganiban, an elementary-school principal and another hopeful applicant, conveyed to Bohannan in 1967: "What interest(s) me most is what we read in the papers, heard over the radio and even saw in the TV's the wonderful job accomplished by this program [Chieu Hoi] in South Vietnam."[40] These sentiments were not mere expressions of Filipinos' blind faith in the positive work of the U.S. military; instead, they reflected the enduring legacies of U.S. colonial benevolence and uplift unfolding in the context of the Philippines's increasing entanglement with the U.S. war in Vietnam.

The same forces that fueled revolutionary nationalism and pulled activists to the streets in the 1960s—namely, rising unemployment, neocolonial dependency, and the escalating war in Vietnam—drove young Filipino men to recruiting stations beginning in 1966. In July, two months after Marcos signed the Vietnam Aid Bill authorizing the deployment of a two thousand–man engineering battalion (PHILCAG), the *Manila Times* beckoned readers: "Do you want to enlist in the Philippine Army and perhaps be one of those sent to South Vietnam?" So far five thousand had applied for enlistment, but the army wanted to recruit three hundred more as replacements. Anyone interested who was a Philippine citizen, "able-bodied," male, single, and between eighteen and twenty-six years old should apply; those with at least six months of military training, including ROTC cadets, would have first priority.[41] To Marcos, enlistment offered a promising solution to the country's socioeconomic problems. He thought that the "hordes of jobless young men cluttering the streets in Manila" could be "a potential manpower source" for PHILCAG. "If these young healthy men are kept busy in Vietnam usefully fighting for freedom and their country instead of being involved in illicit activities," the unemployment problem, ever linked to the problem of internal security, would be solved simultaneously.[42]

The Philippine Army was confident in its ability to secure new recruits, but officials were caught off guard by what came next. In the spring of 1966, as thousands of Filipino citizens stood outside Camp Aguinaldo to volunteer for Vietnam, ten thousand men already enlisted in the Armed Forces of the Philippines (AFP) clamored to join PHILCAG.[43] The massive exodus of AFP soldiers to the recruitment lines sufficiently alarmed Philippine officials. In recent years, the AFP had acquired a reputation for being a largely "undisciplined and demoralized" organization. Sending them to Vietnam, Marcos feared, would "put the reputation of the Filipino fighting man to shame."[44] But AFP soldiers were motivated by obvious financial incentives. In Vietnam, soldiers earned three times the salary as they would in the Philippines. Those who joined PHILCAG, and increasingly those who looked to enlist in the U.S. Army directly, were "enthusiastic about [the] idea of fighting under U.S. auspices in Vietnam and [earning] U.S. army pay scales, allowances, PX privileges, etc."[45]

Positive associations with the U.S. military that were instilled from the colonial era indeed persisted in the 1960s despite the rising anticolonial fervor. PFC Victor Valeriano's experience highlighted the complex dynamics. The son of Napoleon Valeriano, the AFP colonel who had worked closely with Lansdale and Bohannan in the 1950s, Victor Valeriano joined the U.S. Army as an American citizen. Growing up in the suburbs of Northern Virginia had sheltered him from the nationalist upheavals in the Philippines. In 1967, when he met his Filipino school friends in Manila during R&R, "proudly [wearing] his U.S. uniform," he was "shocked by the violence of their verbal attacks on the United States, the U.S. Army, and the American involvement in Viet Nam." What came next surprised him more. Just before he departed Manila, some of these same friends went to him to solicit help in joining the U.S. Army and becoming American citizens. "Can you help me get a job in the United States, even as a waiter?" one asked.[46] Such contradictory expressions point to the complex meanings Filipinos associated with the U.S. military; it was simultaneously a symbol of neocolonial dependency and U.S. imperial violence and a route for personal economic advancement. The desire to become "American," an effect of U.S. colonial rule, continued to delimit the horizon of Filipinos' search for a better livelihood.

Koreans similarly developed a complex understanding of the war, viewing it as both economic opportunity and a reenactment of their colonial subjection under Japan. Their objections to the war were filtered through an anticolonial, anti-Japanese animus rather than directed solely at the United States. "Public opinion has been inflamed," U.S. Ambassador to South Korea Winthrop Brown noted to the State Department in the summer of 1965, "by distorted reports that the U.S. expects flesh and blood from Korea while concentrating its purchases of war materials in Japan to the advantage of that economy rather than the ROK."[47] If the war benefited Japan economically, Korea would pay with the lives of its citizens. Such a rationale lent the notion of South Koreans as "mercenaries"—a charge that was gaining currency among the South Korean public and within the U.S. Congress—a more specific meaning within the context of Japanese-Korean colonial history. During World War II, the incorporation of Koreans into Japan's wartime regime had simultaneously expanded their claims as subjects of the Japanese empire and jeopardized their lives in fighting for it.[48] History seemed set to repeat in 1965 as normalization with Japan and the troop deployment to Vietnam were under way. That these were happening concurrently, Ambassador Brown observed, "creat[es] a situation in which Korea appears to its own people . . . not as an independent and willing contributor [to the war], but as a puppet or vassal" to further U.S. and Japanese interests.[49]

The war might have rekindled anti-Japanese sentiments within South Korean political culture, but to the largely unskilled agrarian population that was being uprooted and mobilized by President Park's industrialization ventures, the war also meant work. Among the young Korean men who were conscripted into military service, most who volunteered to go to Vietnam came from a rural peasant background, attracted to the prospects of higher pay.[50] Korean military personnel in Vietnam earned from $40 to $600 a month, at a time when the GNP per capita in Korea was under $10 a month. These earnings, together with special overseas allowances financed by the United States, including death benefits of $10,000 paid to families of soldiers killed, and American and Japanese commodities acquired and smuggled home from U.S. military commissaries, all contributed to tangible improvements to the everyday lives of Koreans. Between 1965 and 1973, Korean military personnel and civilian workers earned $473.7 million in wages, of which 75–90 percent were remitted to families back home.[51]

Indeed, the mobilization of young Korean men for war in Vietnam was part of a wider phenomenon of migrant labor that characterized the early years of the Park era. This period witnessed the unprecedented movement of peoples from rural areas to urban centers and far beyond the nation's borders, as they sought to take advantage of new economic opportunities opened up by South Korea's integration into the capitalist world economy. At the same time that men were shipped off to war, working-class women found work in the burgeoning camptowns and sex-tourism industries that Park was actively promoting to support the continuing U.S. military presence in South Korea. The exploitation of working-class women's bodies for foreign troops, a state-sanctioned practice carried over from Japan's wartime policy and institutionalized during the U.S. occupation, became further entrenched as part of the state's drive toward militarized development in the 1960s.[52] When Ambassador Lodge told President Johnson that Koreans and other allied troops should "share in the really dangerous work" of the war in Vietnam, he might have been referring to male soldiers; but the expansive military-industrial complex that was beginning to take shape meant that other segments of the population, notably rural and working-class women, were also exposed to the "dangerous work" associated with Park's modernization plan, as they became integrated into the economy through sexualized forms of labor that made them vulnerable to state-sanctioned violence.

By the mid-1960s, then, Vietnam had become a new frontier for working-class peoples in South Korea and the Philippines, men and women who had long experienced the social conditions of living under the U.S. empire. Yoon In-Sik, who recognized that after liberation from Japan "the only possible place to find a job was the American military base," held a job distributing *The Stars and Stripes* and transporting American servicemen around U.S. bases in South Korea; in 1966, Yoon found work in Vietnam as an electrician for Pacific Architects and Engineers, a reputable American contractor, for which he earned $800 to $900 a month.[53] Lucrative opportunities in a variety of skilled and semiskilled work, such as engineering, accounting, carpentry, and plumbing, brought an estimated five thousand Filipinos to Vietnam by 1968. According to *Graphic,* a Philippines periodical, "There are so many good paying jobs in Saigon that even the Filipino dependents are lured to take advantage of the opportunity," as in the case of one Filipina who worked as a teacher alongside her engineer husband, earning $400 a month.[54] The war in Vietnam, in short, provided an outlet for the excess population whose labor could not be sustained within the export-driven economies of the Philippines and South Korea. In Vietnam, collective disillusionment was transformed into individualized promises of upward mobility. As working people risked their lives to pursue economic opportunities and personal advancements, they unwittingly fortified the South Korean and Philippine subempire and the relations of militarized violence that linked the fates of these countries to the United States, Japan, and the capitalist world.

CONSTRUCTING RACE AND NATION

The economic benefits of participating in the war might have been obvious, but Philippine and South Korean officials still sought other justifications that, at the very least, would mitigate the charge that their governments were sending mercenaries to a foreign war. Through the mainstream press and state media outlets, journalists and local government and state officials in both countries contributed to crafting official discourses of racial intimacy that rationalized their roles in Vietnam. The state discourses about PHILCAG and ROK troops were distinctly different, and at times even counterposed one another. Yet together they produced a postcolonial global imaginary that naturalized the conditions of militarized modernity in South Korea and the Philippines and mapped these historical processes onto Vietnam.

The colonial intimacy of PHILCAG manifested through cultural imaginings of Tay Ninh Province, where PHILCAG was dispatched in August 1966. Tay Ninh was located in the southwest region of the country adjacent to the Cambodian border, and had long been a hotbed of communist insurgency. The decision to send troops there made sense: it was where the first Filipinos of Operation Brotherhood had performed their tasks more than ten years ago, and the people there still held "high regard" for them. As a testament to their "long and pleasant association" with Filipinos, the villagers even erected a monument to commemorate the accidental drowning of three Operation Brotherhood doctors in 1955.[55] But Filipinos also had an affinity to Tay Ninh as a physical place. When AFP Chief of Staff Gen. Ernesto Mata visited in July 1966, he noted its resemblance to the lowlands of the Philippines: staple crops and plants native to the Philippines like sugarcane, mangoes, bananas, and rice grew abundantly in Tay Ninh. Even the Black Virgin Mountain, the famed hideout for NLF guerrillas, resembled the Arayat "Huk" Mountain in the Philippines. One *Manila Times* reporter summed up: "Filipino troops stationed here in Tay Ninh will be very much at home."[56]

On August 16, 1966, PHILCAG's advance teams of construction engineers, medics, and community-development workers arrived in Tay Ninh to prepare for the arrival of the larger contingent. Upon landing at Tan Son Nhut Airbase, the PHILCAG commander, Brig. Gen. Gaudencio V. Tobias, stated the purpose of his men to the press: "We are here on a mission of peace and mercy, not to search and destroy, but to keep alive and help reconstruct your war-torn country. We are here to help you build your schoolhouses, your roads and bridges, your resettlement sites, and such projects which can contribute to the socio-economic upliftment [sic] of your country."[57] The message, translated into Vietnamese and distributed by leaflets in the villages, evoked the longer history of Philippine humanitarianism that began with Operation Brotherhood. More concretely, PHILCAG served as part of the broader reorganization of pacification in the countryside. Under the Revolutionary Development program launched in early 1966, the U.S. military sought to implement civic action and security in every hamlet, essentially to contest NLF dominance by adopting its tactics.[58] PHILCAG was to provide the experienced knowledge in waging this "new" kind of war. One Filipino journalist remarked, "Tay Ninh is a test site for the application of a Philippine-inspired counter-insurgency program—and who else could better fit the role of civic actionists?"[59]

PHILCAG's mission entailed clearing six hundred hectares of the Thanh Dien Forest that served as a base area for the NLF, and erecting a refugee-resettlement village in its place. The construction of this "model village" and the civic-action projects it involved were justified through the discourse of racial kinship. "The Vietnamese peasantry which our boys live with every day is no different from the mass of the people in the Philippines," a Filipino reporter noted, "and their very lives, we're sure, are not any different from the lives of the families of many of our soldiers."[60] An affinity of race, place, and culture thus bonded Filipinos and the Vietnamese and enabled the remodeling of Philippine village life in Vietnam. The U.S. military agreed in its assessment: "As Asians, members of PHILCAG are well qualified to understand and communicate with the Vietnamese people. They are not the target of anti-European attitudes among Vietnamese that are a legacy of the colonial period."[61] What racial sameness alone could not communicate, the Filipinos did through medical aid and construction projects that contributed to tangible improvements to everyday life.

PHILCAG's activities recalled those of Operation Brotherhood and the more recent Operation Helping Hand of the 25th Infantry Division. "Our best defense," General Tobias told the press, "is our popularity with the people. All our actions are . . . geared to convincing the people of our sincerity to help them, that we have not come to kill any of them."[62] Younger officers who were at first "gung-ho about getting into combat" had learned to restrain themselves. Scenes of Filipino soldiers dispensing medical aid to villagers and of sergeants performing in a musical trio worked to obscure the war's violence. Even the soldiers' physiques apparently belied a strenuous war. "Looking at the Filipino waistlines, I gathered that the rations are truly ample," Lansdale quipped to General Westmoreland.[63]

Above all, the depiction of PHILCAG as a humanitarian crusade worked to counteract the charge that they were a "mercenary" force, an impression Philippine officials sought to dispel from the outset. Officials and the mainstream press emphasized that these soldiers were "not draftees sent abroad against their will" but were volunteers who chose to go. In doing so, they also distinguished PHILCAG from other allied troops in Vietnam. One *Graphic* correspondent suggested that among PHILCAG troops "there is none of the arrogance that characterizes many foreign soldiers fighting in a strange land." Although the article did not explicitly name these "foreign soldiers," it likely was referencing South Koreans who, besides constituting the largest allied military presence in Vietnam, acquired a reputation as a particularly brutal force.[64]

Like PHILCAG, South Korean troops figured centrally in the state discourses of the postcolonial nation. If Philippine officials and media outlets presented Filipino soldiers as "fellow Asians" who could win the trust of the Vietnamese through their antimilitarist qualities, South Koreans, mobilized as combat soldiers on a far greater scale, were depicted as martial subjects whose dispatch to Vietnam underscored South Korea's emergence as a "mature" and sovereign nation. Indeed, President Park saw Johnson's call for military assistance as an opportunity to rewrite Korea's colonial history by narrating the Vietnam War as a part of the trajectory of South Korea's national development. At the widely broadcast farewell ceremony for the "White Horse" division in August 1966, Park called on the departing soldiers to "bring honor" to the nation, to "demonstrate the bravery of Korean manhood to the world."[65] Speaking after the president, Lt. Lee So-dong invoked a longer national history: "We have coursing through our veins the blood of the *Hwarang,*" the aristocratic male youth corps of a premodern dynasty.[66] Racializing Korean troops as the vanguard of a superior, masculine, and virile race, Park sought to restructure Korea's historical position as a colonized nation vis-à-vis Japan and the United States.

For young Korean men who came of age in the postliberation era of never-ending war, their mobilization to fight in Vietnam as "dutiful nationals" stirred them deeply. "I was excited at the thought of war," one veteran recalled, at once alluding to the vulnerable masculinity experienced by many working-class men at the time. "Men must fight in war, that's how we become men."[67] To these marginalized citizens for whom fighting in the war gave them an opportunity to stake their claim in the nation, Park's rhetoric of overcoming Korea's colonial status through war resonated with their sense of failure as men and as providers for their families. If they were motivated by economic incentives to fight, these soldiers also came to understand violence as a form of currency for demonstrating their worth as citizens and as men. ROK troops learned the tactics of colonial violence first practiced by the Imperial Japanese Army and later by the U.S. military; and in the context of a race war in Vietnam in which Koreans occupied an in-between, semicolonial status, they learned to excel at the dispensation of violence.[68] U.S. military reports routinely described ROK troops as "tough, aggressive, well-disciplined . . . almost faultless."[69] Comparing the allied war effort to an orchestra, the U.S. commander, Gen. Creighton Abrams, remarked that the Koreans "play only one instrument—the bass drum."[70]

ROK marines arrived in Quang Ngai Province in the summer of 1966 as part of the allied pacification campaign. Quang Ngai and neighboring Binh Dinh Province historically occupied the center of Vietnamese revolutionary activity, stemming back to the first armed resistance against French rule in the late nineteenth century and the peasant rebellions of the 1930s. After World War II, the Viet Minh made Quang Ngai a base of its operations. When Diem and his brother, Nhu Diem, launched the Strategic Hamlet Program in 1962, they targeted this area especially as a known NLF stronghold.[71] By the time Korean troops arrived, most villagers had been relocated to the hamlets, leaving behind mainly elders who kept up the family farms, with the occasional help of children and grandchildren who moved between the hamlet and village whenever they could. Many of the elders were once active in the Viet Minh and continued to support the cause of anticolonial nationalism.[72]

The pattern of forced relocation and violence experienced by villagers in Quang Ngai mirrored what would happen in My Lai one year later. On November 9, 1966, fifteen-year-old Anh Hai was visiting his friend in Dien Nien hamlet when he saw the Korean marines approach on foot. He and his friend kept playing, thinking they were Vietnamese soldiers on routine patrol. "By the time we realized these troops were Koreans it was too late to hide even if we'd wanted to," he said. He recounted the scene that followed:

> When they reached the village they ordered all the people into a large group. All they could say in Vietnamese was 'di, di' (go, go). They had no interpreter. They pulled 15 or so old men and boys out of the crowd, lined us up and made us kneel a few yards from the others. They forced a 13 year old boy at one end of the line to stand in front of the group and asked him several questions in Korean. Of course neither he nor any of the rest of us could understand what they were saying. When he didn't reply for several minutes they led him to one side, shot him, and threw his body into a hole.

The soldiers left after this incident, only to return later in the evening. This time, they "again gathered these people into a group. They passed out cakes and candies to the children. Then with machine guns and grenade launchers they killed them all."[73]

Hai's testimony appeared in the 1975 American Friends Service Committee publication *America's Rented Troops: South Koreans in Vietnam*. The exposé was the work of Diane and Michael Jones, two American Quaker antiwar activists who traveled to Vietnam in 1970 and learned about the massacre at Dien Nien and other similar acts of violence committed by South Korean troops. While atrocities at the hands of American GIs had become common knowledge in the United States by the late 1960s, particularly after the revelations of the My Lai massacre, those committed by South Koreans remained far less known. After hearing Hai's story in March 1972, the Joneses conducted forty interview sessions with villagers in Quang Ngai and other surrounding provinces where ROK troops were deployed, to bear witness to the incredible violence the villagers endured. "Our purpose," they stated, "is not to provide absolute proof that certain specific events took place on certain days." Rather, it was to shed light on the broader question of "how ROK troops were used in Vietnam," a question that continued to elude the U.S. antiwar public.[74]

While the Joneses recognized and underscored the violence of South Koreans as systemic, executed with "tactics of deliberate brutality," they did not explain the violence further. The Vietnamese, drawing from experience and knowledge gained through conversations and propaganda, offered their answers. One woman from Quang Nam Province explained to the Joneses, "Korean mercenaries have no ideology. They get paid a lot of money by the Americans to come to Viet Nam and kill people, and the more people they can kill, the more money they will get."[75] Even Filipinos who did not engage in combat were not immune from criticism. According to a sample of public opinion gathered in Tay Ninh in 1967, the people there complained of the "blackmarketeering and womanizing" practices of some PHILCAG members. They were accused of selling stolen PX goods in the local market, as well as their "amorous activities" toward Vietnamese women that made them a sexual threat. Their crimes did not register on the same scale as the South Korean atrocities. Yet they were consistent with the U.S. colonial discourse of Filipino sexual deviance and subversion. As one Vietnamese province chief remarked, the Filipinos were, "after all, only Malays," from a culture far inferior to Vietnam's history of civilization.[76]

These sentiments reveal the extent to which the Vietnamese rejected American claims about the possibilities, or even the desirability, of forging a collective Asian front against communism in Vietnam. Against the discourses of colonial intimacy that connected the Philippines to Tay Ninh and South Korea to Vietnam as twin sites of an anticommunist crusade, the people who bore the brunt of the imperial violence pushed to imagine another world free from war. Beginning in the late 1960s, emerging counterpublics in the Philippines and South Korea took up the task of this critical imagining. Situating the Vietnam War within the longer arc of U.S. imperialism in the Philippines and the unfinished struggle for decolonization in Korea, activists and intellectuals in the two countries pursued a kind of politics that transcended the war.

OTHER VIETNAMS

In February 1968, as the Philippine Congress moved toward approving a bill to extend P35 million to support PHILCAG in Vietnam, the *Weekly Graphic,* a leftist periodical, issued a series of scathing editorials, clarifying exactly what was at stake. Its critiques focused on one of the most salient arguments that had justified PHILCAG from the start: that PHILCAG was a *civic-action* contingent, decidedly noncombatant in nature. "Civic action," one editor clarified, "is *military* civic action." "It means, according to the former Pentagon boss Robert McNamara . . . using indigenous military forces for non-military projects," to present an illusion of benevolence while preserving the "status quo." What's more, the editor noted, Marcos had begun applying this military strategy domestically. The editorial continued, "The Marcos administration is embarked on a counter-insurgency course" in the Philippines, employing "civic actionists" to intensify the war against the Huks. "The mask has fallen from our true intentions in Vietnam," another editor declared. "We are in Vietnam not to help our Asian brothers. . . . Rather we are there to fight the 'initial defense battles' for our country," and "using the people of Vietnam, who we profess to love, as guinea pigs."[77]

These critics shed light on something with far graver repercussions than the pure fact that PHILCAG was complicit in the military violence in Vietnam; they insisted that state violence in the Philippines was deepening with every step of the Vietnam War. The war against the Huks and the war against the "Viet Cong" were essentially one and the same, carried out with the same military tactics and soldiers. By the time the Philippines was fully embroiled in the Vietnam War in 1968, the anti-American fervor that had reverberated for more than a decade merged with a critique against the war, and took on a sharper and more precise tone. "Supposedly we are a beacon light of freedom in these parts (Asia)," noted one *Weekly Graphic* editor. "But can Philcag, which is evidently an American creature in Filipino attire, be the fruit of freedom we should display before the Asian countries we hope to win over to our cause?" The people of Asia could see through the disguise plainly. "Philcag shouts out loud over all Asia, not the realities of Philippine freedom, but the hard facts of American imperialism."[78]

Popular protests against PHILCAG got a welcome boost in the fall of 1969, when a U.S. Congressional Foreign Relations subcommittee held hearings to clarify questions about U.S. military assistance to the Philippines. The hearings, chaired by Senator Stuart Symington (D, Missouri), revealed that in 1966, the Philippine government had received $39 million to equip and dispatch PHILCAG. Senator J. William Fulbright admonished, "This seems to me to be the ultimate in corruption, for us to make deals like this in pursuit of an illusory policy all designed to prove to the world that we have great support in Vietnam, which we do not have at all." When the hearing's transcript was released to the public on November 18, the response was immediate. Some members of the Philippine Congress decried "these grave distortions and slanderous misrepresentations," calling them "a blatant and transparent lie." Antiwar activists welcomed the charges as confirmation of what they had been arguing all along. "Whatever may have been the motives which impelled Messrs. Fulbright and Symington to make those disclosures," the *Weekly Graphic* summarized, "there is no doubt that they did a signal service toward clearing up a lot of hazy things surrounding the sending of the Philippine detachment to Vietnam."[79]

The Symington subcommittee extended its critique of PHILCAG to the issue of U.S. military bases in the Philippines, which remained a contentious point in U.S.–Philippine relations. The subcommittee revealed that the bases cost American taxpayers $270 million annually, and served no useful purpose. The 1959 Bohlen-Serrano Agreement had restricted the use of the bases from American offensive combat missions, thus technically barring their use for the Vietnam War and making them a liability rather than an asset. The bases had no legitimacy. "We are not really there to protect the Philippines," Fulbright charged. "We are there to serve our own purposes, to maintain a base for what we believe to be our forward protection against China or anybody else."[80] Philippine activists echoed and clarified the point: "We need not worry about the terms under which American bases should stay in this country. *They should not stay.*" In the closing weeks of 1969, with the publicity of the Symington hearings and the revelations of the My Lai massacre emerging simultaneously, Filipino activists intensified their protests against U.S. militarism in Vietnam and the Philippines. At antiwar rallies, Filipinos conjured the memory of the Philippine-American War, reminding the public that the current state of violence had deep roots in the history of U.S. empire.[81]

In South Korea, the years after 1965 likewise saw the burgeoning of progressive forces aimed to realize Korea's unfinished democracy. Comprised of university students and an older generation of anticolonial nationalists and postliberation guerrilla fighters, South Korea's popular front seized on the momentum of the anti–Normalization Treaty movement of 1964–65 to mobilize against Park's authoritarian rule. Although critiques of Korea's Vietnam War did not figure prominently at the time, they filtered through other critical discourses about the uneven capitalist development in South Korea and East Asia that were the byproducts of the war. These protests, initially centered on the perceived resurgence of Japanese economic dominance during the time of the treaty, manifested in more locally rooted grievances by the 1970s. In particular, the southern Chŏlla Province that was left largely untouched by economic development as a result of Park's discriminatory industrial policy saw the further impoverishment and radicalization of the population. The Chŏlla region, long a center of anticolonial politics and most memorably the site of the Yŏsu-Sunch'ŏn Rebellion in 1948, experienced a surge of antiauthoritarian activism throughout the 1970s.[82]

In 1980, Chŏlla erupted. Early that year, popular demonstrations rocked the region and spread throughout the country as citizens mobilized en masse to drive out the remnants of Park's authoritarian regime following Park's assassination the previous October. Working peoples across all sectors of society, including miners, textile union workers, students, and left intellectuals occupied cities and university campuses and demanded an end to martial law, better wages, and the general democratization of government and society. On May 15, approximately four hundred thousand people converged at the central Seoul railway station to call for the lifting of martial law, marking one of the largest demonstrations in South Korea to date. Such was the culmination of democratic forces shaped over the course of two decades of militarized modernity, waged by people who bore the brunt of the state's rapid industrialization. And within the longer arc of Korea's post-1945 history, these forces represented the radicalized excess of Korea's unfinished decolonization. The state responded swiftly and violently. In Gwangju, South Chŏlla Province, paratroopers descended on protesters on May 18 in an attempt to quell the uprising with force. For ten days, citizens mobilized to defend the city from the troops, but the firepower was devastating. On May 27, the uprising ended with more than two hundred civilians killed and thousands injured.[83]

The Gwangju Uprising, as the event came to be known, animated South Korean political culture decisively in the coming months and years. The move toward restoring "peace and order" under the military dictatorship of Chun Doo Hwan drove activists underground and led to the purging of thousands of civil servants, teachers, journalists, and politicians. Closing the avenues of political dissent, however, opened up alternative spaces of radical imagination. In particular, literature emerged as a vibrant terrain for the politicization and practice of a counterpublic sphere. Literary writers of working-class backgrounds, many who were targeted by the regime for their dissident activism and writings, took on the difficult task of rewriting the nation's past to imagine a different political present. In this "time of collective dreaming" opened up by subaltern cultural productions, the struggle for economic justice for the proletariat became inseparable from the struggle to reunify the two Koreas against the forces of U.S. capitalist imperialism.[84]

One of these insurgent voices was Hwang Sŏkyŏng, who burst onto the literary scene in the formative years of Park's authoritarian rule. Hwang's literature bears the political force that mirrored his personal life. In 1962, after dropping out of high school at eighteen, he traveled around the country as an itinerant worker, laboring in factories and construction sites that emerged as part of South Korea's industrializing workscape. In 1964, he was imprisoned for dissident activities, and during his incarceration he staged hunger strikes with fellow inmates. Encountering state repression had a radicalizing effect on him, but it was his experience in the Vietnam War that moved him even further to the left. From 1966 to 1969, Hwang was deployed to Vietnam with the ROK marines. Many years later, he reflected on his experience in Vietnam by comparing it to the experiences of the earlier generation of Koreans who fought for Japan in World War II; in both cases, to his mind, Koreans were mobilized as colonial labor in the service of empire.[85] Hwang resumed his activism after the war by organizing factory workers at the Kuro industrial complex in Seoul. At the same time, working and struggling alongside Korea's most marginalized populations sparked his artistic creativity. Throughout the 1970s, he published short stories that captured the plight of workers and their struggles; by the late 1970s, after moving to South Chŏlla, he combined labor activism and cultural expression to empower the people against the violence of the authoritarian state.[86]

Hwang's *The Shadow of Arms*, published in 1985, reflected the political urgency of this time. It represented less a fictionalized account of his actual life experiences than a dissection of the convergent forces that moved him and shaped his politics. Even though it is a story about South Korea's authoritarian development in the 1960s, the place of South Korea is strikingly absent in the novel. Instead, the story takes place in South Vietnam, against the backdrop of the American war. Its physical absence notwithstanding, Korea nonetheless animates the novel through the figure of Ahn Yong Kyu, a Korean soldier deployed to Vietnam. Ahn's reflections about the war, his encounters and conversations with other South Koreans and American and South Vietnamese soldiers, and his constant desire to return "home," brought to life South Korea's participation in the war and the experience of soldiering through the subempire. More than a work of historical recovery, however, the novel excavated the history of Korea and Vietnam as linked sites of colonialism and war, and in so doing sought to situate—and to expand—the struggle for democracy in South Korea as part of a protracted global anti-imperialism. As the first literary work about Korea's Vietnam War, *The Shadow of Arms* locates the war as the site through which to imagine the possibility of Korea's unfinished decolonization.

In this sense, *The Shadow of Arms* is not really a war novel. The story opens with Ahn getting pulled from the trench and reassigned to the Criminal Investigation Division to investigate the black-market activities in Da Nang. The bustle of the black market—of soldiers smuggling and reselling goods on the market, of NLF infiltrators diverting war materials for their cause, of South Vietnamese officials scheming to monopolize and export Vietnam's natural resources—form the pivotal actions of the war, according to Hwang. The economy of the war is no mere sideshow but thoroughly entwined with the war's violence. The PX, Hwang tells us, "is America's most powerful new weapon." "Those who lay hands upon the wealth of America will have the label U.S. MILITARY burned into their brains. Children who grow up humming their songs and eating their candies and chocolates off the streets trust their benevolence and optimism" (66). Indeed, reorienting one's under-standing of the war around the PX presents a different view of the war entirely, one in which Japanese and American goods circulate and constitute the objects of everyday desire, where the "fortress buildings" of American banks tower over GI vice districts in Saigon, and would remain there long after the war is declared over. The war, in short, was making Asia safe for American capitalism. It is also precisely the reason why Ahn is in it: as he states repeatedly, his primary goal was to make some money, then go back home.

"Home" functions as a trope in the novel to mark Ahn's shifting con-sciousness about his place in the war. Ahn positions himself as an outsider, telling an American sergeant on one occasion, "We are here because you asked us to come," and, "We have nothing to do with this filthy war" (246). His constant desire to return home reinforces his conviction that he was there only to make money, nothing more. And yet, the line separating war from "home" gets blurred the longer he remains in Vietnam. Seeing American soldiers flirting with prostitutes outside a bar, for example, brought back childhood memories of the Korean War. "We've long been living in condi-tions like this," Ahn tells a GI deserter, explaining, "Your government parti-tioned our country and occupied it" (399). We find out later in the novel that Ahn's "real home" is in North Korea; thus, when asked again if he wants to go home, he replies: "I have to go back to Korea even if there's no home to go home to" (397). The war in Vietnam, Ahn comes to see "objectively" toward the end, is but a phase of the continuing war in his homeland.

This realization clarifies that Ahn indeed has more of a stake in the war than just to make money, that he is not just a mercenary. The novel thus shifts back and forth between the American war that Ahn is caught in—the war for profits—and the other war, fought by NLF revolutionaries. This other war centers on Pham Minh, an idealistic young man who drops out of medical school to join the front. If fighting was secondary to making money for Koreans and South Vietnamese officials, then for Minh, the war likewise was a means to an end: to serve the people. To juxtapose these two wars, Hwang punctuates the novel with textual fragments that reveal the nature of the two opposing wars: while excerpts of investigation reports on civilian atrocities expose the underlying violence of the American war, an excerpt of an NLF text explains the kind of war that Minh believes in, a war "to win national independence, to secure democracy and to peacefully unify our nation" (507). Even as Ahn recognizes the similar conditions of colonialism that structured the lives of Koreans and Vietnamese, he realizes ultimately a fundamental difference between himself and someone like Minh: "'The guerrillas seem different somehow. Here and here don't seem to be in opposition,' Yong said, pointing to his temple and then striking his chest with his palm" (537). Any remaining hope that Korea's Vietnam War might inspire Koreans to identify with the Vietnamese freedom struggle ends violently when Ahn, near the final scene, kills Minh, a violence that also cuts short the possibility of Korea's unfulfilled decolonization.

Hwang's novel was part of the cultural production of the post-Gwangju era, when South Korean activists revolutionized their struggles against authoritarian rule and began to make explicit the connections between South Korea's dictatorship and the U.S. empire. The Ronald Reagan Administration's support of the brutal crackdown of the Gwangju Uprising, which came as a shock to many who believed the United States would side with the people's democratic struggle, forced open the door to a critical reevaluation of the U.S.–ROK alliance for the first time, which had long been suppressed by the political culture of anticommunism.[87] Korea's Vietnam War, part of this unspeakable history even among left activists in the 1960s and 1970s, began to enter the political consciousness of the left during this time. Even as discourses of Korea's Vietnam remained as vital as ever to the reproduction of anticommunist nationalism in South Korea, those writing and struggling from the margins began charting a different narrative that exposed the colonial violence at the heart of Korea's authoritarian development. In short, these activists described and made visible the subempire, the relations of violence and political economy of the U.S. war in Vietnam that underlay the promise of South Korean and Philippine capitalist development.

CONCLUSION

Radicalizing movements for democracy in South Korea and the Philippines that unfolded in the years after the Vietnam War laid bare the contradictions of the U.S. claim of supporting a "free" Asia for Asians in the age of decolonization. Time and again, American officials exploited this claim for imperial ends. When President Johnson called on these Asian nations to contribute to the U.S. war effort, to show their gratitude and to repay their debt to the U.S. liberating empire, South Korean and Philippine state leaders seized the opportunity. At a time when citizens in these countries escalated their calls for greater economic and political autonomy from a resurgent imperial Japan and the United States, the war in Vietnam appeared to satisfy multiple nationalist desires. Major financial and political concessions secured through troop contributions helped jump-start the Philippine and ROK national economies; at the same time, state officials justified their countries' participation in the war in racializing and nationalist terms, presenting their troops as "fellow Asians" and dutiful nationals. As the war progressed, nationalism and militarism became evermore entwined. By the mid-1960s, these forces worked in tandem to fortify the U.S. military-industrial complex across Asia and the Pacific.

Nationalism and militarism mobilized working peoples in South Korea and the Philippines in unprecedented and largely unforeseen ways. As Philippine and South Korean leaders charted their nations' economic future through the war, unemployed and underemployed men and women found new opportunities for mobility and work within the emerging subempire. Their incorporation into the modernizing nation-state through soldiering and other militarized labor, however, exposed them to increasing state violence that reinforced the precariousness of living and working on the margins of nation and empire. The state's narrowed pursuits of capitalist growth could not ultimately satisfy the people's aspirations for a citizenship free from the exercise of state violence within and beyond the nation. If the search for economic security propelled working peoples to the front lines of the war, then the same desire, coupled with a refusal to accept subempire as the condition for postcolonial freedom and nationhood, drove people to revolt. At issue for the democracy movements in South Korea and the Philippines was never just the war itself, but the conditions of militarized modernity that made participation in the U.S. war a matter of course. Thus, by the 1980s, anti–U.S. imperialism would emerge as an organizing framework for the protracted movements against authoritarian rule in both countries.

These movements tell a complex story of a past still unfolding, of the making of an inchoate social world that had been foreclosed by the rush to decolonization through militarization. People who were conscripted into that modernity, often through their participation in imperial violence, were in a position to radically rethink their relationship to nation and empire by imagining and pursuing relationships with other decolonizing subjects, and to realize a different world altogether. As the next chapter shows, this was true of Asian Americans who were enlisted in the U.S. military during the Vietnam War. Asian American GIs exposed to the inhumanities of race war came back home to testify to the violence against the Vietnamese and connected it to their lives and communities. Their testimonies critically transformed and deepened the Asian American movement in the United States in the late 1960s and early 1970s.

FIVE

Fighting "Gooks"

ASIAN AMERICANS AND THE VIETNAM WAR

PAT SUMI TRAVELED THE WORLD and back in the summer of 1970, traversing distances that eventually took her far beyond her GI organizing work in Oceanside, California. Sumi had been counseling antiwar Marines at Camp Pendleton for some months when Black Panther Party leader Eldridge Cleaver tapped her to join the U.S. People's Anti-Imperialist Delegation. From July to September 1970, Sumi and the ten other members of the delegation, representing the spectrum of the U.S. New Left, toured North Korea, North Vietnam, and the People's Republic of China (PRC). The tour was meant to strengthen solidarity between the U.S. leftists and the communist nations of Asia. In North Korea and the PRC, the delegates visited free clinics, schools, and factories that showcased an alternative form of modernity to Western capitalism, and convinced them that socialist revolution in the United States was wholly within the realm of possibility. In North Vietnam, they witnessed the villagers' determination to survive and defend themselves against the air power of the U.S. military.[1] Sumi was inspired by what she saw on the trip, and it changed her politics. Returning to the United States, she determined that "the Asian American community needed to know more about what was going on in Asia besides the Vietnam War." Leaving the work of GI organizing to others, she committed fully to the Asian American movement.[2]

On May 16, 1971, Asian Americans for Peace, an antiwar group founded in Los Angeles two years earlier, brought Sumi to speak at their "Peace Sunday" rally at the Biltmore Bowl in Los Angeles. Some participants recalled the event as the first major Asian American antiwar rally in Southern California, with over two thousand people in attendance. By then, Pat Sumi had become well known in the Asian American movement, writing and speaking often about her tour in Asia. Alongside other prominent antiwar activists, including actress Jane Fonda, Sumi spoke in resounding terms about the need for Asian Americans to engage in the anti-imperialist struggle that centered in yet exceeded the Vietnam War. The event elevated Sumi's stature within the movement, but it also revealed that her work with GIs was far from over. After her speech, she introduced the crowd to Mike Nakayama, a young Vietnam War veteran whom she had met and befriended while giving a talk in Long Beach. An unknown figure in activist circles and an inexperienced public speaker, Nakayama took the stage nervously. He proceeded to captivate his audience by recounting the horrors of being an Asian American soldier fighting in a racialized war.[3]

Nakayama enlisted in the U.S. Marine Corps in the summer of 1967, not long after the Tet Offensive exposed the failures of the U.S. military and deepened antiwar activism across the country. Born in post–World War II Los Angeles, Nakayama grew up in Crenshaw, a largely working-class neighborhood of black and Japanese Americans, where youth rebellion in the form of gang fights and drug abuse constituted their social world of racialized exclusion from society. Like many of his peers, he saw joining the military as "one of the options for getting out of the environment." As they were often told, they could join the army or go to jail, or end up dead. On June 26, he and a group of friends went to the local recruiting office and volunteered for two-year service. Unbeknown to him at the time, the world he entered was anything but a safer environment. He recalled vividly in boot camp the drill instructor stood him out to instruct the class, "This is what the gook looks like." Like many other Asians and Pacific Islanders in the Marines and army, Nakayama experienced the violence of war long before he ever set foot in Vietnam. Being singled out as a "gook" to his platoon instilled fears about his personal safety, about whether he would "be vulnerable to both sides." As much as he was a part of the dehumanizing boot camp experience that conditioned American GIs to kill the Vietnamese enemies, however, within a month of his tour he "started to see them as human beings." The steady and numbing violence all around him only amplified his sense that "these people kind of look like me."[4]

Nakayama returned to Los Angeles in the fall of 1969, physically intact but forever changed. It was not long after that he met Sumi during one of the activist's public-speaking engagements in Southern California about her tour with the Anti-Imperialist Delegation. As he heard the Japanese American activist preach the gospel of revolutionary Asia, he started to make sense of his own wartime experiences. Their meeting, in a sense, signaled the convergence of two distinct yet kindred experiences of transpacific travel, and it symbolized the beginning of a new revolutionary politics in Asian America. For Nakayama, hearing and meeting Sumi awakened him politically.

Nakayama was one of the estimated 34,600 Asian Americans who fought in the Vietnam War, many who came back to participate in antiwar activism, and many more who never came back at all. Although Asian Americans and Pacific Islanders represented only 1 percent of U.S. forces in Vietnam, their relatively low numbers were offset by the heightened visibility of their racial presence in the military. In this social landscape of violence, "gooks" appeared everywhere. The term "gook," David Roediger reminds us, has a long pedigree in the history of U.S. imperial wars, and it circulated widely among U.S. troops in Vietnam as part of the collective repertoire of fighting a race war.[5] As Nakayama attested, this culture affected Asian American GIs profoundly as they often experienced the taunt from their superiors and fellow soldiers that compounded their sense of danger, that *their* war was fought on two fronts. Indeed, "gook" was never simply an iteration of wartime racism. It was, more precisely, the embodiment of a racial subversion against the U.S. empire that needed to be visualized and kept at bay at all times. The marking of Asian Americans as "gooks" was no mere racist slip of an otherwise normal routine and practice of war making. Rather it fit logically within the ongoing normalization of racial liberalism that figured Asian Americans as exemplary racial subjects (the "model minority") who remained always racially suspect (the "forever foreigner"). As was the case during the incipient U.S. militarization of East Asia in the late 1940s and early 1950s, Asians in the military occupied an indecipherable distinction between asset and peril, between friend and foe, that made them vulnerable and especial targets of state violence.

Asian Americans who came of age after World War II understood the sense of honor, manhood, and redemption that military service meant for their parents' generation, many who had enlisted to prove their loyalty to a nation that deemed them racial enemies. The impossible dilemma that compelled the generation before them to put on the military uniform had transformed by the 1960s into another form of subjection to rational choice: to enlist or to remain captive to their own disaffection and inability to imagine a better world beyond their surroundings. Many were driven by concrete incentives such as the promise of steady pay, money for education, and other types of loans through the GI bill that helped move them closer toward middle-class affluence. For others, the choice was bleaker: go to the military or go to prison. Whatever their reasons for enlisting, the military presented a limited option for young Asian American men to channel their vulnerable masculinity, stemming from the sense of failure to live up to the ideals of male citizenship, into the service of U.S. empire.

Like many other African American, Latino, and Puerto Rican youths who were drawn into the army and the Marines for similar reasons, Asian Americans who found themselves on the front lines in Vietnam experienced the profound contradiction between the promise of liberal inclusion and the war's systemic racial violence. Their collective experience of being racialized as "gook" and fighting an enemy who "looked like them" made palpable their own vulnerability to premature death, and it revealed their complicity with U.S. violence against the Vietnamese. The Selective Service System, many of them reasoned, presented an equal opportunity not to serve but to die for the nation. And as they returned home from war, many began to link the violence in Vietnam to the violence in their own communities, seeing them as parts of a global race war against colonized peoples. In 1971, Nakayama spoke to antiwar veterans, "You've heard of instances of genocide and murder in Vietnam. I'd like to relate a few that have happened in the United States," including the wars against black militants and American Indians that have been ongoing "since the Third World people have lived here."[6] A critical Third World consciousness took shape, reconstituting the humanity of Asian American veterans. This Third World consciousness materialized in grassroots campaigns against racism and structural violence in Crenshaw, Little Tokyo, and other communities. In their day-to-day freedom struggles, Asian American veterans made the violence of empire a central framework in their pursuit of an Asian American liberation politics, one that challenged and exceeded the boundaries of race and nation.

FIGHTING "GOOKS"

Sometime in the late 1960s, President Johnson reportedly told Secretary of Defense McNamara to "go to San Francisco, grab some Chinamen, and drop them into Vietnam." Or so one Filipino American veteran named Doug Luna recalled hearing in passing as he reflected on the racism of the war.[7] If the line appears fantastic in its crude simplicity, it was not entirely off the mark. The Vietnam War, Christian Appy has argued, was a "working-class war," one that conscripted or otherwise compelled to enlist a disproportionate number of young poor and working-class men to risk their lives in combat. Two-thirds of American service persons in Vietnam between 1966 and 1971 lived in impoverished areas, the rural towns, segregated neighborhoods, and colonial peripheries that formed the underside of the nation's post–World War II prosperity. Although many of these young people were enrolled in or had completed high school, the prospects of furthering their education and securing white-collar jobs seemed a distant possibility. The Selective Service System played an important role by "channeling" these men into the military, to satisfy the objectives of the war in Vietnam and the "War on Poverty" simultaneously.[8] Even if military recruiters were not actively picking up "Chinamen" off the streets, as Luna believed, they were certainly present in high school auditoriums and other places selling the promises of the military to these populations.

When Nakayama, Nick Nagatani, and their friends went to the recruiter's office in West Los Angeles, they were driven by a desire to make something of their lives. Like many of their peers, Nagatani and Nakayama joined the Marines because it presented one of the few alternatives to a life on the streets, or in jail. Nagatani recalled, "Back then it was common for the judge to say, 'You want to go to jail or you want to go to the Marine Corps?'" Others who did not face this decision chose the Marines for their martial reputation. Kenji Kudo, a Sansei who grew up in South Central Los Angeles, volunteered for the Marines because he believed he had a "duty to go over there and serve in a combat role," even though he knew the air force and navy presented safer options. Those who came from middle-class backgrounds, to the contrary, tended to see the military as an opportunity for individual career advancements. The Reserve Officers' Training Corps (ROTC) enabled many college students to pursue the military as a career, which often exempted them from combat. James Arima, a Nisei from Seattle who joined the ROTC while enrolled at Seattle University in 1965, pursued Finance Officer Training at Fort Benjamin Harrison after completing his Advanced Infantry Training at Fort Lewis. As these stories attest, Asian Americans' experiences of the Vietnam War varied according to their class background.[9]

Nagatani and Nakayama entered the Marines in the spring and summer of 1967 as part of the buildup of ground troops following the devastation of U.S. forces during the Tet Offensive. In 1968, students at San Francisco State College declared themselves the "Third World Liberation Front" and set course to transform American society. From November 1968 to March 1969, a multiracial coalition of students and protesters around the Bay Area, emboldened by anticolonial revolutions around the world, converged at SF State to demand "self-determination" of their education and to make college more accessible and relevant to their communities. The Third World Liberation Front strike, the longest student-led strike in U.S. history, gave birth to the Asian American movement and politicized a generation of Asian Americans and other people of color far beyond the Bay Area.[10] Nagatani, Nakayama, and others in the military might have been secluded from these politicizing events, but in the military they received an education no less worldly and transformative. For many Asian Americans, being in the armed forces exposed them to a world of race and empire that they never imagined encountering in their lifetimes.

That experience typically began with basic training. Richard Yee, a twenty-one-year-old army draftee from Los Angeles, left California for the first time in 1966 to attend basic training at Fort Polk, Louisiana. "Living in South Central L.A., I got along with the blacks, and Mexicans, and every-body else," he recalled. "I did not know what discrimination was until I went to Fort Polk, Louisiana." There, he witnessed racism in its most blatant forms, particularly at off-base public spaces where African Americans were excluded outright. As an Asian American, he maintained a fragile sense of safety as an observer of social relations organized along a black-white color line. The few other Asian Americans whom he remembered from basic train-ing likewise were shielded from the kinds of overt racism experienced by black servicemen. For a time, his feeling of safety even extended past basic training, for he believed that being Asian exempted him from serving in Vietnam. "At that time they were not sending any Asians over there," he remembered, "because fighting with another Asian, they thought it might be a problem for us." In marked contrast to what Luna remembered about President Johnson's targeting "Chinamen" for military service, Yee believed his race protected him from combat—that is, until depleted troop levels in 1968 necessitated more bodies in Vietnam, including his own.[11]

These contradictory recollections by two Asian American servicemen reveal the insidious dangers of the racialized war they entered, one in which being identified as "Asian" easily meant the difference between life and death. If Yee learned of such dangers through rumors, others experienced them firsthand in basic training. Scott Shimabukuro, for example, recalled hearing his drill instructor remark on the first day of training, "Oh, we have a gook here today in our platoon." Such verbal assaults were part of the dehumanizing process of boot camp, "to break you down physically, mentally, emotionally," to make one "more efficient as a military tool." Racist epithets such as "niggers, boys, and coons" were hurled at black GIs as well, but "gook" worked specifically to visualize the enemy in racial terms. Nakayama explained it this way: "Dehumanizing Vietnamese to being less than human [was essential] so that when you get into the combat situation, you're not in a dilemma about killing human beings. You're killing less than human beings, as if they're insects, you just want to swat a fly, a pest. And that's how you're taught who the Vietnamese are." Basic training stripped recruits of their humanity to enable the more effective work of killing. For Nakayama and others, however, such a process placed them in an impossible dilemma: when forced to stand in front of their platoons as an example of the "gook," they were dehumanized not just to kill but to be killed. "That was not a very good feeling," Nakayama said, but "it made sense."[12]

Many working-class Asian American, black, and Latino men chose to go to war to escape an environment of organized neglect and violence, but found in the military a situation more dangerous than the one they left behind. The compounding effects of state racism that determined their life chances did not end when they entered the military; instead, racism became rearticulated and grafted onto the logic of counterinsurgency. For example, black GIs who were described by social scientists and in the popular media as unattached young men prone to urban violence were deemed "naturally" suited for "jungle warfare."[13] Similar to how Native Hawaiians were made to play the "Viet Cong" in Hawai'i's army training exercises, many GIs of color discovered that military service did not deliver the promise of full citizenship but instead exposed them to heightened violence because of their race. The choice between the military or jail, for many of them, merely preserved their fragile existence within a state of permanent war in which their lives were rendered disposable.

In this heightened state of violence, fighting "gooks" took on a psychological dimension far beyond what the military prepared GIs for. The army certainly was attuned to it, training soldiers to identify the sensory and psychological aspects of fighting the Vietnamese. In 1966, the School of the Americas at Fort Gulick incorporated the smells of "drying fish," burning incense, and cooking "with garlic and other spices peculiar to Southeast Asia" to train soldiers to detect the enemy even when they could not be seen.[14] So focused on honing the senses for killing, the military all but neglected the psychic damage inflicted upon individual soldiers who were indoctrinated into the violence. No one articulated this aspect of the race war more clearly than Robert Jay Lifton, a psychologist who gained prominence in the early 1970s for counseling antiwar veterans. In his seminal work, *Home from the War* (1973), a product of his many "rap" sessions with antiwar Vietnam veterans since 1970, Lifton sought to understand the "psychic-numbing" effects of the war's violence on individual soldiers. He called this condition "the American need for gooks." *Home from the War* was the first sustained study of the "gook syndrome" that would inform a host of studies on post-traumatic stress disorder in subsequent decades.

According to Lifton, the "gook syndrome" was a psychological state that circumscribed the "moral universe" of GIs, dictating their actions and enabling them to commit atrocities with little to no remorse. Like many other antiwar Americans, Lifton was moved by the news of the My Lai massacre, and he sought to understand the war's horrors from the perspective of the GIs. "GIs develop[ed] a hunger not only for an enemy but for a psychological victim," he explained. "Themselves under the constant threat of grotesque death, they must find, in a real sense create, a group more death-tainted than themselves, against whom they can reassert their own continuity of life." American soldiers' survival, in short, depended on "gooks." Lifton's research significantly recast GIs as victims (rather than perpetrators) of the war, and marked a broader effort by some American psychiatrists to popularize the notion of "war-related trauma" as part of the vocabulary of the antiwar movement. So thoroughly did the "gook syndrome" describe the collective experience of American soldiering in Vietnam, Lifton mused, "the fact that black or Indian GIs (or GIs of Japanese, Chinese, or Hawaiian extraction) joined in the gook syndrome is itself somehow American." Killing "gooks" became requisite for soldiers of color to reaffirm their American identity.[15]

For Asian American soldiers, however, the "gook syndrome" meant much more than engaging in a collective mode of savagery or reaffirming their national identity. It also induced a state of vigilance, a feeling of imminent danger that did not ease even when surrounded by one's own troops. Luna recalled being threatened by a fellow soldier, "I won't take any chances and I'll shoot you first and find out the next morning if I was right or wrong." Such verbal threats put Luna on constant edge. He remembered, "A couple of times I had to pull my weapon in situations . . . where I thought somebody was going to try to do me in."[16]

Compounding the dangers, platoon leaders often singled out Asian American GIs to lead reconnaissance missions, insisting that as Asians they could blend in with the enemy. Jose Velasquez, who arrived in South Vietnam in December 1968 as part of G Company, 75th (Ranger) Infantry Regiment, recounted being separated into a smaller team to infiltrate the enemy in the Chu Lai area just south of Da Nang. His team, designated "Team Hawaii" for its multiethnic composition, comprised "two Hawaiians, one Chinese, one Japanese, one American Indian," and himself, a Filipino. "Everyone of us could pass for a Vietnamese, we were all short," he said with some humor. As an added measure of disguise, they draped black cloths over themselves to mimic the "Viet Cong." On the first day of their mission, however, any humor they might have entertained quickly disappeared when they noticed two helicopters with gunners pass them by in the open field, circle around, and hover directly above them. "You talk about [feeling] scared, I have never been so scared than at that time," Velasquez remembered; "we just didn't know what to do because these are your . . . your own guys." They frantically waved their radio handsets and tore off their black garments, which was about all they could do at that moment to preempt their own deaths. To their relief, the helicopters left without incident.[17]

Chris Taga also related a similar experience. Like many of his contemporaries, the Japanese American from Los Angeles enlisted in the army in 1966 to find a sense of direction in his life. "I would see guys returning from the service, and they seemed like they knew what they wanted to do with their lives; I didn't have a clue," he said. He dropped out of Los Angeles City College after his first semester, determined that the army "was the way to go." As soon as he started basic training at Fort Bliss, Texas, however, he knew he "made a mistake." He was singled out constantly as a "gook" by the drill instructor, and the racism did not subside. When he deployed with the 101st Airborne Division to the I Corps region in September 1966, to counter North Vietnamese incursions along the Lao border, Taga was selected to "walk point" for his reconnaissance platoon. He clarified, "it was not a desirable position," for the point man "usually is the first guy to get shot at, to trip a booby trap, or whatever." Nonetheless, he did it for six months. One day, when the platoon approached an intersection at the trail, his platoon leader ordered Taga and an African American GI to take the trail on the right. As they walked, they sensed something wasn't right. They returned and told their sergeant, "Hey, I don't think we should be walking up this trail, there are signs that it's been disturbed." But the sergeant was insistent. As Taga recalled, "The sergeant started calling me a fucking gook, why am I insubordinate, walk up the trail! And I told him, 'no, it's crazy, it's suicide.'" Unable to persuade Taga, the sergeant took the trail himself. Ten minutes later, they heard an explosion. When they found the sergeant, he "is laying on the trail, his intestines are hanging out of his guts," but alive. "I didn't even feel bad for the guy," Taga reflected. "His thing was, I was an expendable guy. To him I was just like the enemy or something."[18]

Stories like Taga's and Velasquez's circulated among Asian American GIs in Vietnam as tacit knowledge about the kinds of dangers they faced. From the Army Special Forces, Luna had heard that the NLF targeted Asian American soldiers especially because of their ability to blend into the population. He learned that "[e]ach month, several Asian American GIs would get killed," usually from being strangled from behind while riding around town in cyclos.[19] Even Lansdale related a story of his own. In a memo to his "old team" describing the frenzied atmosphere in Saigon following the Tet Offensive, he described the experiences of Mike Yaki, "a fine youngster from Los Angeles of Japanese descent" who had been working for the U.S. Agency for International Development. According to Lansdale, Yaki was helping at a Vietnamese relief center when the Saigon police barged in with their weapons pointed at him. "He got marched out into the street, hands in the air, and stood there with guns at his back while he tried to explain that he was an American." When U.S. military patrols drove by the scene, "our GI's gawk[ed] at the sight, some snapping pictures of the Vietnamese allies giving such a husky-looking VC as Mike his just dues." "It was just a psychologically-shattering moment for Mike," Lansdale sympathized. To prevent another such episode of mistaken identity, USAID subsequently assigned a "red-headed youngster ... [who] looks true Yankee" to accompany Yaki on his rounds. "If Mike is shot at now, at least it will be as an American."[20] Such irony might have humored Lansdale, but it did little to comfort Yee when he learned of his own brother's death at the hands of American troops. Forty years after his brother was killed by "friendly fire" in Vietnam, Yee still wondered whether being Asian American played a part in his death. Indeed, his torment about his brother's death may have led him to believe that Asian Americans were initially kept away from Vietnam because of their race. What had seemed a mistaken fact on Yee's part, after all, made sense.[21]

Rumors, stories, and speculations such as these capture the sense of elusive safety that Asian American GIs shared during their tours in Vietnam. In the absence of archival records to document their encounters on the ground, such anecdotes acquire a kind of materiality, however fragile and incomplete, to grasp the dangers and feelings of fear they experienced day to day. They do not merely fill in the gaps of "what happened" to enable a more complete account of the war. Rather, these stories and the acts of telling them constitute a production of knowledge about race and its affective embodiment through state violence. That the events themselves may or may not have occurred is not ultimately important. The novelist Tim O'Brien reminds us about the messiness of telling war stories: "A thing may happen and be a total lie; another thing may not happen and be truer than the truth."[22] Thus, although President Johnson's quote about snatching up "Chinamen" cannot be verified, and Velasquez's "Team Hawaii" exists nowhere in the historical record, and Yee may never know why his brother died, what matters is that these are the stories that remain, that circulate. As stories, speculations, and rumors, they possess an "illegitimate historicity," yet it is precisely as such that they acquire disruptive power to challenge official representations of military racism as an aberration of individual pathology or of wartime exigencies.[23] These unofficial accounts, in short, attest to the thoroughgoing anti-Asian violence that pervaded U.S. military culture and indelibly shaped the experiences of Asian American GIs.

From stories, too, we glean the possibility of alternative affinities practiced between GIs and Vietnamese. These are the quotidian encounters that register as everyday nonevents, but endure as fleeting moments of humanity worth remembering. For Larry Wong, a Chinese American Marine deployed to Da Nang in February 1968, the sight of domestic life inside the village that he patrolled brought him home to his family farm in Yakima Valley. "I remember looking at a hooch," he said, "and seeing a pot of hot rice and some veggie[s] cooking . . . just the essence reminded me of Grandma cooking at the kitchen."[24] If the army sought to weaponize the sense of smell to make soldiers more effective in the work of killing, it did not account for its unintended and potentially subversive effects. Beyond stimulating nostalgia for home, food also enabled human interactions with the Vietnamese that exceed most accounts of American soldiering. According to another Asian American veteran, the sights and scents of food interrupted his constant state of searching for "gooks": ". . . when we go into a village, and [face turns into a big smile, laughing] noodles, noodles! Okay! Hey, and chopsticks! . . . And the Americans looking at me, 'Why is this guy with the Vietnamese eating their food?' They say, 'don't touch that, man. They got booby trap or poison in there. You gonna get sick, they gonna kill you.'" The warnings did not faze him. "Hey, I just grind [eat]," he said. "I don't care. Hey, I'm one of them." For another Asian American soldier, eating at a Chinese restaurant in Saigon occasioned a lively and unexpected conversation with an NLF guerrilla about how the Americans were "wrong being in this country."[25] Such momentary social interactions eluded official accounts of the war, and yet preserve in their retelling the possibility of a different outcome of events.

Such interactions between Asian American GIs and the Vietnamese did not simply stem from a primordial sense of affinity based on essentialist notions of race and culture. Indeed, they could never be divorced from the wider race war that partly depended on the weaponization of intimacy. If socializing with the Vietnamese offered GIs reprieve from the war's numbing brutality, that feeling was never far removed from the actual dangers of being booby-trapped, poisoned, or outright shot by the "Viet Cong." The violence of race war meant that deviating from the "gook syndrome" only heightened one's exposure to death. And as the war dragged on, these interactions became increasingly politicized. By the late 1960s, for example, NLF leaflets targeting black GIs were common sightings: "Your real enemies are those who call you 'Niggers'—your genuine struggle is on your native land; GO HOME NOW AND ALIVE!"[26] Whether these were genuine expressions of affinity remained indecipherable. And yet, it was within this space of uncertainty, and the acts of risking one's life amidst such uncertainty, where GI resistance became possible.

Nagatani was nearing the end of his tour in Vietnam in early 1969 when whispered rumors set him adrift to uncertain safety.[27] One day as he was getting his haircut at the barbershop on base, the Vietnamese woman cutting his hair told him what she heard about his Marine unit's next assignment. Rather than move out with the unit and risk his life, he had an alternative. She told him, "You're going to go to such-and-so village and stay there for so many days, then you're going to go to some other district, and you'll stay there for so many days, and some other place for a couple more days, and then you'll be back in eight days." "By the way," she cautioned, "if you wear a yellow kerchief around your neck, you will be recognized as being opposed to the war in Vietnam, and no one will shoot at you." Weary of endless war but aware of the uncertain dangers of this alternative, Nagatani must have wavered over his options. No doubt the idea of respite finally enticed him. He related the plan to his buddies, and together they proceeded just as the barber had told him, quietly from one village to the next, with their yellow kerchiefs in plain sight. And just as the barber said, they returned to the base within days, unharmed. "I understand that you heeded my warning about wearing the yellow kerchiefs," the barber said to Nagatani when they saw each other again. Following her advice turned out to be a good move, for his unit "had taken some really heavy casualties." In the end, the words of one Vietnamese woman saved his life.

Nagatani and Nakayama returned home separately to Southern California in the fall of 1969, to a world neither of them remembered. "When I left, and when I came back were two different worlds," Nakayama said. "People had long hair, they wore fringe leather jackets."[28] In this world, the spectacular story of Nagatani's AWOL in Vietnam took on a new life. He must have recounted his experience to Sumi shortly after he met the Nisei activist in 1970, for more than twenty-five years later she still recalled his anecdote with passionate clarity.[29] In Sumi's rendering, the story was not one of mere survival but a testament to GI opposition against the war. His tale of seditious intimacy, like many other stories told by Asian American veterans, resonated with the antiracist and anti-imperialist tenor of the times, and attested to the global reach of Asian American resistance. As movement activists gravitated to the figure of the Asian American GI to further their political agenda, veterans returned home to participate in activities that mattered to themselves and their communities. Still carrying the psychic burdens of a not-so-distant race war, many Asian American veterans channeled their energies toward the local struggles of the Asian American movement, and began the process of reconstituting their personhood.

ASIAN AMERICANS AND THE THIRD WORLD LEFT

"[We were] out in the jungle on Saturday, and by Friday we were here," Nagatani said, remarking on their swift transition home. "There was no depressurization, no transition or anything." Their jarring return did not keep them from being swept into the political fervor. Three months after returning home, Nakayama followed his friends to enroll at Long Beach State College, where he took courses in Asian American studies and attended some antiwar protests. "That's pretty much the first time I got involved [in activism]," he reflected. When word spread on campus that a prominent Asian American activist was scheduled to speak about the war, he invited Nagatani to attend. "Mike took me down to Long Beach to hear a woman speak, it turned out to be Pat Sumi." Meeting Sumi for the first time and hearing her speak that day transformed them. "She talked about the concept of Asian American, or Asian," Nagatani remembered, "all that blew by me all these years. So after hearing about her being in Vietnam, being a guest of the PRG [Provisional Revolutionary Government of the Republic of South Vietnam], and coming back and sharing her experiences with us, that was, in a lot of ways it was like an awakening."[30]

Their "awakening" was the product of a rising political militancy that took hold around the country in the late 1960s. As Nagatani and Nakayama were off fighting the Vietnamese in 1967–69, groups like the Red Guard Party, the Chicano nationalist Brown Berets, and the Puerto Rican Young Lords came into formation. In form and substance, these groups stylized themselves after the Black Panther Party, which formed in Oakland in 1966 to mobilize and empower black youth against the organized state violence they experienced daily. These groups linked the everyday violence of living and surviving in America's ghettoes to the militarism of the U.S. empire. By the late 1960s, the tenet of the mainstream civil rights movement that African Americans could integrate successfully into the nation had given way to a more critical vocabulary and politics of anti–U.S. imperialism. In this view, racial minorities in the United States had more in common with the Vietnamese than with Americans on the basis of a shared, global struggle against the racial exploitation of American capitalism.[31]

This Third World consciousness that transformed and radicalized the civil rights movement had roots in anticolonial struggles preceding the 1960s. It was expressed most poignantly at the historic meeting of nonaligned Asian and African states in Bandung in 1955. As the United States intervened in the processes of formal decolonization around the globe, in Vietnam, Korea, Congo, Palestine, Cuba, and elsewhere, anticolonial revolutionaries expanded the horizon of national liberation beyond the founding of independent nation-states to tackle the new forms of colonialism being enforced by U.S. power. These global struggles deepened the imagination of race radicals in the United States. Black activists including Malcolm X and Robert F. Williams, the NAACP organizer from Monroe County, North Carolina, who exiled to Cuba in 1961, applied the symbols of anticolonial revolution to expand the meaning of the struggle against U.S. racism. By the late 1960s, as the civil rights imperative appeared to close the door on meaningful democratic change, radical activists articulated the links between racial inequalities in the United States and U.S. imperial violence abroad more clearly and with greater urgency.[32]

Sumi's activism exemplified the global expansiveness that defined Third World activism during these years. Before her sojourn with the anti-imperialist delegation elevated her to the pantheon of the Third World left, Sumi took part in the civil rights movement in the South. In 1966 and 1967, she spent time in Mississippi and Atlanta, organizing black voters, attending demonstrations, and getting educated "about what racism really means" by working alongside the grassroots activists of the Student Non-Violent Coordinating Committee (SNCC) and the Congress of Racial Equality (CORE). The black radical tradition taught her to see race as a structuring force of inequality both within and beyond U.S. national borders. After getting pulled briefly into pacifist resistance against the Vietnam War, she returned to California in 1969 and deepened her antiwar activism. She turned to Marine Corps Base Camp Pendleton as a site of struggle. The Marines at Camp Pendleton who were predominately black, brown, and working-class, she believed, "were people who not only understood the war from the inside, but who might understand America from the inside." Her work with the Marines led her to cofound the first chapter of the Movement for a Democratic Military (MDM) in Oceanside. It was the first GI organization to oppose the war based on an antiracist and anti-imperialist solidarity between black and brown GIs and "Vietnamese freedom fighters."[33]

In their approach to GI organizing, Sumi and other MDM members were drawn to the concept of intercommunalism developed by the Black Panther Party. Intercommunalism, according to Black Panther Party cofounder Huey Newton, described the shared experiences of surviving and resisting against state violence across the global expanse of the U.S. empire. Oakland and other black communities in urban America were the products of uneven capitalist development—"internal colonies"—and in this sense shared much in common with Vietnam, Cuba, and other decolonizing nations.[34] MDM made these global connections explicit. It forged relations with other Third World nationalist formations including the Black Panther Party, the Chicano Moratorium, and the Brown Berets, drawing parallels with the experiences of different racialized groups and linking them to the Vietnamese national liberation struggle. Those black, brown, and working-class GIs, Sumi clarified, "are the ones who are the cannon fodder, the ones taking the casualties, the ones who are expected to kill." Thus, they were also the ones with the best potential to see the relationship between racial oppression in the United States and the imperial violence they took part in, and to bring a swift end to the war.[35]

Sumi's involvement with MDM ended in 1969, but she continued to work with antiwar Asian American GIs like Nakayama and Nagatani, helping to broaden their political networks. A milestone achievement for the GI movement occurred from January 31 to February 2, 1971, when the Vietnam Veterans Against the War (VVAW) launched the "Winter Soldier Investigation" to publicize the litany of American war crimes in Vietnam before the U.S. media. When Sumi heard about the upcoming event from Jane Fonda, the actress and fellow GI organizer at Camp Pendleton who funded the event, she urged Nakayama to attend. Sumi was certain that Nakayama would have something important to add to the testimony. He hesitantly agreed.

In late January, Nakayama flew to Detroit with his unlikely companions, including Fonda, the activist attorney Mark Lane, and actress Sue Lyon. Despite arriving with a celebrity contingent, he never saw them again over the conference's duration, and became an anonymous face among more than one hundred veterans.[36] Over the first two days, he saw individuals getting up to the front of the cramped conference room at the Holiday Inn, one by one testifying to the atrocities they witnessed as part of the U.S. military in Vietnam. Even the psychologist Lifton, who had recently started speaking with veterans at the VVAW in New York, spoke about the war's psychological effects on soldiers.

By the last day, Nakayama had heard enough. When it was his turn to speak, he went straight to the point: "The thing that bothered me about this investigation is that it seemed as though people were trying to cover up the issue of racism, which I believe is one of the definite reasons why we are in Vietnam. We talked a lot about atrocities, but the systematic and deliberate genocide of all Asian people through the use of racism cannot be allowed any longer." Encouraged by someone in the audience telling him to "take your time . . . you're telling the truth," he continued: "The things that the brothers are relating have been happening in the United States since the Third World people have lived here." As one striking example, he drew a parallel between the "relocation of Vietnamese from their homes" to strategic hamlets and the relocation of "my parents and grandparents" to concentration camps. "We've been hearing about trying to get this war over, investigations . . . into genocide. I'd like the people to get behind trying to end the genocide here and get behind some people like Angela Davis and free ourselves over here." Using the language of Black Power he cultivated from his campus activism and from Sumi, he concluded, "I'd like to say Free Angela, and All Power to the People."[37]

Nakayama offered his testimony as part of the "Third World" panel to address the issue of military racism. His lesson about the global nature of U.S. state repression and Third World unity, however, mostly went unheard.

By the time Nakayama and the other nonwhite panelists spoke, all members of the press had packed and gone, leaving just a few people in the audience.[38] The largely emptied room only amplified Nakayama's point about the failures of antiwar veterans to theorize the "systemic" nature of racism, which drew Asian Americans like himself to the black freedom struggle and bound the fates of "Third World" peoples in the United States with those overseas. The connections he made between the Vietnamese, Japanese Americans, and African Americans may have seemed marginally relevant to a group of veterans preoccupied with ending the war, but such were precisely the kind of intercommunal politics that drove and sustained the Asian American movement in the late 1960s and early 1970s.[39]

If the GI movement seemed uninterested in his message, Nakayama found receptive ears among Asian American activists. When he returned to Los Angeles, he continued his political education and, when the opportunity came, spoke his views about the war. In April 1971, as hundreds of antiwar veterans descended on the National Mall in Washington, D.C. to cast away their war medals—a symbolic moment for the GI movement—Nakayama accompanied Sumi to Vancouver, BC, to attend the Indochinese Women's Conference. The conference introduced Nakayama to revolutionary women from North and South Vietnam and Laos, and to many more women activists from across North America who were committed to the project of "global sisterhood" and demilitarization in Southeast Asia. In May 1971, he took the stage at the Asian Americans for Peace rally at the Biltmore Bowl and spoke before two thousand antiwar demonstrators. His testimony about his racialized experiences in Vietnam drew the attention of *Gidra,* the influential Asian American movement newspaper, which gave him space in that month's issue to recount his story for its approximately five thousand readers. "I was doing stuff that I didn't think I was going to do," Nakayama reflected decades later, still surprised by all he accomplished in those few short months.[40]

Nakayama found his political voice in a movement that, for the most part, understood him and other GIs as victims of state racism, whose disposable lives primed them to "kill or be killed." Nakayama's testimonies of being equated with a "gook" and of his sense of danger in the war only served to reinforce this image of the victimized GI. Thus, it stands to reason that draft counseling became one of the important activities of the Asian American movement. In November 1968, the Asian American Political Alliance (AAPA) at UC Berkeley began conducting draft counseling to help young Asian

FIGURE 8. Mike Nakayama speaking at Peace Sunday at the Biltmore Bowl in Los Angeles, May 16, 1971. (From *Gidra,* June 1971.)

American men avoid going to war. "Concerned with the large percentage of youth in exploited areas who are inducted into the Army because they lack information on their rights to deferment and alternative service," AAPA opened a counseling center in San Francisco's Chinatown in early 1969, providing "services for all Asian-American draft-age young men." With an office space at the Chinatown Legal Aid Society and a bilingual staff, the Chinatown Draft Help Center directed its service to the "Asian ghetto dweller," who remained "culturally isolated" and for whom "many of the alternatives and deferments provided by the SSS [Selective Service System] are culturally and institutionally deprived." By 1970, the group expanded its services to four days a week, and renamed itself "Chinatown-Manilatown Draft Help" to reflect its expanding constituents.[41]

The Chinatown Draft Help Center was rooted in local community-based struggles that linked the systematic abandonment of American ghettos to the "overrepresentation" of black and brown people fighting in the war. Similar to the draft-counseling centers that served Chicano and black youths in Oakland and other cities, Chinatown Draft Help became a space to theorize state violence and its impact on communities of color, particularly the conscription of young men to do the work of killing. "The rich of this country are now using the have-nots of this country to fight the have-nots of Vietnam," the organizers of Chinatown Draft Help explained in the February 1970 issue of *Getting Together,* a monthly bilingual newspaper of I Wor Kuen, a Marxist-Leninist collective based in New York City. They emphasized that the draft served a double function: "by picking primarily on the sons of the have-nots in this country, [it] keeps young angry men off the street and in the army where they can be controlled." They saw the draft as a crucial tool of "maintaining 'law and order.'"[42]

Taking "young angry men" off the streets and putting them in the military, however, wrought a different kind of problem: some rebelled from within the military. Two months after this article appeared, *Getting Together* published an interview with Sam Choy, an Asian American GI who was court-martialed for threatening to shoot his superiors in response to the racism he encountered in Vietnam. "Sam is a hero," the editor emphasized. "He is one of the few people who had the self-respect and courage to *defend himself from racists*." As the links between racism and military violence became clearer to Asian American GIs, many found ways to resist against their exploitation and complicity in the violence. Increasingly, they came to understand the work of soldiering to entail the labor of protest and opposition to their own formation. "Wait till Japanese-Americans and Chinese-Americans really wake up," one veteran had told Lifton during the psychologist's field research; "some of them who fought in Vietnam are the angriest guys I know."[43] Indeed, as these images of Asian American GIs' victimhood and resistance circulated within the Asian American movement, actual veterans came home and inserted themselves into the political landscape.

ASIAN AMERICAN VETERANS ORGANIZING

In the summer of 1971, Nakayama and Nagatani began reaching out to Asian Americans they knew who had served in the war. They were determined that as a group, Asian American veterans who opposed the war could make a positive impact on their community. They coined themselves Asian Movement for Military Outreach, or AMMO. In the August 1971 issue of *Gidra,* they stated their aim: "The power of the U.S. military has been deemed necessary for the safety and well being of *all American* people. Yet this is the institution that uses our Asian brothers in the service as examples of what Vietnamese look like, calls them Gooks, Japs, Chinks, and other racist terms, degrades the character of Asian women, regards Asian people as being less than human and having no regard for human life." Against such institutionalized dehumanization, concrete things could be done. "We feel we can serve the community," they asserted, "by giving righteous draft counseling to brothers not in the service; by counseling, informing and corresponding with brothers currently in the military through a newsletter; by relating to veterans and their experiences of alienation and dehumanization; and by educating the community about the nature of the military through speaking engagements." "We are not just an anti-war group," they clarified. While they recognized antiwar and GI movement activists as important allies, they emphasized their distinctive agenda to support "our Asian brothers" and to "serve our community."[44]

AMMO represented a critical formation within the Asian American movement. It gave GIs and veterans an outlet to testify to their subjection to racism and militarism, and it nurtured a space for them to become political activists. In doing so, AMMO distinguished itself from the longstanding Asian American political tradition that equated military service with the struggle for civil rights. If putting on the military uniform was once a political statement about the right to fight and die for the nation, especially for Japanese Americans during World War II, then AMMO explicitly called into question the racial violence that such claims to citizenship entailed. AMMO harnessed and expanded the critique of the U.S. Third World left that linked the production of racism to U.S. imperial wars abroad. Participation in U.S. wars, AMMO insisted, was never a solution to mitigating racial exclusion.

Not all Asian American veterans gravitated to antiwar activism, but few opposed it outright. Indeed, AMMO drew people first and foremost by the concrete support that it offered to veterans and GIs. Kenji Kudo, who knew Nakayama from school before joining the Marines, connected with the group because he understood personally the isolation faced by most GIs in Vietnam. "We felt it was important to let the guys know in service that, although we are against the war as veterans, we understand how they feel, because we were in their position." Sometime during Kudo's second tour in Vietnam in 1969, a friend from Los Angeles sent him a copy of *Gidra,* to inform him of the protests happening back home. It was his first exposure to the antiwar movement, and it shattered him. He reflected, "You kind of take it personal, you think the demonstrators are blaming you." To counter such feelings of ostracism and to show support, Kudo took the lead in publishing AMMO's monthly newsletter. "We would explain who we were, what our purpose was," mainly "to support the guys over there." During the year and the run of the newsletter, Kudo recalled getting two replies from GIs that were "positive." To him it was worth all the effort.[45]

AMMO grew slowly by word of mouth, pulling people who related similar experiences of racial violence and trauma from the war. Chris Taga was one of its first members. When Taga returned home from active duty, his first conscientious act of protest was to urge his own brother and friends not to join the military. A coworker introduced him to Nagatani in the summer of 1971, and he was roped in quickly. "We all had problems adjusting back to civilian life," Taga said. "It's kind of like an instant bonding." For him, the group provided an outlet to share his experience of being a point man in his platoon, which continued to haunt him long after he came home.[46]

Some nonveterans also found a place in AMMO. Mike Yanagita became involved in draft counseling while undergoing his own appeal process against the draft. A transplant from Ann Arbor, Michigan, where he participated in the peace movement, Yanagita came to see the war differently after meeting Nagatani and Nakayama and hearing their stories. "They were talking about the racism they experienced in the military, and how their commanding officer would stand them up in front of the squadron and talk about this is what the enemy looks like," he recalled. For Yanagita, meeting the veterans in AMMO opened him up to "this other aspect" of the war. When it was time to update his draft appeal, he scribbled a new line for his reasoning for refusing to serve: "I don't want to kill my Asian brothers and sisters." His appeal process dragged on for two years, but by then the war was nearing its end.[47]

AMMO had roughly twenty regular participants, but the numbers belie their deeper significance and impact in the community. The group met regularly at the office of the Japanese American Community Services (JACS) in Los Angeles's Little Tokyo, which was home to a number of other grassroots collectives, including the Pioneer Center, which advocated for low-income housing for elderly Issei, and other programs related to mental health and drug abuse. Started by a group of mostly third-generation Japanese Americans, JACS drew inspiration from the Black Panthers and the Young Lords to serve the most marginalized segment of their community. JACS was funded by the Neighborhood Youth Corps, a Great Society program intended to put youth to work through job training, but whose effects far exceeded the scope and vision of Johnson's War on Poverty. AMMO rooted its identity and activism firmly within this grassroots network in Little Tokyo, intimately connected to its multifaceted struggles. "We weren't just organizing on an island," Nagatani emphasized, "because we were part of a larger movement" that was concerned about other issues besides the war. Telling young men not to go into the war was one thing, "but don't go in and do what? That was a greater challenge."[48]

Thus, aside from draft counseling and conducting teach-ins against the war, those in AMMO immersed themselves in other forms of community organizing. Nagatani was particularly active in JACS's youth and drugs program, which waged a massive campaign against the pharmaceutical company Eli Lilly in 1971. "Eli Lilly was saturating our communities with these red pills called barbiturates, that young people were overdosing on at the time," he said. At the same time, it was also manufacturing weapons "used in Vietnam and killing people over there."[49] The link between the violence of the war abroad and the killing of young people of color at home could not have been clearer. Kathy Nishimoto Masaoka, a Sansei activist who was recruited into the youth and drugs program shortly after graduating from Berkeley and moving home to Los Angeles, recalled that in one recent year thirty-one young people from the community "high school age or younger" died from drug overdose. The devastating loss compelled her to act; she felt "we had to do something." Along with Nagatani and others, she became involved in teach-ins and educational programs with students and parents about drug prevention.[50] In 1971, Nagatani also cofounded Yellow Brotherhood in his neighborhood of Crenshaw. Similar to JACS, Yellow Brotherhood utilized federal funding from the Neighborhood Youth Corps and created meaningful and substantive action by mobilizing former drug abusers, ex-gang members, ex-convicts, and Vietnam veterans to do drug-prevention outreach. Within six months, it succeeded in eliminating drug trafficking and gang activity in the community.[51]

The veterans carried out their day-to-day activism beneath the radar of the mainstream antiwar movement, but occasionally their activities captured headlines. On August 20, 1972, AMMO interrupted the annual festivities of the Nisei Week Parade in Little Tokyo with a contingent of Asian American youths, whom Nagatani and others had helped organize that summer through their antiwar and drug-prevention work. The Nisei Week Parade, a tradition started in 1930 to celebrate Japanese American civic inclusion, had never been a place for subversive politics, and the planners that year made sure of it by specifying a "no politics" policy. However, it did nothing to stop the intrusion. Dubbing themselves the Van Troi Anti-Imperialist Youth Brigade, the group of 150 high school students and other participants marched down the parade route, boldly declaring their solidarity with the Vietnamese freedom fighters. They named themselves "Van Troi" after a young Vietnamese martyr who had been executed eight years before by the South Vietnamese government for his antiwar resistance. Clad in uniform dark jeans, white tees, and hachimaki headbands, the Van Troi Youth Brigade marched in a disciplined, militarized formation as they chanted in unison, "go left, go right, now pick up the gun!"[52]

The spectacle was an unwelcome disruption to the typically peaceful celebration in Little Tokyo, "much to the dismay of the Nisei Week community." Organizers had invited special guests to act as parade marshals, including the Japanese consul general in Los Angeles, the president of the Japanese Chamber of Commerce, and Mike Masaoka, the Japanese American Citizens League (JACL) lobbyist in Washington, D.C. The presence of these "community leaders" made the disruption an especial affront. Nisei Week officials called in the police to disperse the protesters. But before they did, the youth capped off their performance by burning an effigy of President Nixon and the Japanese "Rising Sun" flag in protest against the reversion of Okinawa from U.S. military control to Japan and the resurgence of Japanese militarism. "We oppose Japanese militarism just as we oppose U.S. imperialism," the Van Troi Youth Brigade printed in their statement that was leafleted at the parade. "Japan has worked hand in hand with the U.S. in perpetuating the war. Furthermore, Japan is currently expanding her own armed forces and is expected to actively aid in construction, technology, and manpower needed for the war."[53]

Protesting Japanese militarism presented no contradiction for the Japanese American youths of the Van Troi Brigade. In the past several months, they had become acutely aware of events in Okinawa and Japan, particularly around the Okinawan reversion that had taken place in May 1972. Throughout the summer, *Gidra* and other movement newspapers had been reporting on

FIGURE 9. Van Troi Anti-Imperialist Youth Brigade burn Rising Sun Flag and interrupt Nisei Week Festival in Los Angeles's Little Tokyo, August 20, 1972. (From *Gidra*, September 1972.)

the antiwar and anti-imperialist struggles of Okinawans and editorializing about the broader ramifications of Japan's resurgence in deepening imperial violence in Asia. To the Van Troi Brigade organizers, the Nisei Week Parade was a perfect time and place to make explicit the connections between these international struggles and "our struggle in our communities." "Because we are Asian Americans," another contingent of activists involved in the protest explained, "and because we believe in the necessity and possibility of uniting broadest segments and classes within the Japanese-American community as an internal colony, *all the more* do we see the necessity to hit hard against the primary enemy of all Asian people both in our home continent and here in America, namely Japanese militarism and imperialism."[54]

In their day-to-day organizing, from draft counseling, to fighting youth drug addiction, to protesting Japanese militarism, the veterans of AMMO made the violence of empire central to their political engagement. Their anti-imperialist sensibility connected them to other movements far beyond the Asian American community in Los Angeles. In the spring of 1973, members of AMMO and the JACS office made the trip to the Pine Ridge Indian Reservation in South Dakota to support the American Indian Movement and the occupation at Wounded Knee. Eighteen to twenty people comprised this Asian American contingent, including Kathy Masaoka, Mo Nishida, Dennis Kobata, and others.[55] Taking its name literally, AMMO delivered five thousand rounds of assorted ammunition to the American Indian activists as they waged their bloody struggle against federal marshals.[56] As Nakayama reflected, "There are so many parallels between the Native Americans and their struggles and the Vietnamese, as another Third World nation." To go from one movement to another, "it wasn't a big stretch." Their activities drew the attention of the FBI's counterintelligence program (COINTELPRO). Although AMMO did not suffer the fate of other organizations that bore the full brunt of the FBI's counterinsurgency, at least one informant infiltrated the group. "We were never raided," Nagatani recalled, but exaggerated reports from the informant, including claims of a plot to assassinate the police, resulted in some arrests.[57]

Asian American veterans came home from the war and became immersed in a range of local and national activities that fueled the project of Third World liberation. And as they did, they grappled with the contradictions of their own complicity in U.S. state violence, which inevitably steered them right back to the war that changed them. In the fall of 1972, AMMO initiated a medical-supply drive to raise donations for the PRG to contribute medical aid for the Vietnamese. "When we go on speaking gigs we would pass around a hat" to collect donations, Nagatani said. "Part of this whole drive was to really educate about the war on genocide being perpetuated upon Asian peoples, the Vietnamese people," and to recognize the human toll of the war. Their efforts quickly spread to other parts of the country. On December 30, 1972, representatives from the Bay Area Asian Coalition Against the War, the New York Asian Coalition Against the War, and AMMO met in San Francisco to kick off a national medical drive to show "concrete" support for the Vietnamese and "to strengthen ties of friendship between Asians in the United States and Vietnam."[58] Asian Veterans Against the War, a group similar to AMMO formed recently in the Bay Area, followed with its own fundraiser in San Francisco's Japantown.[59] These symbolic and material acts of solidarity reaffirmed Asian American veterans' common humanity with the Vietnamese.

"War," Nakayama said, "it's a day-to-day trauma that you have to go through. It's not something that happens just once in your life."[60] Indeed, for Nakayama and countless other Vietnam veterans, the war never left them. Memories of the war continued to haunt them years later, as many continued to relive the horrors routinely and intimately. For Asian American veterans, their post-traumatic stress was often related to the racialized violence they experienced in wartime. Two decades after the war, one Chinese American veteran told his psychiatrist of recurring dreams of being beaten up in the shower by fellow white GIs, who shouted at him, "If we ever catch your gook ass in our shower again, we're going to kill you!" Some months after describing this event, the veteran reported nightmares of being choked to death, and only then recalled the assailants had thrown a laundry bag over his head and tugged the drawstring so tightly around his neck that "I couldn't shout or scream. I couldn't even breathe."[61]

In 1980, the American Psychiatric Association added "Posttraumatic Stress Disorder" (PTSD) to its *Diagnostic and Statistical Manual of Mental Disorders,* giving official language to name and comprehend the persistence of war's trauma for veterans. The recognition of PTSD in American culture was a product of multiple converging forces that took shape in the years after the war's end, including the push by conservative politicians to reinforce the image of the "good" veteran that had been tarnished by the antiwar movement.[62] Less remembered, however, was its origins in the GI movement. Lifton, the psychiatrist who wrote extensively about the "gook syndrome" and participated in VVAW activities in the early 1970s, was perhaps the most public figure who sought to expose the dehumanizing effects of the war on American soldiers, and who continued that work through the 1970s by advocating for veterans and their rehabilitation needs. If the recognition of PTSD had roots in the GI movement and the imperative of ending the war, it was swiftly severed from this moment. PTSD offered no explanation or critique of the systemic violence of militarism, but instead focused on the individualized and psychic harm suffered by veterans.

It is easy to forget that long before the experiences of the war's violence became subjected to individualized diagnosis, they shaped and mobilized a more radical project of Third World liberation. Asian American veterans came home from the war in the late 1960s and early 1970s and became swept into the grassroots struggles of their communities, engaging in draft counseling, advocating for the elderly, and doing youth drug prevention, all facets of the broader struggle to end the war and to undo the violence of U.S. empire. Asian American veterans came back from war and confronted state violence at home, seeing the war in Vietnam as a stage of a continuous U.S. war against racialized and colonized subjects. Thus, they emerged as part of an antiracist and anti-imperialist vanguard that connected the struggles of one community to another—across racial and national divides—in Los Angeles, the Bay Area, and elsewhere in the United States. As we shall see, these connected movements to end the U.S. imperialist war stretched across Asia and the Pacific.

By the late 1960s and early 1970s, the Vietnam War had entered a critical phase marked by the intensification of aerial bombardments in North Vietnam and neighboring Laos and Cambodia. On and near U.S. bases in Okinawa, Japan, and the Philippines where the air war was being waged, the issues of war and empire became ever more inseparable. The renewal of the decolonizing Pacific in the final years of the Vietnam War created the space for new forms of internationalism to emerge, and it is to this space that we now turn.

SIX

A World Becoming

THE GI MOVEMENT AND THE DECOLONIZING PACIFIC

IN OCTOBER 1971, THE U.S.S. *Coral Sea* was preparing for its departure from the Alameda Naval Complex in San Francisco Bay for the South China Sea when the sailors on board pursued other plans. On October 11, seven crewmembers organized a press conference on behalf of thirty-seven others on board and announced their refusal to go to Vietnam. Asserting a "moral obligation to voice [their] opinions," they collected over 1,300 signatures in a petition to publicize the crew's objection to the war and demands to keep the carrier docked. The Bay Area community responded swiftly in support. Antiwar activists protested in front of the naval air station, and churches provided sanctuary for deserters. On November 12, after a month of struggle and anticipation, the *Coral Sea* finally departed San Francisco Bay. All told, 250 men abandoned the ship. From San Francisco, the deserters issued a statement of solidarity with the other crewmembers and with U.S. military service persons in general: "Just as we have left the Coral Sea, we know that increasing numbers of brothers and sisters in the military will find the courage to resist the intimidation of their commanding officers, and refuse to fight."[1]

As antiwar activists resumed struggle in the Bay Area, the *Coral Sea* continued into the Pacific, docking at bases in Okinawa, Japan, and the Philippines, en route to Vietnam. When the carrier arrived at these bases over the next two months, a diverse group of activists, including GIs, American peace activists, base workers, and antibase and anti-imperialist activists, welcomed the disaffected sailors. The *Coral Sea* had transported the crew across the waters to another world of radicalism, one that they had heard much about but had not experienced firsthand. In the closing months of 1971, a wave of labor strikes led by Filipino base workers had brought U.S. military operations at Clark Air Base to a near standstill. In their demands to the U.S. military for equal pay and their rights to work and to strike, the base workers found unlikely alliances with the GIs stationed there, some who joined the strikers at the picket lines. "The Filipinos are my brothers," an American airman proclaimed against orders to disperse the strikers. "I will not fight them. Theirs is a legitimate cause."[2] When the *Coral Sea* docked in Subic Bay in January 1972, GIs there were ready to organize. They handed out copies of underground newspapers as the sailors disembarked, and acquainted them with the wider movement unfolding around them.

The movement of the *Coral Sea* in 1971–72 symbolized a new phase of the war under President Nixon's Vietnamization policy. Vietnamization was sold to the public in 1969 as the phased withdrawal of U.S. combat troops and the "handing over" of the fighting to the South Vietnamese Army. Meant in part to quell antiwar dissent on the home front, Vietnamization had the unintended consequence of expanding—and radicalizing—the antiwar movement across the Pacific. Antiwar activists were quick to point out the deception. Vietnamization, they knew, signaled not an end to the war but a strategy that both increased the utilization of South Vietnamese forces *and* intensified aerial bombardments that reactivated the chain of U.S. bases in Asia and the Pacific. In 1970, the Pacific Counseling Service (PCS), a pacifist organization that had provided legal aid to GIs and draft resisters in the Bay Area, expanded its operation to Japan, Okinawa, and the Philippines. At these places, the PCS organizers opened "GI centers" in proximity to U.S. air and naval bases, the arsenal of Nixon's escalated air war, to counsel American servicemen and to nurture a political space for those who no longer wished to participate in the war.

In expanding antiwar activism across the Pacific, the PCS organizers did not expect to get pulled into "other streams of internationalism" that would redefine their political struggle.[3] At these locales, American activists and GIs were introduced to a different kind of antiwar politics, one that approached the Vietnam War as a phase of longer histories of colonialism and U.S. militarism in the region. In Okinawa and the Philippines, in particular, protests against the Vietnam War were part and parcel of the insurgent politics around the reversion of Okinawa to Japan and the continuation of martial law in the Philippines. These were the imperial dynamics and colonial legacies that were unfolding at the time, and that reinforced the precariousness of living and surviving under the U.S. empire. GIs and their organizers became integrated into these political landscapes. The unlikely coalitions they forged and sustained with base workers and antimilitary and anti-imperialist activists deepened and transformed their antiwar activism, creating an emergent internationalism through shared experiences of race and empire. In this other world, Third World liberation seemed wholly possible.

Such practices of internationalism were not invented anew, but built on the infrastructure of older left internationalist alliances. When GIs, communist workers, and labor organizers of the International Longshore and Warehouse Union protested the buildup for permanent war at the end of World War II with demobilization campaigns in Hawai'i, the Philippines, Guam, and other places, they were continuing the popular front activism that spanned the globe in the 1930s and 1940s. Two and a half decades later, the internationalizing war in Vietnam reactivated these networks once again. U.S. military and local state authorities kept a close watch on the GIs and GI organizers, mindful that their efforts to end the war posed a threat to the U.S. empire and its international alliances. By 1973, as the war drew to an end, GI organizers returned stateside, many of them deported from the Philippines during martial law, and pursued different channels to continue their anti-imperialist work. What follows is a story of a short-lived but remarkable insurgency that rocked the U.S. empire at the end of the Vietnam War, a phase of the making of the decolonizing Pacific that revealed a glimpse of a decolonized future yet to come.

PACIFIC COUNSELING SERVICE AND THE NEW LEFT

The Pacific Counseling Service began its first GI project in Monterey, California, in March 1969, amid the largest concerted rebellion to shake the U.S. military in recent memory. A Marine colonel assessed two years later, "The morale, discipline and battle-worthiness of the U.S. armed forces are, with a few salient exceptions, lower and worse than at any time in this century and possibly in the history of the United States."[4] A culture of GI dissent flourished as part and parcel of the antiwar movement in the late 1960s and early 1970s, driving soldiers, sailors, and Marines to rebel from within the military. In individual and coordinated instances, GIs went absent without leave, deserted, rioted, refused or shirked combat, and committed "fragging" against their superiors.

GI rebellion during the Vietnam War reflected the imperatives of the era's antiwar movement, but it also marked a critical moment in the longer formation of the U.S. empire. In the decades after World War II, unbridled militarism and racialized class inequalities proceeded apace to transform the U.S. military into a budding site of antiracist working-class resistance. More than just a "working-class war" that pulled disproportionate numbers of poor people into the ranks, the war in Vietnam was, at root, a colonial conflict that exposed the limits of American claims to democracy and racial equality. As the previous chapter showed, Asian American GIs who were drafted or compelled to enlist witnessed a kind of racial violence in Vietnam that rang all too familiar in their own lives. By the time their communities at home began to radicalize the agenda of the antiwar movement, transforming the call from "bring home the troops" to "stop killing our Asian brothers and sisters," GIs of color likewise drew upon the symbols of Third World liberation to proclaim racial and anticolonial solidarity with decolonizing subjects of the U.S. empire.

The San Francisco Bay Area occupied a key site of these political transformations. Home to several major military installations, including the Alameda Naval Air Station, Fort Ord, the Presidio, and the Oakland Army Base, the Bay Area was well situated for antiwar activists to confront the war machine directly. On April 27, 1968, a group of forty active-duty servicemen headed an antiwar demonstration in San Francisco, marking the first GI-led civilian peace rally in the country. Two and a half months later, nine AWOL servicemen publicly took "sanctuary" at a local Presbyterian church and announced their resignation from the military, an event that galvanized media attention around the fledgling GI movement. In these instances of early GI resistance, GIs and their supporters emphasized their moral opposition to the war, a pacifist stance encouraged by the religious left. Thus, when Sidney Peterman, a Unitarian minister in Monterey and a longtime member of the peace organization the American Friends Service Committee, proposed the establishment of a GI legal-counseling office by the name of West Coast Counseling Service, he found receptive ears among the local churches and religious groups. With a group of GI organizers, Peterman opened the PCS office to provide legal counseling to servicemen.[5]

PCS was rooted in the peace activism of the Bay Area but was also part of the wider GI movement spreading across the country. Beginning in 1968, New Left activists opened GI coffeehouses near military bases to offer a space for GIs to gripe openly about the military and to cultivate their antiwar consciousness. Loosely affiliated and localized, the coffeehouses brought GIs and antiwar civilians together and nurtured their camaraderie beyond the

FIGURE 10. Active-duty GIs and civilians march for peace in San Francisco, September 1968. (Courtesy of GI Press Collection, Wisconsin Historical Society.)

confines of military life. New Left activists saw the coffeehouses as an important space to further the antiwar movement. In their view, GIs were not simply victims of the draft but were political actors in their own right who could be mobilized to bring a swift end to the war. The GI coffeehouse, like the Honolulu Labor Canteen that brought together GIs, plantation workers, and labor organizers in the mid-1940s, became a thriving ground for GIs and civilian activists to sow the seeds of rebellion within the military.[6]

Peterman was inspired by these developments when he proposed his GI counseling office in Monterey. Peterman had engaged in some GI counseling work through his church, but it was time to commit more fully. With funding secured through the Unitarian Universalist Association, the Unitarian Service Center, the Clergy and Laymen Concerned About Vietnam, and a handful of organizers including some Vietnam veterans, clergy, and conscientious objectors, PCS opened its doors near Fort Ord in the spring of 1969. Alan Miller was among this initial cadre. A white Presbyterian cleric from Minnesota, Miller had spent the early 1960s taking part in the civil rights movement in the South before moving to the Bay Area in 1965. In San Francisco, he worked with local college ministries as an administrative person, took part in student antiwar activism, and helped conscientious objectors find alternative service through the church. Miller's theological background, his experience working with GIs, and his broad commitment to social justice were precisely the qualities Peterman was searching for. Together, the PCS organizers promptly went to work. In the first six months, they handled more than 700 legal cases involving GI rights at Fort Ord, and helped 120 soldiers obtain conscientious-objector status.[7]

The Seaside Police Department began infiltrating the PCS office and compiling reports of its activities during this time. In September 1969, the DOD issued a "Directive on Dissidents," the most comprehensive policy to date for "handl[ing] dissident and protest activities among members of the armed forces." It outlined regulations about the possession and distribution of print materials, off-post gathering places, and on- and off-post demonstrations. Although admitting to the legality of most of these activities, the directive also gave base commanders wide discretion in implementing the guidelines.[8] The DOD policy allowed the PCS activists to continue their work but portended the repression to come.

PCS expanded on the West Coast at the end of 1969, about the time that the GI movement as a whole steered further left. With a dozen or so organizers, PCS opened offices in Oakland, San Francisco, San Diego, and Tacoma. In Tacoma, PCS aligned with the GI-Civilian Alliance for Peace, the local GI collective that had just concluded an unprecedented campaign to rally GI support for the United Farm Workers Union and their boycott of nonunion grape growers. Dale Borgeson, an army draftee from Minnesota who became a GI organizer at Fort Lewis during this time, soon joined the PCS ranks. Borgeson would play an important part in the PCS expansion to Asia within the year.[9]

The extension to San Diego coincided with the December 14 moratorium demonstration at nearby Oceanside and the founding of the Movement for a Democratic Military. In the largest demonstration in the country on that day, an estimated one thousand service people converged with a crowd of four thousand to rally near Camp Pendleton. GIs carried signs that read, "Bring our brothers home, keep us here!" and "End racism through solidarity!" The historic demonstration galvanized a multiracial coalition of GIs under the banner of Third World unity, and broadly signaled the GI movement's departure from its pacifist roots. It was the kind of revolutionary politics that PCS organizers increasingly pursued. Miller and others explained in their 1970 report, "Because of the racist patterns in American society and the fact that draft counseling services are primarily available to white, middle class young people, a disproportionately high number of service personnel are ... members of the black, brown, or third world communities." Hence, "much of the work of PCS is directed on behalf of non-white GIs." Third World movement publications such as the *Black Panther* and the San Francisco–based *New Dawn* soon directed black and Asian draftees to PCS offices, acknowledging the important service they offered to their communities.[10]

The formation of PCS in 1969 took place at a critical juncture in the transformation of the U.S. New Left. As the Students for a Democratic Society, the leading New Left organization, fractured in 1969 and drove some disillusioned activists away from radical politics, many stayed committed and searched for inspiration elsewhere. Taking their cue from the Asian, Chicano, and Black Power movements, the largely white middle-class activists of the New Left had learned to look beyond national boundaries in pursuit of new models of building socialist democracy. In 1969, the New Left exemplified this shift by forming the Venceremos Brigade, a group of American activists who went to Cuba to harvest sugarcane with Cuban workers and to show their solidarity with the Cuban Revolution. For GI organizers, the tenor of global struggle meant that the pursuit of a strictly antiwar politics no longer sufficed; they needed also to instill an antiracist and anti-imperialist consciousness among the servicemen.

The PCS organizers met this challenge by turning toward Asia. Expanding their projects to Asia, they thought, would allow them to organize GIs abroad and to politicize them around issues beyond the war. In the spring of 1970, Peterman embarked across the Pacific and renamed the group by replacing "West Coast" with "Pacific," making it the Pacific Counseling Service. Meanwhile, in Monterey the PCS staff invited Pat Sumi to speak to the soldiers at Fort Ord. Sumi had returned recently from her tour of North Korea, North Vietnam, and the People's Republic of China with the U.S. People's Anti-Imperialist Delegation. The PCS organizers thought her presence in Monterey would captivate the GI audience, especially if she could speak about "Cuba and socialism."[11]

Peterman made his first of many trips to Asia at the invitation of some Japanese antiwar activists in Tokyo. Responding to their request to open a GI counseling office in Japan, the PCS founder went for two months to survey the situation. His trip confirmed what he knew about Beheiren (the Citizens' Federation for Peace in Vietnam), a loosely organized collective of former Communist Party members, artists, intellectuals, students, and workers that was at the forefront of Japan's antiwar movement. Beheiren was founded in 1965 by Oda Makoto—a popular writer and left critic—and other left intellectuals committed to the broad goals of ending Japan's complicity in the war and securing peace and self-determination for the Vietnamese. The group was deliberately nonsectarian, opting to function independently rather than to adhere strictly to political party lines. As such, it drew concerned citizens across all strata of society, including professionals, housewives, shopkeepers, and the elderly, fostering their grassroots politics. Local chapters emerged all across Japan, with members engaging in petition drives, teach-ins, and protests near military bases.[12]

Beheiren sought alliances with American activists and GIs from its inception. With increasing numbers of soldiers passing through Tokyo on R&R, in 1965 the group launched the Japan Technical Committee for Assistance to Anti-War U.S. Deserters, which garnered international attention two years later for helping four U.S. sailors escape to Sweden. In December 1969, in concert with the moratorium demonstrations in the United States, Beheiren helped Marines at the U.S. Marine Corps Air Station at Iwakuni start a chapter of the American Servicemen's Union, one of the largest and most influential GI organizations at the time. Given Beheiren's remarkable history of organizing American servicemen, its outreach to PCS seemed logical. In April 1970, Peterman returned to Tokyo for an "indefinite period," with a budget of six hundred dollars a month to establish a GI center in the building that was also home to Beheiren's central office.[13]

Word spread quickly about the new GI center in Tokyo, and before long, U.S. military personnel on R&R and from surrounding areas in Japan made their way to the office to seek legal support. Beheiren was indispensable to PCS's early transition to Japan, helping expand its work to nearby bases. On July 4, 1970, when thirteen imprisoned Marines at Iwakuni led a rebellion against the "brutal and dehumanizing conditions" in the brig, PCS and Beheiren came to their support. With a joint defense team, they helped turn the "Iwakuni 13" into a symbol of GI resistance in Asia.[14] Later they worked with the Iwakuni Marines to found the Hobbit coffeehouse, where Marines could interact with and learn from Japanese activists. As one organizer put it, the coffeehouse enabled the GIs to develop "a friendship [with the Japanese] that's not a monetary exchange with a 'sweet cream' lady." Put differently, the coffeehouse served as a demilitarized space that radically disrupted the racialized, gendered, and sexualized relations of the U.S. military empire in Asia. In this space, GIs and Japanese activists practiced solidarity based on a shared antiwar sensibility.[15]

Their success did not go unnoticed by the local and base authorities. Responding to their "proselytizing" of GIs around the base towns, the U.S. military discontinued all R&R flights to Tokyo in 1971. That year, the Japanese government initiated steps to deport the American activists. By the summer of 1972, following a series of raids, the military police at Iwakuni declared the Hobbit "off-limits" to American military personnel.[16] The GI movement in Asia posed a new kind of problem unforeseen by U.S. military and state officials, to which they responded swiftly and aggressively.

VIETNAMIZATION AND THE NIXON DOCTRINE

The transpacific journeys of the American activists reflected the transformation of the New Left, but the routes were not solely of their making. On November 3, 1969, President Nixon announced his "Vietnamization" policy, partly to mollify the growing antiwar public. The phased withdrawal of U.S. ground troops from South Vietnam had begun in June and would be completed on a steady schedule "as the South Vietnamese become strong enough to defend their own freedom," the president told Americans.[17] Contrary to what the name implied, however, Vietnamization both intensified the war by other means and internationalized it anew. The policy underscored Nixon's intention to prosecute the war from afar, ostensibly beyond the view of the dissenting home front. In effect, after 1969 the air force and the navy assumed an unprecedented role in the war by carrying out escalated aerial campaigns, with direct consequences for U.S. bases in Asia and the Pacific. Instead of suppressing the GI movement, Vietnamization set the stage for its proliferation across the Pacific.

The increased military operations at the Pacific bases renewed international tensions and debates about U.S. base policies. In Japan, Okinawa, and the Philippines, antiwar activists denounced the U.S. violation of bilateral base agreements, which disallowed the use of the bases for military operations in Vietnam and elsewhere without the prior consent of their governments. Protests in these countries and territories erupted almost spontaneously in the wake of Nixon's escalated war. To base workers and others who had long lived in the shadow of the U.S. empire, the Vietnam War both represented an act of imperial aggression in a neighboring country and served to remind them of the limits of their own sovereignty. In these militarized countries and territories where the United States continued to exercise political and economic influence, antiwar politics proved inseparable from a broader critique of U.S. imperialism.

The radical politics at these locales would come to transform the GI movement. In an unprecedented instance in the spring of 1972, the PCS organizers and GIs from several bases met in Tokyo for a joint press conference to issue an antiwar statement. The statement began, "We protest the United States' claim of 'winding down the war' and 'Vietnamization,' . . . for this fabrication now entails renewed massive bombing raids causing the genocide of the Vietnamese." Going one step further, they read, "We most strongly protest the United States' military's mockery of the Japanese-American security treaty, openly violating the provision that no troops be transferred to the Republic of Viet Nam without prior Japanese approval."[18] Antiwar GIs and GI organizers had learned to identify with the politics of those who shared a different and more entangled relationship with U.S. imperialism, namely base workers and other antibase and labor activists for whom the Vietnam War was but a phase of a larger and more intractable problem.

U.S. officials also understood the broader implications of the war. Marshall Green, the Assistant Secretary of State for East Asia and Pacific Affairs, stated at the time, "Our Vietnam policy must be viewed in a wide context." Green reminded State Department officials that Vietnamization was not new but was a continuation of the post–World War II strategy of training and utilizing allied forces. The "striking Asian examples of successful modernization" in countries such as South Korea, Japan, and Taiwan were indicative of the benefits of the long-term investments in the allied military programs, he noted, but that very "success" also meant that it was time to scale back. Especially with mounting discontent over American power globally, the United States needed to allow Asian allies to assume greater responsibilities, to find "Asian solutions to Asian problems."[19] Vietnamization, by replacing U.S. troops with U.S.-trained South Vietnamese forces, was one manifestation of this wider shift in U.S. policy toward Asia at the start of the 1970s.

This policy shift was known as the Nixon Doctrine. Announced by the president in July 1969, the Nixon Doctrine elaborated the U.S. intent to share the burdens of regional security and Third World capitalist development with other "modernized" Asian nations. Japan was key in this formulation. In November 1969, Prime Minister Eisaku Sato explained Japan's new role within this imperial realignment in a speech at the National Press Club in

Washington, D.C. Sato declared the dawning of a new era, the "New Pacific Age," when Japan would "take the leading role . . . towards nation-building efforts of the Asian countries." Assured by a quarter-century of U.S. tutelage, the prime minister spoke confidently as a junior partner: "Japan, in cooperation with the United States, will make its contribution to the peace and prosperity of the Asian-Pacific region and hence to the entire world."[20] Japan's erstwhile colonial ambitions in the name of the Greater East-Asia Co-Prosperity Sphere thus materialized through the Nixon Doctrine. As the end of the Vietnam War came into sight, the United States and Japan already began working to secure Japan's role in the rehabilitation of Southeast Asian economies after the war.

As Sato and Nixon met to renew their alliance, concerns about Okinawa's future mounted. A Japanese colonial prefecture since 1879, Okinawa emerged from World War II not as an independent nation but as yet another colonized territory, this time under the U.S. military. When Japan regained sovereignty in 1952, Okinawa remained an occupied territory administered by the United States, primarily for the purpose of stationing troops and maintaining its nuclear arsenal. The violence associated with the U.S. military presence, including crimes committed by GIs and the environmental and health impact of base operations, had driven Okinawan protests since the early 1950s. In the 1960s, these protests intensified and coalesced around the demand for "reversion"—that is, to restore Okinawa's Japanese prefectural status and to end the American occupation.[21]

In November 1969, Sato and Nixon signed a joint communiqué that paved the path for Okinawa's reversion to Japan in 1972. By this time, however, it had become clear to Okinawans that reversion was not the answer to their problems. They realized that even after Okinawa was returned to Japan and the U.S. occupation formally ended, the United States would still be allowed to keep bases there for as long as it deemed necessary. Reversion would not mean the end of military buildup but its escalation so long as the war continued. Thus, as Sato and Nixon signed their agreement, Okinawans descended upon U.S. bases to call for the immediate and unconditional removal of all U.S. military personnel, bases, and nuclear weapons from the island. Oda Makoto, then on his U.S. speaking tour, rallied antiwar activists in Washington, D.C. and denounced the resurgence of Japanese imperialism.[22] As the United States and Japan reaffirmed their "common political and security interests in the Pacific," antiwar and anti-imperialist protests intensified in the two countries.[23]

Reversion signaled a cause for ongoing political engagement among Okinawan base workers. In December 1969, after the U.S. military declared its intent to fire 2,400 base workers as part of the move toward reversion, the workers responded swiftly. Zengunro, the base workers' union, promptly passed a strike vote demanding the removal of all U.S. bases from Okinawa; but they clarified that as long as the bases remained they would be entitled to retain their jobs. Thirty-five thousand base workers struck for five consecutive days in January 1970, fired by visions of an unfulfilled democracy centered on peace, jobs, and justice. With a firm grasp of their complex subordination as workers and as colonized subjects, the base workers did something more unexpected: they reached out to GIs for support. They handed out translated leaflets and posters to GIs, which PCS noted had an "immediate and positive" impact. GIs smuggled posters back to the base and plastered them on barrack walls, and affirmed their solidarity by swapping "V" signs and power salutes. Some GIs even initiated meetings with Zengunro leaders "to exchange views on racism, imperialism, third world liberation, and on the possibilities of joint action."[24]

These expressions of solidarity were forged deliberately against the unequal relations of power in U.S.-occupied Okinawa. Indeed, for Okinawans the violence of the U.S. military occupation was not a metaphor but a lived reality. Sexual violence against women and other acts of violence committed by GIs were routine experiences within the base town's economy built on sex and pleasure. These relations of violence came to a head in December 1970 in Koza. On December 20, an American driving under the influence of alcohol struck an Okinawan pedestrian, prompting a spontaneous rebellion. Within an hour, a gathering crowd of protesters had swelled to more than one thousand; people descended onto the streets, overturned American-owned cars, and set fire to them. They threw rocks at the military police who tried to fight them back with tear gas and fire hoses. Women who worked in the bars joined the rebellion by filling cola bottles with gasoline to fuel the fires.[25]

The Koza Uprising was a colonial revolt in which the participants, many of them displaced migrants from other parts of Okinawa and the former Japanese colonies, knew firsthand the power of the U.S. military over their lives. They developed a complex and worldly understanding of race and colonialism, which was made clear by their deliberate refrain from harming black GIs during the revolt.[26] Many Okinawans recognized and drew on the symbols of black liberation as they waged their own struggles against the military's economic exploitation and racial discrimination. Black GIs

FIGURE 11. Black GIs show support for Okinawan base workers' strike in 1971. (Courtesy of GI Press Collection, Wisconsin Historical Society.)

reciprocated the gesture. In May 1971, on the heels of the signing of the Reversion Treaty, Okinawans went on a general strike to protest the terms of the agreement and won the firm support of GIs. At a public rally in Koza, GIs leafleted statements of solidarity on the streets, which read in Japanese and English, "We are moved by the sight of the Okinawan people fighting. . . . Brothers and sisters, your struggle is beautiful. We must crush American imperialism through our solidarity!"[27]

Worlds removed and yet brought together by shared circumstances as working peoples of the U.S. military, GIs and Okinawan base workers found common ground in the events surrounding Okinawa reversion. If Vietnamization had brought the PCS activists abroad, then the Nixon Doctrine transformed and radicalized the work of GI organizing. Borgeson, the GI organizer in Tacoma who went to Tokyo in December 1970 and then to Okinawa, learned to appreciate the revolutionary potential of such unlikely alliances between GIs and Asians. While struck by the same "spontaneous anti-military, antiwar sentiments among the GIs" in Japan and Okinawa as anywhere else he had seen in the States, Borgeson also saw the possibility "to educate the GIs about what was going on in Okinawa," to broaden their understanding of the U.S. military and the war within the framework of imperialism.[28] Building solidarity with Zengunro base workers, in this case, would help channel the GIs' antimilitary sentiments into an anti-imperialist struggle against the United States, Japan, and their interimperial alliances.

These emergent coalitions and threats to empire did not elude authorities. Indeed, they drew the collaborative surveillance of U.S. base officials and local police forces. When U.S. military officials in Koza banned PCS organizers from entering a stockade to counsel imprisoned GIs, for example, they filed trespassing complaints with the Japanese Self-Defense Forces that effectively granted the latter authority to enforce the ban.[29] Dissident GIs and American activists in Okinawa thus came to be targeted as radicalized subjects of the U.S. empire, subjected to political repression the origins of which proved increasingly difficult to pinpoint.

PCS pushed onward, expanding projects to wherever U.S. military activities and GI resistance demanded. In August 1971, less than a month after Borgeson arrived in Okinawa, Miller, then the administrative coordinator working from San Francisco, assigned him to the Philippines. The political crisis surrounding an impending declaration of martial law had grown increasingly desperate, and the time was ripe for a new GI project. If organizing in Japan and Okinawa in 1970–71 had introduced the American activists and GIs to another world of radicalism, events in the Philippines the following year would test their political commitments against state violence of a different scale.

CLARK AND SUBIC BAY UNDER MARTIAL LAW

Borgeson arrived in the Philippines on August 22, 1971, the day after a bomb ripped through a political rally held by the opposition Liberal Party in downtown Manila, killing ten people. The attack marked the latest in a string of violence under President Marcos's rising dictatorship, and reminded Borgeson of the palpable dangers that confronted dissidents such as himself. Upon arrival, Borgeson met Melinda Paras, a young Filipina American activist from Wisconsin who recently had gone to the Philippines to participate in the national democratic movement. A member of the Venceremos Brigade to Cuba in 1969 and Kabataang Makabayan (KM), a nationalist youth organization affiliated with the Communist Party of the Philippines, Paras would become instrumental in forging collaborations between Americans and Filipino activists in the coming year.[30]

Paras knew the political landscape, and she imparted her knowledge to the Americans. In November 1971, just before Jane Fonda's antiwar troupe arrived to perform for GIs at Clark and Subic Bay, Paras warned the performers about the dire political situation in the country. Their "political vaudeville," already performed before thousands in the United States under the banner of "Free—or Fuck—the Army" (FTA), would not sit well with Philippine authorities, she cautioned. "Countless" leaders of KM had been "incarcerated . . . kidnapped and murdered" by the Philippine Constabulary; and given the FTA's mission of "arousing just dissent among the puppet troops of the U.S. imperialists, and in support of our liberation struggle, your groups may also fall prey to the harassment of the Marcos fascist puppet regime." The bleak political climate notwithstanding, Paras affirmed her faith that the FTA would pull off a successful event, particularly if they could build positive relations with the media. "The press can be a very valuable asset in resisting the suppressing of the people's democratic rights and civil liberties," thus "good relations with the mass media [must] be maintained at all times during your tour." On the eve of the greatest antiwar GI demonstration ever staged overseas, the Americans received firm reassurance that they had the support of KM, a gesture that convinced them of the vital place of GI organizing with the national democratic struggles in the Philippines.[31]

The FTA show opened on the evening of November 28, 1971, outside Clark Air Base. Before 1,500 U.S. airmen, military dependents, and Filipino civilians, the FTA launched the first of its four performances in the Philippines much as it had done in the United States—by denouncing U.S. militarism, the Vietnam War, and the racial and gendered oppressions of the military. But an ocean away from home, the cast deviated from their usual program. They enacted skits depicting the history of U.S. colonialism in the Philippines and the exploitation of resources and people, explicitly linking the oppressing of Filipinos with that of African Americans in the United States. During one performance, a group of Filipino students interrupted by shouting, "Down with U.S. imperialism!"—a rejoinder welcomed by the performers. Over the next few days, the FTA performed to ten thousand more people, many of them Filipinos, and drove handfuls of GIs to the newly established GI center near Clark.[32] The show gave the PCS organizers just what they needed to jumpstart their activities.

Anticipating the subversive nature of the FTA shows, the DOD dispatched some officials to report on the event. The DOD observers, sitting among rowdy audiences, appeared more amused than alarmed. In their reports they indicated the shows were "amateurish" in quality, their substance "an insult to the intelligence of most persons attending."[33] Their trivializations, however, only reflected wider disillusions about U.S. colonialism's racial legacies in the Philippines. In 1970, for example, when a senior military official called for the closure of the Manila R&R site in response to increasing "anti-American" sentiments, some argued against it, suggesting that "there is a firm rapport between the Negro servicemen and Filipinos that leaves Manila free of racial problems experienced elsewhere."[34] Such a foolhardy statement, coming not long after General Westmoreland declared racial conflicts the preeminent problem confronting the U.S. armed forces, reflected less a reality than the colonial fantasy about Filipinos' enduring support for the U.S. military presence. Little did U.S. officials know that the racial "rapport" between blacks and Filipinos was the outcome of an anticolonial and antiracist internationalism long in the making, and that was now being reactivated.[35]

On a broader level, the FTA shows exploded the myth of the Philippines as a "showcase of democracy." The former U.S. colony's ongoing economic dependence on the United States and complicity in its war in Southeast Asia belied this claim. It turned out that by this time, even some U.S. leaders were ready to cast the slogan aside. In 1969, the Senate Foreign Affairs Committee sent a team of U.S. state officials to the Philippines to investigate the political situation. The mission's findings confirmed that "flagrant corruption and fraud in certain areas of the government," coupled with escalating unemployment in the provinces, had contributed to "the rebelliousness of the young people." The country was swept up in "nationalistic fervor," which in turn was "exploited by a small Communist element to stir revolutionary zeal among some of the youth." By their admission, the Philippines seemed to have reverted to an unbridled nationalism that threatened to cast the nation beyond the "free world." Marcos's inability to institute necessary reforms to reverse the current trend "could spell the end of democracy in the Philippines."[36] Their assessment proved all too prescient.

If the U.S. model of democracy in Asia appeared to be waning, Borgeson and other American activists arrived in time to reclaim the slogan. In January 1971, just as PCS planned to start a GI project in the Philippines, Eric Seitz of the National Lawyers Guild (NLG) also expressed interest in expanding the guild's work there. An organization of progressive lawyers with a long history of labor and civil rights activism, NLG had committed firmly to the antiwar movement; by 1970, it established military law offices in Japan and Okinawa to work alongside PCS. In the spring of 1971, Seitz toured the

Philippines and met with students and base worker union leaders, including some GIs who were "militant, working class, many of them black and brown," who all convinced him of the need for the guild's presence.[37]

Seitz and a team of five lawyers solicited the help of Borgeson and Paras to open an office in Manila in September 1971. Although slow to start, their workload picked up with the momentum gathering around the FTA shows. The GI newspaper at Clark introduced the airmen to the NLG lawyers, next to a spread about the FTA. The enthusiasm generated from the FTA shows cemented the reputation of NLG and PCS among American servicemen. By December, the two groups moved their offices from Manila to Angeles City and Olongapo, within the vicinity of Clark Air Base and Subic Naval Base, respectively. Over the next two months, Borgeson and the NLG lawyers kept a "very busy pace" at the GI centers, handling thirty-five cases involving courts-martial and other nonjudicial punishments, and even opening the space to discuss Philippine politics with the GIs. "Crowded with GIs from early in the morning to late at night," the GI centers became the hub of the GI movement in the Philippines.[38]

Their successes alerted Philippine and U.S. authorities. In February 1972, base officials at Subic began denying base passes to the NLG attorneys, typically an ordinary courtesy for the Americans. The increase in conscientious-objector applications being filed at Clark also led the staff judge advocate there to complain to the Philippine Immigration Office about the American activists, which prompted Bureau of Immigration officials to visit the GI center on February 12. Typical harassments of this sort tended to get resolved when U.S. citizens showed their valid documentation. But their apparent intransigence led authorities to pursue more serious charges and confrontational tactics.

On March 15, armed with a lead from immigration authorities that PCS and NLG were involved with local "subversive groups," the Philippine Constabulary and the military police jointly raided the GI center at Clark. With no one present at the time, they left and returned the next month. This time, under the pretext of searching for an escaped American convict, the armed agents seized PCS and NLG files, and concluded the raid by arresting one GI counselor on a false charge of having an invalid visa. Upon hearing of these incidents, Miller notified Congressman Ronald Dellums, a longtime civil rights advocate, urging him to help protect the GIs and American civilian workers. Dellums fired off a cable to the Clark Air Base commander and to the U.S. ambassador to the Philippines, demanding an explanation for the police attacks. Before either had time to respond, however, the Constabulary and American agents attempted another raid. Without a search warrant this time, they garrisoned the house with armored vehicles for two hours, intimidating the Americans with a display of force. They left without incident, but the event left the activists shaken and fearful that "the next one may well result in the death of several people."[39]

As Philippine and U.S. military authorities intensified their efforts to suppress the GI movement, the PCS's and NLG's appeals to elected officials became more frequent and urgent. Miller wrote to Dellums and three senators that "matters have now reached an extreme situation," and he urged them to start an investigation to "protect the freedoms of both civilian PCS counselors and GI's stationed at Clark." Prompted by the call, U.S. Senator Sam Ervin Jr., the chairman of the Subcommittee on Constitutional Rights, wrote to the Secretary of Defense to inquire into the matter. To no one's surprise, the response was unfavorable. Based on its own investigation, the DOD found that the NLG attorneys had received the "full cooperation" of the staff judge advocate when they first arrived at Clark. Despite efforts "to establish [a] good professional working atmosphere, NLG relations with the military have not always been a model of felicity." Not only did the lawyers seek to "create dissension and disloyalty" among servicemen, but they also had "fallen into disfavor with the Philippine Government" by their open support of KM and criticisms of the Marcos regime. In short, NLG engaged in work that fell beyond legitimacy, and that undermined both governments. The DOD concluded, "Activities of this nature will not be sanctioned."[40]

The DOD seemed to grasp the full implications of the subversive activities. In their day-to-day organizing, PCS and NLG activists sought to expose GIs to the realities of Philippine life beyond the U.S. bases, to cultivate their awareness about the nationalist struggles unfolding around them. At the GI center, for example, they read and discussed the writings of the popular nationalist historian Renato Constantino, which introduced the GIs "to a different way of looking at the U.S. presence there" by raising questions about the legacies of U.S. colonialism and the role of the U.S. bases. What they could not comprehend entirely through reading they got to see with their own eyes. On several occasions, the PCS and NLG activists organized excursions that brought GIs to Manila to witness anti-Marcos demonstrations. In turn, the Filipino people got a glimpse of the GI movement at Clark and Subic. In May 1972, Constantino interviewed Borgeson about PCS and NLG and wrote an article for the *Manila Chronicle* that "gave us very terrific coverage." The article, Borgeson believed, helped cement the GI movement in the political consciousness of the national democratic movement.[41]

Press coverage of the GI movement increased through May as Filipino activists focused their struggle on U.S. bases and their role in the escalation of the Vietnam War. U.S. Ambassador Henry Byroade sought to placate public concerns by insisting that the U.S. government had not misused the bases for the war, a statement backed by Marcos and other Philippine officials. The claim did not satisfy skeptics. Instead, it translated into a call for unified action. On May 17, some GIs from Clark and Subic planned to hold a press conference in Manila to divulge the true nature of the bases to the Philippine public. But authorities caught wind of the plan, and the evening before, the military police raided the GI center at Subic and arrested the two GIs scheduled to speak. The "kidnapping" did little to intimidate other GIs, however. The next day, the press conference went on as scheduled, with two sergeants from Clark stepping in to cover for "their missing Navy brothers." Before the Philippines media, Staff Sgt. Wayne Evans and Sgt. Tom Andric disclosed information about U.S. military operations at Clark and its direct involvement in the Vietnam War. An NLG lawyer stated later that their testimony was "very well received by the press, and the coverage here was excellent."[42]

The two men revealed that a squadron of F-4 fighter-bombers had been recently deployed from Clark Air Base to Thailand, along with more than five hundred support personnel, as part of the resumed bombing of North Vietnam. The revelations confirmed what critics knew, but some Philippine legislators wanted to hear more. That afternoon, Senator Benigno Aquino invited Evans and Andric to testify before a closed session of the Philippine Senate Committee on Foreign Relations, where the two further revealed Clark and Subic as staging areas for the war. When asked why they chose to testify, Evans replied, "We came to this committee to let the Filipino people know the great danger to them in allowing Clark Air Base and Subic Naval Base to be used in the war in Vietnam. We fear the people of the Philippines are in grave danger of reprisals if the situation in Vietnam worsens." Senator Aquino praised their courage and thanked them on behalf of the Filipino people, "for telling the truth about the use of the U.S. bases here." After their testimony, base authorities immediately confined Evans and Andric, pending criminal investigation. But the two had accomplished their task. According to a Filipino columnist, they had "served their noble purpose," telling "the truth about the use of the U.S. bases in the Philippines—and none of these uses are for either defense or peace." Their statements further damaged the credibility of the U.S. embassy and Marcos, and won the favor of the Philippine public. "The issue is now one of credibility, whether to believe the two American servicemen who have been involved in the operations of these bases, or the President." The overwhelming answer came three days later when approximately ten thousand Filipino workers and students besieged the U.S. embassy on the international day of protest against U.S. aggression in Vietnam. The demonstrators demanded an immediate end to all U.S. bombing, before being violently dispersed by the police.[43]

The events surrounding the press conference and the Senate hearing marked the culmination of the GI movement in the Philippines. They confirmed the worst fears of U.S. officials: that PCS and NLG organizers, "under a cover [and] front of GI counseling and legal defense," had worked "to reach service personnel for the purpose of subversion and political indoctrination; to provide a link between service personnel and indigenous leftist movements; and . . . to destroy the effectiveness of the U.S. armed forces in furtherance of the 'socialist revolution' in the United States."[44] Their political activities appeared to have spiraled beyond control. But before long a solution presented itself. On September 21, 1972, Marcos declared martial law. The president immediately ordered the arrests of political dissidents and oppositional leaders, suspended habeas corpus, and unleashed a reign of terror throughout the country. PCS and NLG activists did not escape unscathed.

On October 16, the Philippine Constabulary raided the GI center outside Subic one last time and arrested the two remaining organizers. An NLG lawyer initially escaped the incident but was apprehended the next day from the putative safe confines of the U.S. military base. By this time, the base commander was all too ready to dispense with his legal responsibility to protect the American lawyer and aided the Constabulary to bring a swift end to the problem. Over the next few days, the staff of the NLG and PCS offices in San Francisco worked frantically to develop a strategy to deal with the crisis, enlisting the help of the media, members of Congress, the American Civil Liberties Union, and the State Department for the release of the American civilians. By the end of the week, without pressing formal charges, the Marcos regime deported the three American activists back to the United States. With the remaining defense cases at Clark abandoned, and just as the U.S.S. *Kitty Hawk* docked at Subic Bay with a new crew of weary and agitated sailors, the GI movement in the Philippines came to an abrupt end.[45]

Doug Sorensen, Bart Lubow, and Gene Parker, the three deported NLG and PCS activists, may have left their work unfinished in the Philippines, but they continued to rally against martial law upon returning to the United States. When they arrived in San Francisco on October 27, they immediately convened a press conference to shed light on the situation. "The Philippines' struggle for national democracy," they urged, "must not become another Vietnam War." Their message found receptive ears among local Filipino activists, including Kalayaan, the San Francisco–based anti-imperialist coalition that was then at the forefront of the anti-eviction movement at San Francisco's International Hotel. After the declaration of martial law, Filipino activists in the Bay Area formed the National Committee to Restore Civil Liberties in the Philippines (NCRCLP), a coalition that would play an active role in organizing opposition against Marcos over the next two years. On October 28, the NCRCLP invited the GI organizers to testify at their symposium. "These two brothers talked about U.S. involvement in the Philippines and the miserable life and poverty of the people, but more importantly, of the people's heroic struggle against the Marcos regime," according to an article in *New Dawn*. For several more weeks the deported organizers continued speaking across the country before getting reassigned to other GI projects in Hawai'i and Okinawa.[46]

As they returned to GI organizing and the NLG lawyers moved on to different progressive legal work, Paras and Borgeson stayed in the Bay Area to engage further in Filipino anti-imperialist politics. The two had arrived in San Francisco just before the others, with Paras likewise having been deported and Borgeson having escaped the emergency by being in Japan at the time. After getting politicized around the Vietnam War in the Midwest three years earlier, the two had traveled the world and back, returning to a political community that neither had started from but that both now found a home in. Their time in the Philippines, according to Borgeson, had strengthened their "ties with the Philippine activist movement" such that to get "pulled from one movement into another" only seemed natural. In February 1973, Borgeson left the Bay Area for Seattle, to rejoin his friends from his antiwar activist days at Fort Lewis. As a "departing gift," Paras and other Filipino activists gave him a copy of Carlos Bulosan's *America Is in the Heart,* which he read on his train ride up the Pacific Coast. "I was very moved by it," Borgeson recalled, at once aghast at the violent history endured by an earlier generation of Filipino workers and empowered by their resolve to build a labor movement. Reading Bulosan as he traveled along the same route as the venerable activist had done decades earlier, Borgeson got a glimpse of the history of Filipino labor activism whose relevance to contemporary struggles would become clear soon enough. When he arrived in Seattle, Borgeson linked up with young Asian American activists amid their ongoing struggles for Filipino cannery workers' rights and for the preservation of the International District. Charged to help spread the message against martial law, Borgeson became immersed in the local politics of yet a different imperial metropole.[47]

Just as he had witnessed in Okinawa and in the Philippines, Borgeson found in Seattle a group of dedicated activists who understood the linkages between "domestic" working-class struggles and global revolutions against the U.S. empire. His anecdotes about his political encounters in the Philippines captured the imagination of people like Gene Viernes and Silme Domingo, who at the time were leading a class-action discrimination lawsuit on behalf of nonwhite cannery workers against their employer. In the fall of 1973, Borgeson helped initiate the Seattle chapter of the Katipunan ng mga Demokratikong Pilipino (Union of Democratic Filipinos; KDP), an organization started in the Bay Area earlier that summer by Paras and other Filipino activists, with the twin goals of ending racism in the United States and martial law in the Philippines. Racism and fascism were roots and branches of the U.S. capitalist empire, the KDP founders insisted, and the struggle against one necessitated the struggle against the other, guided by a broader internationalist vision of democracy.[48]

Nowhere was this "dual program" more dramatically exemplified than in the labor struggles of the Pacific Northwest in the 1970s, where the efforts to democratize Local 37—the Filipino cannery union of the International Longshore and Warehouse Union with a long tradition of transpacific radicalism—eventually exposed the connections between the U.S. empire and the Marcos dictatorship and the dangers therein. In 1981, shortly after Viernes traveled to the Philippines to speak with activists about workers' conditions under martial law, he and Domingo were gunned down outside their Seattle union office by agents of the Marcos regime.[49] In the end, and as ever before, a threat to the Philippine government was a threat to the U.S. empire, a fact that the Viernes-Domingo murders would come to epitomize for Filipino activist communities in the United States and in the Philippines.

The Viernes-Domingo murders remain a critical event in the annals of Asian American labor activism; yet that the story of the GI movement in

Asia should end here is no anomaly. If these episodes appear irrelevant to one another, contained by their respective historiographies, they nonetheless bear the traces of deeper connections forged through kindred acts of revolutionary dreams and travels. Like the Filipino migrants who traversed the Pacific and the Pacific Coast before them, the GI activists traveled on imperial routes sedimented over long histories of U.S. militarism in Asia. They went overseas in 1970, propelled by Nixon's call to "Vietnamize" the war, and came back with an altered view of the war entirely. Organizing GIs across the vast U.S. military empire had exposed the organizers to issues that far exceeded the Vietnam War, including Okinawa reversion and martial law in the Philippines, which reframed their approach to the GI movement beyond the scope and period of antiwar politics.

Indeed, while Borgeson deepened his work with KDP in the mid-1970s, PCS continued to recruit new organizers to work in Okinawa. There, the effects of ongoing U.S. militarism at the close of the Vietnam War remained starkly transparent. As PCS reported in 1974, the recent transition of the U.S. military to an "all-volunteer" force had led to bases in Okinawa comprising "more than 50% Black and Third World" GIs, even as "the military remains as racist an institution as it ever was." These men and women in the military, aside from being subjected to military racism and sexism, provided the personnel for a post-Vietnam military that was invested in maintaining a "constant near-war situation" to wage new wars in ensuing decades.[50] Although PCS folded in 1976, having lost much of its funding from progressive organizations that had moved to other concerns, its short career reveals a history of imperial and anti-imperial circuits that spanned the Pacific in the long twentieth century, the connections that at once made the U.S. empire and global dreams of revolution possible.

Conclusion

THOUGH THE ALLIES DECLARED VICTORY in August 1945 and World War II officially came to an end, the battles of the presumptive global superpower did not. The United States has been at war, continuously, ever since. The U.S. military extends around the world but has animated the colonial histories of Asia and the Pacific with particular vehemence and contradiction. From the dissolution of the Japanese empire in 1945 to its steady resurgence as a subempire over the next three decades, the United States sought to secure the region from the spread of communism, and much of this labor fell upon former colonial subjects. Soldiers, counterinsurgents, and civilian workers from the Philippines, South Korea, and the United States all took part in this long war, living and fighting and dying across two continents. And yet, despite their sizeable presence circulating and laboring in diaspora, these Asians and Asian Americans remain a mere footnote in our understanding of the second half of the twentieth century. I have sought to recount aspects of their lives to shed light on how they came to be, and the histories of race and empire that they illuminate. These Asians, I argue, emerged as a particular labor force, essential to—and sometimes torn between—both the building of postcolonial nation-states and the furthering of U.S. empire; their participation in the military was vital to their inclusion into the nation in the age of decolonization. At the same time, soldiering through empire brought formerly colonized peoples into proximity, spurring fleeting alliances that exposed—if only briefly—the limits of these state endeavors and the horizons of their unfinished struggles for democracy.

In the post–World War II decades, the United States relied on a growing network of decolonizing states and territories to function as the periphery of the capitalist world system. I have traced the links within this imperial geography via the long grasp of the military, and the soldiers and workers who traversed it. We have seen South Korean and Taiwanese military trainees learning to be modern soldiers in U.S. schools; Filipino doctors, nurses, and retired guerrillas teaching the techniques of freedom to the South Vietnamese; and citizen-soldiers from South Korea, the Philippines, and Hawai'i carrying out search-and-destroy and other combat missions in the South Vietnamese countryside. In each of these instances, colonial legacies and individual desires were mobilized and channeled into the service of U.S. empire. The transition from colony to liberated nation was a messy process that unfolded unevenly across Asia and the Pacific; but in nearly all cases, the military was pivotal. As former colonial subjects were enticed by the possibilities afforded by the military, these newfound nations and territories became further integrated into the U.S. imperial project.

The military labor of these citizens, we have seen, reinforced their symbolic value as "free Asians" for the United States. Indeed, though white supremacy lost credibility during World War II, race remained central to the project of U.S. globalism, albeit in a more complex form. One of the aims of the book has been to underscore the parallel between the liberal inclusion of Asians as national citizens and their deployment as racialized embodiments of freedom who could attenuate and justify state violence. Scholars have tended to view Asian American inclusion after World War II as a complex story of domestic racial progress, unfolding against the backdrop of the vicious cold war in Asia and the budding of the civil rights movement in the United States. As should be clear by now, we must revise this interpretation. Asian inclusion occurred in lockstep with the ever-widening U.S. war and its ever-evolving tactics to secure Asia from communism. The inclusion of Asians via the military, moreover, was always partial: at times it reinforced suspicions of their "subversive" intents; at other times they were seen as "gooks," becoming the racial targets of state violence. Enlisted to liberate Asia from colonialism and communism, Asians in the military simultaneously expanded the power of the U.S. government to demarcate and police the boundary between "good" and "bad" Asians. It became an endless exercise and a repertoire of the United States's permanent war after 1945.

The trajectories of these Asian soldiers were the product of multiple historical forces that converged in the middle decades of the twentieth century. I have called this space—as conceptually rich as it is geographically various—the decolonizing Pacific. The end of World War II spawned what would become a continuous struggle for democracy in the former colonial world, the beginnings of what would become, by the mid-1950s, a global clamor for decolonization. U.S. officials, determined to crush these insurgencies and to secure the "free world" through militarization, pursued the integration of different regions in Asia into the global capitalist economy; the goal, they claimed, was to overcome the colonial past, to usher in an "Asia for Asians." In coopting the decolonization project for imperialist ends, the U.S. empire birthed unintended consequences. The resistance to colonial control did not end, despite the promise of freedom through capitalism; that anticolonial spirit persisted among workers, soldiers, and other colonized peoples. As they soldiered through empire, the subjects at the heart of our story became inextricably linked to this larger tide of resistance. The foment opened up a critical space to imagine and pursue an alternative future. This collective imagining was forged through a series of distinct yet connected struggles, against both militarism and imperialism, from Hawai'i to the Philippines, from South Korea to Okinawa and elsewhere across the United States; the result radicalized the decolonizing Pacific.

Our exploration ends in the mid-1970s, but obviously the story of soldiering through empire doesn't end there. The U.S. military's failure in Vietnam presented yet another moment for the United States to recalibrate empire in the name of freedom and opportunity. Critical to this effort was the institution of the All-Volunteer Force (AVF). In 1973, the United States officially ended military conscription, following years of public upheaval against racist state violence at home and abroad that had centered on the draft. Abolishing the draft allowed the army to rebrand itself as an "equal opportunity" employer whose benefits were open to all regardless of race, class, and gender. The AVF, a putatively race-neutral institution driven by the forces of the free market, with the incentives of competitive pay and benefits, achieved multiple aims. It enticed greater numbers of black and brown working and unemployed peoples, the populations who had been rendered in excess by the diminishing welfare state, to enlist in the army, seeing it as an avenue for personal advancement. At the same time, framing military service as employment and an individual choice worked to silence dissent both within the armed forces and among the American public.[1]

The AVF played a key part in revitalizing U.S. military culture after the shakeup of the Vietnam War, transforming the military into a symbol of national cohesion, and making American military interventions more palatable to the public. A racially inclusive military tackled the problems of racial strife and military decline and sought to resolve them simultaneously. Yet when we take a more expansive view—against the long arc of the decolonizing Pacific—we see that this rebranding of the military is not unique to the post–Vietnam War era but a continuation of U.S. imperial statecraft since World War II. The AVF, in this sense, should be seen as an instantiation of the decades-long project of securing an Asia for Asians. Just as the post-1945 militarization of Asia and the Pacific mobilized the desires of colonial subjects through military service, the United States after Vietnam, reeling from an insurgent decade, tried to contain the racial crisis at home by drawing people on the fringes of the postindustrial economy into the military. The result, as in the past, was a military force made up of the most marginalized and potentially disruptive segments of society, yet whose deployment came to signify the U.S. commitment to racial equality and freedom at home and abroad.

And as in the past, this combination carried deadly consequences. The "loss" of Vietnam prompted successive presidents to reassert America's global strength through military aggression. In 1981, the Reagan Administration ramped up counterrevolutions in El Salvador, Guatemala, and Nicaragua, and continued to support authoritarian regimes around the world, determined to eliminate leftist governments and insurgencies and to ensure the vitality of global capitalism. In 1983, Reagan shocked the world when he ordered a full U.S. military invasion of the small Caribbean island of Grenada, toppling its Marxist government and installing a pro-U.S. regime. As ever before, the maintenance of capitalist freedom required the brunt force of U.S. state violence. The period between 1980 and 1986, in fact, saw the largest buildup of the U.S. military and its nuclear arsenal since the end of World War II;[2] unbridled militarization, however, did little to dampen American claims to supporting freedom and democracy. Speaking before Congress in 1986, Reagan repeated the tired mantra of post-1945 U.S. globalism, declaring the United States an "ardent champion of decolonization."[3]

The revival of American militarism and nationalism during the Reagan years partly depended on recrafting the dominant narrative of soldiering that was tarnished by the antiwar movement. In 1980, the same year that the American Psychiatric Association officially recognized Posttraumatic Stress Disorder among veterans, the army adopted the slogan "Be All You Can Be" as part of its renewed marketing blitz to attract higher quality recruits. It was part of the ongoing effort since the implementation of the AVF to present the military as an avenue of boundless individual fulfillment. Recruitment for the AVF had floundered in the late 1970s but was reinvigorated through the massive increases in military spending during Reagan's first term. Speaking to veterans and elected officials in Columbus, Ohio, in 1982, Reagan boasted, "We've improved our strategic forces, toughened our conventional forces, and—one thing that's made me particularly happy—more and more young Americans are proud again to wear their country's uniform."[4]

Numerous factors contributed to an increase in army enlistments, not least of which was the economic recession of the early 1980s that saw youth unemployment rise to 17.4 percent (35.2 percent for black youth aged sixteen to nineteen).[5] But these were extraneous factors, according to the president and army officials. America's modernized army and the men and women who "proudly" served in it worked to regenerate the image of the patriotic soldier in American culture.[6] This image summoned Americans to fulfill their patriotic duty of "supporting our troops," a slogan that became widely circulated by the start of the new decade when the United States launched the Gulf War.

The U.S-led coalition against Iraq that began in the fall of 1990 was the first major U.S. deployment since the Vietnam War, involving close to 500,000 American troops and 200,000 troops from allied nations. The official justification was to protect Saudi Arabia's and Kuwait's sovereignty from Iraq, and to ensure the continued supply of oil from the Persian Gulf to the United States and the Western world. Lasting from August 1990 to February 1991, the war occurred at two key historical junctures. The first was the end of the cold war and, with that, the perceived end of America's justification to maintain its global military presence; the second was the growing concerns among neoconservative politicians and commentators about the threat of multiculturalism and its potential to fracture (or "balkanize") the nation. The insecurities of race and empire, once again, were partially resolved through representations of the military. Television images of the buildup and the war, showcasing the awesome effects of precision bombs and the military's advanced technology, worked alongside the war's commodification—through the display of American flags and yellow ribbons to show support for the troops, for example—to galvanize public support for the war and to stifle antiwar dissent.[7] At the same time, news reports also highlighted the racial diversity of the armed forces, justifying U.S. military interventions as a moral crusade to spread American freedom and democracy.[8] Indeed, little seemed to have changed from the past. As before, racial inclusion came to signify—even became synonymous with—U.S. globalism. If racial liberalism attenuated the violence of U.S. militarism in the mid-twentieth century, multiculturalism similarly thrived in the 1990s alongside a reinvigorated U.S. military power.

These were some of the legacies of the decolonizing Pacific. The permanent war that was engineered to contain the "communist" menace after 1945 continues into the present, now largely to contain the blowback of U.S. militarization accumulated over the half-century.[9] Once again, citizens from nations that had borne the brunt of colonial violence were compelled to take part in this long war. When President George W. Bush launched the War on Terror in 2003, he mobilized the international community for military and political support. What Bush called the "Coalition of the Willing," a faint echo of President Johnson's Free World Military Assistance Program, obscured the disproportionate burden of the fighting and dying among Pacific Islanders, many of whom had enlisted in the U.S. military. In 2007, out of the fifty-four U.S. states and territories, Guam ranked number one for recruiting success in the Army National Guard; once again, the apparent enthusiasm among Chamorros for enlistment was matched by their exceptionally high death toll. As it had been during the Vietnam War, the people of Guam (alongside Micronesia) suffered the highest killed-in-action rate per capita compared to other states and territories in the wars in Iraq and Afghanistan.[10]

The gift of American freedom, memorialized annually in Guam on Liberation Day, accrues a debt that has compelled generations of Chamorros to send their young men and women to fight and die on behalf of their "liberator."[11] For colonized subjects and noncitizens living under the U.S. empire, imagining freedom beyond the military remains a difficult task. The military continually generates incentives to attract people whose lives have been rendered precarious by histories of war and displacement. For example, the Military Accessions Vital to National Interest (MAVNI) Recruitment Program, implemented by the DOD in 2009, offered expedited citizenship for legal noncitizens, prioritizing those with "critical skills" useful to the military such as "physicians, nurses, and certain experts in language with associated cultural background."[12] The MAVNI Program was part of the revival of counterinsurgency in the War on Terror, championed by senior military officials who had studied the "lessons" of Vietnam obsessively. Similar to the civic-action campaigns of Operation Brotherhood and the Freedom Company in the 1950s, the "armed social work" in Iraq and Afghanistan relied on the labor of noncitizen soldiers, many who carry with them the traces of America's violent imperial past and present.[13]

Yet it is precisely the act of imagining freedom beyond war that has been the other legacy of the decolonizing Pacific. The aspirations of colonized subjects, we have seen, could never be contained by the military and satisfied by promises of inclusion into the nation. Indeed, this other story also continues, with the 1980s marking a critical turning point. As the Reagan Administration returned the military to the center of U.S. foreign policy, progressive movements across Asia and the Pacific were ascendant. In South Korea and the Philippines, people's democratic movements drove out longstanding dictatorships and ushered in a new age of democracy. In Hawai'i, Guam, the Northern Marianas, the Marshall Islands, Okinawa, and other islands in the South Pacific, movements for sovereignty converged with renewed calls against nuclear buildup and testing and for complete demilitarization, giving rise to the People's Charter for a Nuclear Free and Independent Pacific Movement in 1983. These movements, reminiscent of the Vietnam War era, built strategic alliances across national and regional borders, connecting the fates of different groups throughout the decolonizing Pacific, and inspiring solidarity movements in the United States, Australia, and other parts of the First World. In short, the unfinished movements for decolonization sparked once again amidst the revival of U.S. militarism, giving rise to another insurgent decade.[14]

In the shadow of a long war with no end in sight, we would do well to heed the demands of these radical movements and those leading the fight against the structural and day-to-day violence of U.S. militarism, though there is no resolution to celebrate. The U.S. military remains firmly rooted in Asia and the Pacific, and indeed across much of the planet. And as the United States continues to wage its open-ended war in the name of freedom, it continues to coopt the energies of progressive movements, offering partial remedial gestures. At various times and in various places, this has meant everything from apologizing for past wrongs, to closing certain bases and expanding others, to declaring wars many times over only to continue them by other means. Liberalism has obscured the human toll of militarism—even deemed it acceptable—by equating military might with development, modernization, humanitarianism, and the free market; and it is on these terms that we must reckon with the ongoing effects and legacies of colonialism. In the middle decades of the twentieth century, the inclusion of "liberated" Asians into the military enabled the United States to expand its capitalist empire, even as it spawned countermovements, fleeting alliances, and an ongoing effort to realize a decolonized Pacific. Now firmly ensconced in the twenty-first century, those post-1945 machinations seem both a world away and surprisingly prescient, as we continue to live with the violence of the waning American empire. Yet again, a decolonizing Pacific is ever on the horizon.

NOTES

INTRODUCTION

1. Mike Nakayama and Nick Nagatani, interview with author, September 19, 2009. On the racial and class politics of Crenshaw in the 1960s, see Scott Kurashige, *The Shifting Grounds of Race: Black and Japanese Americans in the Making of Multiethnic Los Angeles* (Princeton, NJ: Princeton University Press, 2008), 249–58.

2. "Nisei" refers to "second generation" Japanese born in the United States, Canada, and Latin America.

3. 313th Intelligence Detachment, Unit History, 1945, Box 4825, Entry 37042, RG 338. Also see Eiichiro Azuma, "Brokering Race, Culture, and Citizenship: Japanese Americans in Occupied Japan and Postwar National Inclusion," *Journal of American-East Asian Relations* 16, no. 3 (2009): 183–211.

4. Nakayama and Nagatani, interview with author, September 19, 2009.

5. On post–World War II racial liberalism, see Mary L. Dudziak, *Cold War Civil Rights: Race and the Image of American Democracy* (Princeton, NJ: Princeton University Press, 2000); Nikhil Pal Singh, *Black Is a Country: Race and the Unfinished Struggles for Democracy* (Cambridge, MA: Harvard University Press, 2004); Daniel Martinez HoSang, *Racial Propositions: Ballot Initiatives and the Making of Postwar California* (Berkeley: University of California Press, 2010); Jodi Melamed, *Represent and Destroy: Rationalizing Violence in the New Racial Capitalism* (Minneapolis: University of Minnesota Press, 2011); Cindy I-Fen Cheng, *Citizens of Asian America: Democracy and Race during the Cold War* (New York: New York University Press, 2013); Ellen D. Wu, *The Colors of Success: Asian Americans and the Origins of the Model Minority* (Princeton, NJ: Princeton University Press, 2014); Naomi Murakawa, *The First Civil Right: How Liberals Built Prison America* (Princeton, NJ: Princeton University Press, 2014).

6. Kurashige, *The Shifting Grounds of Race,* 249.

7. Christina Klein, *Cold War Orientalism: Asia in the Middlebrow Imagination, 1945–1961* (Berkeley: University of California Press, 2003), 224.

8. On the entanglements of liberal inclusion and state violence, see Mahmood Mamdani, *Good Muslim, Bad Muslim: America, the Cold War, and the Roots of Terror* (New York: Pantheon, 2004); Chandan Reddy, *Freedom with Violence: Race, Sexuality, and the U.S. State* (Durham, NC: Duke University Press, 2011); Melamed, *Represent and Destroy;* Nikhil Pal Singh, "Racial Formation in an Age of Permanent War," in *Racial Formation in the Twenty-First Century,* eds. Daniel Martinez HoSang and Oneka LaBennett (Berkeley: University of California Press, 2012), 276–301; A. Naomi Paik, *Rightlessness: Testimony and Redress in U.S. Prison Camps since World War II* (Chapel Hill: University of North Carolina Press, 2016).

9. Foreign Nationals Trained in U.S. under Military Assistance Program (FY50–FY60); Box 2, Folder MAP Training #10 (1), U.S. President's Committee on Information Activities Abroad (Sprague Committee) Records, 1960–61, Eisenhower Library.

10. On the history of postcolonial nation building in South Korea, see Gregg Brazinsky, *Nation Building in South Korea: Koreans, Americans, and the Making of a Democracy* (Chapel Hill: University of North Carolina Press, 2009); Seungsook Moon, *Militarized Modernity and Gendered Citizenship in South Korea* (Durham, NC: Duke University Press, 2003). On the national memory of South Korean soldiers, see Viet Thanh Nguyen, *Nothing Ever Dies: Vietnam and the Memory of War* (Cambridge, MA: Harvard University Press, 2016), 129–55.

11. Robert M. Blackburn, *Mercenaries and Lyndon Johnson's More Flags: The Hiring of Korean, Filipino, and Thai Soldiers in the Vietnam War* (Jefferson, NC: McFarland, 1994); Frederick Logevall, "'There Ain't No Daylight': Lyndon Johnson and the Politics of Escalation," in *Making Sense of the Vietnam Wars: Local, National, and Transnational Perspectives,* eds. Mark Philip Bradley and Marilyn B. Young (New York: Oxford University Press, 2008), 91–107.

12. Singh, "Racial Formation in an Age of Permanent War"; Keith P. Feldman, *A Shadow over Palestine: The Imperial Life of Race in America* (Minneapolis: University of Minnesota Press, 2015); Murakawa, *The First Civil Right;* Elizabeth Hinton, *From the War on Poverty to the War on Crime: The Making of Mass Incarceration in America* (Cambridge, MA: Harvard University Press, 2016).

13. Frederick Cooper and Ann Laura Stoler, eds., *Tensions of Empire: Colonial Cultures in a Bourgeois World* (Berkeley: University of California Press, 1997); David B. Abernethy, *The Dynamics of Global Dominance: European Overseas Empires, 1415–1980* (New Haven, CT: Yale University Press, 2000); Bruce Cumings, *Dominion from Sea to Sea: Pacific Ascendency and American Power* (New Haven, CT: Yale University Press, 2009); Jun Uchida, *Brokers of Empire: Japanese Settler Colonialism in Korea, 1876–1945* (Cambridge, MA: Harvard University Press, 2014); Matt K. Matsuda, *Pacific Worlds: A History of Seas, Peoples, and Cultures* (New York: Cambridge University Press, 2012).

14. Odd Arne Westad, *The Global Cold War: Third World Interventions and the Making of Our Times* (New York: Cambridge University Press, 2005); Keith L. Camacho, *Cultures of Commemoration: The Politics of War, Memory, and History in*

the Mariana Islands (Honolulu: University of Hawai'i Press, 2011), 39–58; Matsuda, *Pacific Worlds*, 278–92.

15. Vijay Prashad, *The Darker Nations: A People's History of the Third World* (New York: The New Press, 2007); Gary Wilder, *Freedom Time: Negritude, Decolonization, and the Future of the World* (Durham, NC: Duke University Press, 2015).

16. Thomas J. McCormick, *America's Half Century: United States Foreign Policy in the Cold War and After,* 2nd ed. (Baltimore: Johns Hopkins University Press, 1995); Melvyn P. Leffler, *A Preponderance of Power: National Security, the Truman Administration, and the Cold War* (Stanford, CA: Stanford University Press, 1992).

17. McCormick, *America's Half Century;* William S. Borden, *The Pacific Alliance: United States Foreign Economic Policy and Japanese Trade Recovery, 1947–1955* (Madison: University of Wisconsin Press, 1984); Cumings, *Dominion from Sea to Sea*; Ellen Meiksins Wood, *Empire of Capital* (London: Verso, 2003), 129–30.

18. C. T. Sandars, *America's Overseas Garrisons: The Leasehold Empire* (New York: Oxford University Press, 2000); Sasha Davis, *The Empires' Edge: Militarization, Resistance, and Transcending Hegemony in the Pacific* (Athens: The University of Georgia Press, 2015); Martha Smith-Norris, *Domination and Resistance: The United States and the Marshall Islands during the Cold War* (Honolulu: University of Hawai'i Press, 2016).

19. McCormick, *America's Half Century;* Borden, *The Pacific Alliance.*

20. I explain subempire in chapter 4. On theorizations of subimperialism, see Kuan-Hsing Chen, *Asia as Method: Toward Deimperialization* (Durham, NC: Duke University Press, 2010); McCormick, *America's Half Century*, 186–90.

21. Paul Kramer, *Blood of Government*, 87–158; Singh, "Racial Formation in an Age of Permanent War"; T. Fujitani, *Race for Empire: Koreans as Japanese and Japanese as Americans during World War II* (Berkeley: University of California Press, 2011); Jodi A. Byrd, *The Transit of Empire: Indigenous Critiques of Colonialism* (Minneapolis: University of Minnesota Press, 2011).

22. Cedric J. Robinson, *Black Movements in America* (London: Routledge, 1997), 135.

23. Quoted in Feldman, *A Shadow over Palestine,* 61.

24. Shigematsu and Camacho, *Militarized Currents*, xxi; Chen, *Asia as Method.*

25. Derek Gregory, *The Colonial Present: Afghanistan, Palestine, Iraq* (Malden, MA: Blackwell, 2004), 20.

26. Guam had the highest killed-in-action rate per capita during the Vietnam War. See Michael Lujan Bevacqua, "The Exceptional Life and Death of a Chamorro Soldier: Tracing the Militarization of Desire in Guam, ~~USA~~ should have a strike through, as it appears in the title.," in *Militarized Currents,* 35; Hwang Sok-Yong, *Shadow of Arms,* trans. Chun Kyung-ja (New York: Seven Stories Press, 2014).

27. My work builds on recent scholarship on labor and empire. See Daniel E. Bender and Jana K. Lipman, eds., *Making the Empire Work: Labor and United States Imperialism* (New York: New York University Press, 2015).

28. Christian G. Appy, *Working-Class War: American Combat Soldiers and Vietnam* (Chapel Hill: University of North Carolina Press, 1993); Jin-Kyung Lee, *Service Economies: Militarism, Sex Work, and Migrant Labor in South Korea* (Minneapolis: University of Minnesota Press, 2010).

29. Brazinsky, *Nation Building in South Korea;* Edward Miller, *Misalliance: Ngo Dinh Diem, the United States, and the Fate of South Vietnam* (Cambridge, MA: Harvard University Press, 2013).

30. My conception of soldiers as intermediaries is informed by a growing body of work on the social and cultural histories of empire. See, for example, Jana K. Lipman, *Guantanamo: A Working-Class History between Empire and Revolution* (Berkeley: University of California Press, 2009); Julie Greene, *The Canal Builders: Making America's Empire at the Panama Canal* (New York: Penguin, 2010); Uchida, *Brokers of Empire;* Michelle Moyd, *Violent Intermediaries: African Soldiers, Conquest, and Everyday Colonialism in German East Africa* (Athens: Ohio University Press, 2014).

31. See for example, Fujitani, *Race for Empire.*

32. Kimberley L. Phillips, *War! What Is It Good For? Black Freedom Struggles and the U.S. Military from World War II to Iraq* (Chapel Hill: University of North Carolina Press, 2012).

33. Dudziak, *Cold War Civil Rights;* Cheng, *Citizens of Asian America.*

34. Wu, *The Color of Success;* Madeline Y. Hsu, *The Good Immigrants: How the Yellow Peril Became the Model Minority* (Princeton, NJ: Princeton University Press, 2015).

35. Fujitani, *Race for Empire;* Feldman, *A Shadow over Palestine;* Moon-Ho Jung, "Seditious Subjects: Race, State Violence, and the U.S. Empire," *Journal of Asian American Studies* 14, no. 2 (June 2011): 221–47; Jodi Kim, *Ends of Empire: Asian American Critique and the Cold War* (Minneapolis: University of Minnesota Press, 2010); Kramer, *The Blood of Government;* Melamed, *Represent and Destroy;* Murakawa, *The First Civil Right;* Reddy, *Freedom with Violence;* Singh, "Racial Formation in an Age of Permanent War"; Seema Sohi, *Echoes of Mutiny: Race, Surveillance, and Indian Anticolonialism in North America* (New York: Oxford University Press, 2014).

36. Lansdale, "Our Battleground in Asia," speech delivered at the reunion of Nieman Fellows, Harvard University, June 19, 1957. Box 80, Folder 296, Edward Geary Lansdale Papers, Hoover Institution.

37. I'm influenced by Lisa Lowe's method of reading across archives. In *The Intimacies of Four Continents,* Lowe writes, "In pursuing particular intimacies and contemporaneities that traverse distinct and separately studied 'areas,' the practice of reading across archives unsettles the discretely bounded objects, methods, and temporal frameworks canonized by a national history invested in isolated origins and independent progressive development." Lisa Lowe, *The Intimacies of Four Continents* (Durham, NC: Duke University Press, 2015), 6.

38. Ibid., 4.

39. Kim, *Ends of Empire,* 3; Robinson, *Black Movements in America,* 137; Heonik Kwon, *The Other Cold War* (New York: Columbia University Press, 2010).

1. Case of Hsuan Wei, July 7, 1954, Box 1, Entry A1 3069, Subject and Country Files, 1941–1962, Office of the Assistant Legal Advisor for Far Eastern Affairs, Office of the Legal Advisor, RG 59.

2. Foreign Nationals Trained in U.S. under Military Assistance Program (FY50–FY60); Box 2, Folder MAP Training #10 (1), U.S. President's Committee on Information Activities Abroad (Sprague Committee) Records, 1960–61, Dwight D. Eisenhower Presidential Library; Chi-Op Lee and Stephen M. Tharp, *Call Me 'Speedy Lee': Memoirs of a Korean War Soldier* (Seoul: Wonmin Publishing House Company, 2001), 41.

3. Michael E. Robinson, *Korea's Twentieth-Century Odyssey: A Short History* (Honolulu: University of Hawai'i Press, 2007), 97.

4. Notes on the Wake Conference, compiled by General of the Army Omar Bradley, Chairman of the Joint Chiefs of Staff, October 13, 1950; Truman Library. I thank Jessie Kindig for bringing this source to my attention.

5. Moon-Ho Jung, "Seditious Subjects: Race, State Violence, and the U.S. Empire," *Journal of Asian American Studies* vol. 14, no. 2 (June 2011): 228–29. The Treaty of Peace, Amity, Commerce, and Navigation, signed between the United States and Chosŏn Korea on May 22, 1882, allowed the United States to appoint diplomatic representatives and offered protections for U.S. trade vessels and citizens in Korea.

6. John W. Dower, *Embracing Defeat: Japan in the Wake of World War II* (New York: W. W. Norton, 1999), 73–78; Sheila Miyoshi Jager, *Brothers at War: The Unending Conflict in Korea* (New York: W. W. Norton, 2014), 16, 27–28.

7. Bruce Cumings, *Korea's Place in the Sun: A Modern History* (New York: W. W. Norton, 2005 [1997]), 190–92; Arnold quoted in Jager, *Brothers at War,* 31.

8. Benninghoff to State Department, September 15, 1945, in *FRUS* (1945), vol. 6, 1050.

9. Petition to CIC by Korean Contingent, May 3, 1946. Box 1, Folder 000.1, Assistant Chief of Staff, G-2, General Correspondence 1946, RG 554.

10. Memo to MacArthur, Increase of Japanese Police Force, October 9, 1946. Box 1, Folder 014.12, Assistant Chief of Staff, G-2, General Correspondence 1946, RG 554.

11. Petition to CIC by Korean Contingent, May 3, 1946.

12. Benedict J. Kerkvliet, *The Huk Rebellion: A Study of Peasant Revolt in the Philippines* (Berkeley: University of California Press, 1977).

13. 441st CIC Detachment, Summary of Information, Communist Party Activity in Okinawa, July 11, 1947. Box 1, Folder 014.33 (Repats) 1946, Assistant Chief of Staff, G-2, General Correspondence 1946, RG 554.

14. Hodge quoted in Cumings, *Korea's Place in the Sun,* 198.

15. Hodge to Commanding Generals, USAFIK, November 6, 1946. Box 50, Folder Military Discipline 1946; General Correspondence (Decimal Files), Entry 1378, USAFIK Adjutant General, RG 550.

16. Benninghoff to State Department, September 15, 1945, in *FRUS* (1945), vol. VI, 1050.

17. Langdon to Secretary of State, November 1, 1946, in *FRUS* (1946), vol. VIII, 754.

18. Pauley to Truman, June 22, 1946, in *FRUS* (1946), vol. VIII, 706–9.

19. Allan R. Millett, "Captain James H. Hausman and the Formation of the Korean Army, 1945–1950," *Armed Forces and Society* 23, no. 4 (Summer 1997): 510.

20. USAFIK History of G-3 (Operations) Section, August 1945–June 1948. Box 12, USAFIK G-3, Subject Files, 1945–1948, Entry 1376, RG 554.

21. Hodge quoted in Cumings, *Korea's Place in the Sun,* 200.

22. Bryan R. Gibby, *The Will to Win: American Military Advisors in Korea, 1946–1953* (Tuscaloosa: University of Alabama Press, 2012), 29–31; Brazinsky, *Nation Building in South Korea,* 73–74.

23. Gibby, *The Will to Win,* 48.

24. Muccio to Secretary of State, October 28, 1948, in *FRUS* (1948) vol. VI, 1317–18.

25. Gibby, *The Will to Win,* 31, 42.

26. Quoted in Interview with You, Chung Nam, 28 October 1948; USAFIK, G-3, Subject Files, 1945–1948, Entry 1376; Box 12, Folder Misc. G-3 Reports and Messages 20 Oct–4 Nov 1948; RG 554.

27. Quoted in Jager, *Brothers at War,* 52.

28. G-2 Periodic Report, Yosu Rebellion; USAFIK, G-3, Periodic Reports, 1946, 1948, Entry A1 1372; Box 5, Folder Periodic Report, October 1948; RG 554. This account of Yŏsu-Sunch'ŏn rebellion is pulled from "History of the Rebellion of the Korean Constabulary in Yosu and Taegu, Korea," USAFIK, Adjutant General, General Correspondence (Decimal File), 1948–49, Entry 1378; Box 15, Folder 000.5 Reports 1947–48; RG 554.

29. Quoted in "A House Divided: Photos from Korea's 1948 Yeosu-Suncheon Rebellion," Life.com. Accessed January 14, 2015.

30. Cumings, *Korea's Place in the Sun,* 218; Millett, "Captain James H. Hausman and the Formation of the Korean Army," 522.

31. Cumings, *Korea's Place in the Sun,* 222–23.

32. "History of the Rebellion of the Korean Constabulary in Yosu and Taegu, Korea," USAFIK.

33. Millett, "Captain James H. Hausman and the Formation of the Korean Army," 527.

34. Thomas J. McCormick, *America's Half-Century: United States Foreign Policy in the Cold War and After* (Baltimore: Johns Hopkins University Press, 1995), 88; William S. Borden, *The Pacific Alliance: United States Foreign Economic Policy and Japanese Trade Recovery, 1947–1955* (Madison: University of Wisconsin Press, 1984).

35. Masuda Hajimu, *Cold War Crucible: The Korean Conflict and the Postwar World* (Cambridge, MA: Harvard University Press, 2015), 38.

36. Technical Manual on Counter Intelligence Investigations (TM 30-218) (Washington D.C.: Department of the Army, 1947).

37. Disposition of Subversive and Disaffected Personnel, November 30, 1948. Box 773, Folder: Alien Enemies and Rights of, 1948, Entry 1481, General Correspondence Files, 1947–56, Ryukyus Command, Adjutant General Section, RG 554.

38. War Department Memorandum, "Communist Infiltration of and Agitation in the Armed Forces," February 6, 1946. Container 33, Folder: 2F011029, Entry A1 134-A, Office of th Assistant Chief of Staff for Intelligence, G-2, RG 319.

39. Ibid.

40. Nelson Peery, *Black Fire: The Making of an American Revolutionary* (New York: The New Press, 1994), 292–93.

41. "4,000 Manila Yanks Demonstrate When Ship Is Canceled," *Chicago Daily Tribune,* December 26, 1945, 1.

42. "Soldiers in Philippines Assail War Secretary in Demobilization Plea," *The Sun,* January 9, 1946, 1.

43. DA Pamphlet 20-210, "History of Personnel Demobilization in the United States Army," July 1952, 166.

44. Ibid., 293.

45. Quoted in "Identify Red as Sparkplug of GI Protest," *Chicago Daily Tribune,* January 24, 1946, 7. David Livingston at the time was a president of Wholesale and Warehouse Workers Union of America, Local 65. See Erwin Marquit, "The Demobilization Movement of January 1946," *Nature, Society, and Thought* 15, no. 1 (2002): 11.

46. "Soldiers in Philippines Assail War Secretary," 1.

47. "RAF Crews Strike Over Slow Return," *New York Times,* January 25, 1946, 2.

48. "Vital Issue Raised by Bombay Mutiny," *New York Times,* February 22, 1946, 3.

49. "GIs Protest," *New York Times,* January 13, 1946, E1.

50. "Communist Infiltration of and Agitation in the Armed Forces," February 6, 1946.

51. Weekly Report #65, Summarization of Intelligence Trends, March 10, 1947, 1135th Counter Intelligence Corps Detachment, Container 21, Folder: Weekly Report #65/March 1947, Entry 134A, Office of the Assistant Chief of Staff for Intelligence, G-2, RG 319.

52. Takashi Fujitani, *Race for Empire: Koreans as Japanese and Japanese as Americans during World War II* (Berkeley: University of California Press, 2011); Kimberley L. Phillips, *War! What Is It Good For? Black Freedom Struggles and the U.S. Military from World War II to Iraq* (Chapel Hill: The University of North Carolina Press, 2012), 22.

53. Office of the Adjutant General, Assignment of Military Personnel of Japanese Ancestry, September 4, 1946, Box 52, Folder: 291.2 Minorities (Military Personnel), 1946, General Correspondence (Decimal Files), Entry 1378, Adjutant General, USAFIK; RG 554.

54. Grant Ichikawa, "Original Women 'M.I.S.' Linguists Were Dept of the Army Civilians," n.d. http://www.javadc.org/women%20DAC%20linguists.htm, accessed December 4, 2016.

55. Summary of Information (Subject Kuwaye, Misao), November 18, 1947, Military Intelligence Section, General Staff. Box 1, Folder: 014.33 (Repats) 1946,

General Correspondence, Co-ordination (Executive) Division, Assistant Chief of Staff, G-2, RG 554.

56. On the Honolulu Labor Canteen, see Marquit, "The Demobilization Movement of January 1946," 7–11.

57. Summary of Information (Subject Kuwaye, Misao), November 18, 1947.

58. Memorandum to Chief of Staff (subject: Kuwaye, Misao) November 14, 1947. Military Intelligence Section, General Staff. Box 1, Folder: 014.33 (Repats) 1946, General Correspondence, Co-ordination (Executive) Division, Assistant Chief of Staff, G-2, RG 554. Emphasis original.

59. Ibid.

60. Report on Calvin Kim, Box 142, Folder: Kim, Calvin, Entry 47-B, Declassified NND 73402, RG 319.

61. On the persecution of Diamond Kimm, see Cindy I-Fen Cheng, *Citizens of Asian America: Democracy and Race during the Cold War* (New York: New York University Press, 2013), 137–47.

62. Disposition of Subversive and Disaffected Personnel, April 22, 1954, Office of the Assistant Chief of Staff for Intelligence G-2, Records of the Investigative Records Repository, Intelligence and Investigative Dossiers, Entry 134-A, Container 33, RG 319.

63. The State Department also at times recognized his name as "Lee Sa Min," and his alias, "Kyong-son Yi." In the translated text of his news conference statement, his name is "Lee Sam In." Telegram, U.S. Embassy, Seoul, to Department of State, "Translated Text of Pyongyang Radio Broadcast," December 20, 1949, enclosure to "Biographical Information on Yi Sa Min," January 14, 1950; Central Decimal File 795.521/1-1450; Box 4297; RG 59.

64. Letter, Korean Consul General to J. Edgar Hoover, February 24, 1955. Obtained through the Freedom of Information Act.

65. Telegram, U.S. Embassy, Seoul, to Department of State, January 14, 1950.

66. Arleen de Vera, "Without Parallel: The Local 7 Deportation Cases, 1949–1955," *Amerasia Journal* 20: 2 (1994): 1–25; Mae M. Ngai, *Impossible Subjects: Illegal Aliens and the Making of Modern America* (Princeton, NJ: Princeton University Press, 2004), chapter 6.

67. McCormick, *America's Half-Century,* 89, 92.

68. Stanley L. Scott, "The Military Aid Program," *Annals of the American Academy of Political and Social Science* vol. 278 (November 1951): 47–55.

69. Statement by President Harry S. Truman, January 27, 1950, Public Papers of the President, Harry S. Truman Library and Museum.

70. McNamara quoted in Stephen Rosskamm Shalom, *The United States and the Philippines: A Study of Neocolonialism* (Philadelphia: Institute for the Study of Human Issues, 1981), 106.

71. Records regarding Individuals, 1941–56, Office of Assistant Chief of Staff, G-2, Box 138, Entry 1847-B, RG 319.

72. Letter, Secretary of Defense Marshall to Senate Armed Services Committee, January 17, 1951, quoted in Report of the Committee on Armed Services to Accom-

pany S.1, Universal Military Training and Service Act, submitted by Lyndon Johnson, February 21, 1951. 82d Congress, 1ˢᵗ Session.

73. Phillips, *War! What Is It Good For?* 125–26.

74. Cumings, *The Korean War,* 13–14.

75. Report of the Committee on Armed Services to Accompany S.1, Universal Military Training and Service Act.

76. "Universal Military Training: A Foundation of Enduring National Strength," First Report to the Congress by the National Security Training Commission, October 1951; Box 1, Folder UMT; Manpower Requirements File, 1951–53; Office of Manpower Requirements; Manpower, Personnel & Reserve; Assistant Secretary of Defense; RG 330.

77. Phillips, *War! What Is It Good For?* 134–43.

78. Ibid, 140.

79. Korean War Personnel Problems, August 15, 1952, Box 66, Folder: History of the Korean War—Personnel Problems, Vol. III, Part 2, Military Historian's Office, Organizational History Files, RG 550.

80. Ibid.

81. Staff Memorandum, Program of Research on the Utilization of Native Military Manpower in Korea, August 5, 1953, Box 66, Military Historian's Office, Organization History Files, RG 550.

82. Hearing before the Senate Committee on Armed Services on S. 273, "A Bill To Provide for the Enlistment of Aliens in the Regular Army," July 11, 1949. 1ˢᵗ Session, 81ˢᵗ Congress, p. 7. Before 1952, eligibility for citizenship was restricted to "free white persons." Ian F. Haney Lopez, *White by Law: The Legal Construction of Race* (New York: New York University Press, 1996).

83. Memorandum, Secretary of the Army to Haislip, November 7, 1950. Addendum to Army General Staff, G-1, Utilization of Foreign Nationals, November 15, 1950; Military History Institute.

84. Ibid.

85. NSC 108, Note by the Executive Secretary to the National Security Council on "Utilization of Manpower of Other Nations for Military Purposes," April 17, 1951; Box 34, Folder Military programs (1); Disaster File; White House Office, National Security Council Staff: Papers, 1948–61.

86. Ibid.

87. Army General Staff, G-1, Utilization of Foreign Nationals, November 15, 1950.

88. NSC 108.

89. On modernization theory, see Michael E. Latham, *Modernization as Ideology: American Social Science and "Nation Building" in the Kennedy Era* (Chapel Hill: The University of North Carolina Press, 2000).

90. James Van Fleet, "25 Divisions for the Cost of One," *Reader's Digest,* February 1954.

91. Ibid.

92. Foreign Nationals Trained in U.S. under Military Assistance Program (FY50–FY60); Box 2, Folder MAP Training #10 (1); U.S. President's Committee

on Information Activities Abroad (Sprague Committee) Records, 1960–61; McNamara quoted in Shalom, *The United States and the Philippines,* 106.

93. KMAG officer quoted in Brazinsky, *Nation Building in South Korea,* 90.

94. Memorandum, S. L. Scott to Thomas D. White, "Reports re: Training of Foreign Nationals under MDAP," May 10, 1951; Box 111, Folder Training Program-1950-Army, Navy & Air Force; Office of Military Assistance; Statistical Section Subject File; International Security Affairs; RG 330.

95. "Collateral Benefits Derived from Military Assistance and other DOD Training Programs," April 20, 1960; Box 2, Folder MAP Training #10 (2); U.S. President's Committee on Information Activities Abroad (Sprague Committee) Records, 1960–61.

96. Guidebook for Visiting Military Students, Aug 1, 1959; Box 2, Folder MAP Training #10 (1); U.S. President's Committee on Information Activities Abroad (Sprague Committee) Records, 1960–61. Dwight D. Eisenhower Presidential Library.

97. Allied Officer Sponsor Program, Fort Leavenworth, July 7, 1959; Box 2, Folder MAP Training #10 (1); U.S. President's Committee on Information Activities Abroad (Sprague Committee) Records, 1960–61.

98. Hospitality Program for Foreign Trainees, U.S. Naval Training Center, November 16, 1957. Box 2, Folder: MAP Training #10 (1); U.S. President's Committee on Information Activities Abroad (Sprague Committee) Records, 1960–-61.

99. "The ROK's Learn to Be an Army," *New York Times,* June 22, 1952, 11.

100. Quoted in Brazinsky, *Nation Building in South Korea,* 95.

101. Letter, C. S. Thomas to Secretary of State, July 7, 1954; Box 1, Folder China: Desertion Cases including Hsuan Wei—Chinese Lieutenant; Entry A1 3069; Subject and Country Files, 1941–62; Office of the Assistant Legal Advisor for Far Eastern Affairs; Office of Legal Advisor; RG 59.

102. "Delay Flight So Chiang Foe Can Be Heard," *Chicago Daily Tribune,* July 6, 1954, 1.

103. Letter, C. S. Thomas to Secretary of State, July 7, 1954.

104. Memorandum of Conversation re Hsuan Wei, July 7, 1954; Box 12, Folder Defense; Records of the Bureau of Far Eastern Affairs relating to Southeast Asia and the Geneva Conference, 1954; RG 59.

105. Ibid.

106. Case of Hsuan Wei, July 7, 1954; Box 1, Folder China: Desertion Cases including Hsuan Wei—Chinese Lieutenant; Entry A1 3069; Subject and Country Files, 1941–1962; Office of the Assistant Legal Advisor for Far Eastern Affairs; Office of the Legal Advisor; RG 59.

107. In April 1957, there were seven Chinese nationals known to the State Department who had refused to return to Taiwan at the end of their military training. Telegram, Department of State to U.S. Embassy, Taipei, April 25, 1957; Central Decimal file 211.9311/3-1157; Box 867; RG 59.

108. Ngai, *Impossible Subjects,* 237–39; "Protecting Deportable Aliens from Physical Persecution: Section 243(h) of the Immigration and Nationality Act of 1952," *The Yale Law Journal* vol. 62, no. 5 (April 1953): 845–52.

109. Letter, Francis E. Walter to John F. Dulles, April 20, 1956; Central Decimal file 211.9311/4-2056; Box 867; RG 59.

110. "Whatever Happened?" by Robert Goldsborough, *Chicago Tribune,* January 1, 1967, E3.

111. Madeline Y. Hsu, *The Good Immigrants: How the Yellow Peril Became the Model Minority* (Princeton, NJ: Princeton University Press, 2015).

CHAPTER TWO

1. Acheson quoted in Marilyn B. Young, *The Vietnam Wars, 1945–1990* (New York: Harper Perennial, 1990), 43.

2. Memorandum, Lansdale to Draper Committee, "Civic Activities of the Military, Southeast Asia," March 13, 1959; Box 45, Folder 1271; Edward G. Lansdale Papers; Edward G. Lansdale, *In the Midst of Wars: An American's Mission to Southeast Asia* (New York: Harper & Row, 1972), 48, 50–51.

3. Memorandum, "Civic Activities of the Military, Southeast Asia," March 13, 1959.

4. Letter, Lansdale to Edward Rowny, February 14, 1963; Box 49, Folder 1373; Lansdale Papers.

5. Lansdale, *In the Midst of Wars,* 57.

6. See for example, Young, *The Vietnam Wars,* 43–46; Richard Drinnon, *Facing West: The Metaphysics of Indian-Hating and Empire-Building* (Minneapolis: University of Minnesota Press, 1980). Recent historians have begun to unpack these connections. See Colleen P. Woods, "Bombs, Bureaucrats, and Rosary Beads: The United States, the Philippines, and the Making of Global Anti-Communism, 1945–1960" (PhD diss., University of Michigan, 2012), chapter 3; Daniel Immerwahr, *Thinking Small: The United States and the Lure of Community Development* (Cambridge, MA: Harvard University Press, 2015), chapter 4.

7. Young, *The Vietnam Wars,* 35; Vijay Prashad, *The Darker Nations: A People's History of the Third World* (New York: The New Press, 2007), 119; Roderick Bush, *The End of White World Supremacy: Black Internationalism and the Problem of the Color Line* (Philadelphia: Temple University Press, 2009), 161.

8. Kathryn C. Statler, *Replacing France: The Origins of American Intervention in Vietnam* (Lexington: The University Press of Kentucky, 2007), 95–107.

9. Memorandum, Charlton Ogburn to Everett Drumright, U.S. Policy Toward Indochina, June 10, 1954; Box 46, Folder 306.1, U.S. Policy Toward the Far East; Records of the Office of Chinese Affairs, Numerical File, 1949–1955; RG 59.

10. Dulles quoted in Young, *The Vietnam Wars,* 46; "U.S. Inspires Whole Orient, Says Romulo," *Chicago Daily Tribune,* June 22, 1946, 9; Letter, Carlos Romulo to Dean Acheson, March 2, 1950; Box 3, Folder Philippine Relations with Indonesia; Records of the Officer-in-Charge of Philippine Affairs, 1948–1957; RG 59.

11. Verbatim Proceedings of the 6ᵗʰ Plenary Session, September 8, 1954; Box 10, Folder Manila Conference (2); Records of the Bureau of Far Eastern Affairs relating to Southeast Asia and the Geneva Conference, 1954; RG 59.

12. "VP for Closer Ties with Asia," *The Manila Times,* June 13, 1955.

13. Statement, Delegate of the Philippines, 5th Plenary Session; Box 10, Folder Manila Conference (2); Records of the Bureau of Far Eastern Affairs Relating to Southeast Asia and the Geneva Conference, 1954; RG 59.

14. Woods, "Bombs, Bureaucrats, and Rosary Beads," 189–90.

15. Christina Klein, *Cold War Orientalism: Asia in the Middlebrow Imagination, 1945–1961* (Berkeley: University of California Press, 2003).

16. Raul Manglapus, "Our Recognition of South Vietnam," July 18, 1955; Box 86, Folder 360; Entry 3100-A; General Records, 1946–61; U.S. Embassy, Manila; RG 84 (emphasis original).

17. Telegram, U.S. Embassy, Manila to Secretary of State, July 25, 1955; Box 86, Folder 360-Government; Entry 3100-A; General Records, 1946–61; Philippine Islands, U.S. Embassy, Manila; RG 84.

18. Ibid.

19. Dorothy B. Fujita-Rony, *American Workers, Colonial Power: Philippine Seattle and the Transpacific West, 1919–1941* (Berkeley: University of California Press, 2003); Catherine Ceniza Choy, *Empire of Care: Nursing and Migration in Filipino American History* (Durham, NC: Duke University Press, 2003); Yen Le Espiritu, *Home Bound: Filipino American Lives Across Cultures, Communities, and Countries* (Berkeley: University of California Press, 2003), 28–29; Robyn Magalit Rodriguez, *Migrants for Export: How the Philippine State Brokers Labor to the World* (Minneapolis: University of Minnesota Press, 2010).

20. Lansdale, *In the Midst of Wars,* 168.

21. William J. Lederer and Eugene Burdick, *The Ugly American* (New York: W. W. Norton, 1999 [1958]); Neil Sheehan, *The Pentagon Papers: The Secret History of the Vietnam War* (New York: Bantam Books, 1971); Cecil B. Currey, *Edward Lansdale: The Unquiet American* (Washington, D.C.: Brassey's Inc., 1998); Jonathan Nashel, *Edward Lansdale's Cold War* (Amherst: University of Massachusetts Press, 2005).

22. Edward Miller, *Misalliance: Ngo Dinh Diem, the United States, and the Fate of South Vietnam* (Cambridge, MA: Harvard University Press, 2013), 86.

23. Memorandum, Charles Bohannan to Felix Jabillo, September 26, 1953; Box 35, Bohannan Papers; Text of "Manual for the Philippine Constabulary, 1915"; Box 19; Bohannan Papers.

24. Miller, *Misalliance,* 97–99.

25. USOM Community Development Activities in Vietnam, July 25, 1954; Box 20, Folder Refugees—Plans for North Vietnam; Entry 1435; Agriculture & Natural Resources Division; Subject Files, 1951–57. On Community Development in the cold war, see Immerwahr, *Thinking Small.*

26. Antonio Velasco quoted in Vincente G. Martinez, "Free Vietnam Looks Up," *The Evening News,* September 13, 1955.

27. Operation Brotherhood, A JCI Assistance Project, n.d; Folder Voluntary Agencies, 2 of 2; Entry 1452; Resettlement and Rehabilitation Division Subject Files, 1953–58; RG 469.

28. "Free Vietnam Looks Up," *Evening News.*

29. Letter, William H. McKeldin to Thomas E. Nauhten, January 7, 1955; Box 7, Folder Voluntary Agencies 1955–56; Entry 1455; Classified Subject Files, 1954–58; Resettlement and Rehabilitation Division, Field Service; RG 469.

30. Memorandum for the Record, "Pacification" in Vietnam, July 16, 1958; Box 42, Folder 1201; Lansdale Papers.

31. Ibid.; Rufus Phillips, *Why Vietnam Matters: An Eyewitness Account of Lessons Not Learned* (Annapolis, MD: Naval Institute Press, 2008), 44–45.

32. Phillips, *Why Vietnam Matters,* 46–47.

33. Memorandum for the Record, "Pacification" in Vietnam, July 16, 1958.

34. Memorandum, Richard C. Parsons to Thomas J. McCormick, March 17, 1955; Box 7, Folder Voluntary Agencies, 1955–56; Entry 1455; Classified Subject Files, 1954–58; Resettlement and Rehabilitation Division, Field Service; RG 469.

35. Memorandum for the Record, "Pacification" in Vietnam, July 16, 1958.

36. Letter, McKeldin to Nauhten, January 7, 1955.

37. Josefina Pablo, telephone interview with author, January 24, 2010.

38. Phillips, *Why Vietnam Matters,* 44.

39. Record of Conversation, Alfred Cardineaux with Commissioner General for Refugees, November 24, 1956; Box 7, Folder Voluntary Agencies, 1955–56; Entry 1455; Classified Subject Files, 1954–58; Resettlement and Rehabilitation Division, Field Service; RG 469.

40. USOM Report on Operation Brotherhood, n.d.; Box 2, Folder Operation Brotherhood; Entry 1438; Community Development Division, Subject Files, 1954–57; RG 469.

41. On the complexities of the U.S.–SVN alliance in the 1950s, see Miller, *Misalliance;* Jessica M. Chapman, *Cauldron of Resistance: Ngo Dinh Diem, the United States, and 1950s Southern Vietnam* (Ithaca, NY: Cornell University Press, 2013).

42. Quoted in Memorandum, T. J. Farrell to M. H. B. Adler, April 30, 1956; Box 2, Folder Operation Brotherhood; Entry 1438; Community Development Division, Subject Files; RG 469.

43. Ibid.

44. Report on Operation Brotherhood, Volunteer Agencies-Operation Brotherhood, November 13, 1955; Box 3, Folder Voluntary Agencies, 1 of 2; Entry 1452; Resettlement & Rehabilitation Division Subject Files; RG 469.

45. Agreement between the Government of Viet-Nam and Junior Chamber International, August 9, 1955; Box 2, Folder Operation Brotherhood; Entry 1438; Community Development Division, Subject Files; RG 469.

46. USOM Report on Operation Brotherhood, n.d.

47. "PVL Chief Leaving for Saigon Today," *The Manila Times,* December 6, 1954; "PVL Bid Accepted," *Daily Mirror,* January 5, 1963; "World Vets Plan Housing Program," *The Manila Times,* June 25, 1954.

48. Colleen Woods, "Bombs, Bureaucrats, and Rosary Beads," 175.

49. Freedom Company, Philippines, Report of the Secretary to the Membership, November 15, 1954. Charles T. R. Bohannan Papers, Hoover Institution Archives.

50. Quoted in Woods, "Bombs, Bureaucrats, and Rosary Beads," 185.

51. Telegram, Frisco San Juan to Curtis Campaigne, January 1955; Box 28, Folder Misc. Vietnam; Bohannan Papers.

52. Memorandum, Lansdale to Collins, December 23, 1954. Box 28, Folder: Lansdale, Edward G (2). J. Lawton Collins Papers. Dwight D. Eisenhower Presidential Library.

53. Memorandum, J. D. Handley to M. H. B. Adler, November 5, 1955; Box 4, Folder Reports—Field (General Classified); Entry 1455; Classified Subject Files, 1954–58; Resettlement and Rehabilitation Division, Field Services; RG 469. On the significance of Cao Dai, Hoa Hao, and Binh Xuyen in South Vietnamese politics, see Chapman, *Cauldron of Resistance.*

54. Freedom Company Team Report No. 2, January 19, 1955; Box 28, Folder Misc. Vietnam; Bohannan Papers, Hoover Institution.

55. Memorandum, Plans for March 1955 Demobilization, March 1955; Box 2, Folder National Security—Disengaged Service Personnel; Entry 1438; Community Development Division, Subject Files, 1954–57; RG 469.

56. Memorandum for the Record, TRIM, May 12, 1955. Box 3, Folder: Proposed Veterans Benefits; Entry 1438; Community Development Division, Subject Files, 1954–57; RG 469.

57. Douglas Valentine, *The Phoenix Program: America's Use of Terror in Vietnam* (New York: Morrow, 1990), 27.

58. On Diem's National Revolution, see Miller, *Misalliance,* 129.

59. "PVL Annual Convention Set," *The Manila Times,* June 4, 1955; Letter, Carlos P. Garcia to VVL, June 15, 1955; Box 28, Folder Misc. Vietnam; Bohannan Papers, Hoover Institution; "VP For Closer Ties with Asia," *The Manila Times,* June 13, 1955; "Seeks Nod for S. Vietnam," *The Manila Times,* June 22, 1955; Letter, Enriquez et al. to Macario Peralta, July 13, 1955; Box 28, Folder Misc. Vietnam; Bohannan Papers, Hoover Institution.

60. Telegram, Palmer to USOM Manila, June 7, 1955; Box 36, Folder Technical Assistance—3rd Country Training (Classified); Entry: UD 1366; Classified Subject Files (Classified Central Files), 1951–60; Mission to the Philippines; RG 469.

61. Telegram, Prentice to USOM Saigon, June 12, 1955; Box 36, Folder Technical Assistance—3rd Country Training (Classified); Entry: UD 1366; Classified Subject Files (Classified Central Files), 1951–60; Mission to the Philippines; RG 469; Woods, "Bombs, Bureaucrats, and Rosary Beads," 176.

62. Philippine Constabulary Annual Report, 1955--56. Box 48, Folder 1351. Lansdale Papers.

63. JUSMAG Philippines, MDAP Country Statement, Republic of the Philippines, January 1, 1957; Box 9, Folder 091.7; Entry 242; Security Classified General Correspondence, 1941–1961; Adjutant General's Section; Joint U.S. Military Advisory Group to the Republic of the Philippines; RG 334.

64. Telegram, JUSMAG Philippines to MAAG Saigon, August 1955. Box 4, Folder: 35.3; Entry 242; Security Classified General Correspondence, 1941–1961; RG 334.

65. British Training of Filipinos in Jungle Warfare, ca. November–December 1957. Box 10, Folder 353; Entry 242, Security Classified General Correspondence Files, 1941–1961; RG 334.

66. Cable, CINCPAC to Chief, MAAG Indochina and Chief, JUSMAG Philippines, December 1955; Box 4, Folder: 35.3; Entry 242; Security Classified General Correspondence; RG 334.

67. Letter to Ramon Magsaysay, July 18, 1955. Subject Files, Vietnam National Army. Ramon Magsaysay Center.

68. Lansdale Notebook, n.d.; Box 72, Folder 1954; Lansdale Papers.

69. Recto quoted in telegram, U.S. Embassy, Manila to Secretary of State, July 25, 1955.

70. Freedom Company Manager's Report, January 5, 1956. Box 28, Folder: Freedom Company Philippines, 1954–1957. Bohannan Papers, Hoover Institution.

71. Stephen Rosskamm Shalom, *The United States and the Philippines: A Study of Neocolonialism* (Philadelphia: Institute for the Study of Human Issues, 1981), chapter 2.

72. Proposed Program for Philippines Psychological Warfare Training Center, November 14, 1955; Box 7, Folder 353; Entry 242; Security Classified General Correspondence, 1941–1961; Adjutant General's Section; Joint U.S. Military Advisory Group to the Republic of the Philippines; RG 334; Memorandum of Conversation, Department of State, December 28, 1955; Box 3, Folder Manila Pact; Entry 1216; Office Files, 1948–1957; Office of Southwest Pacific Affairs; Office of the Officer in Charge for Philippine Affairs; RG 59.

73. Memorandum, Walter Robertson to Richards, June 10, 1957; Draft Agreement between U.S. and Philippine Governments on Counter-Subversion Program for Southeast Asia, Request to Conclude Agreement on Counter-Subversion School, August 19, 1958; Box 4024, Folder 796.52/5-2357; Central Decimal File; RG 59.

74. Quoted in Renato Constantino, *The Making of a Filipino: A Story of Philippine Colonial Politics* (Quezon City, Philippines: Malaya Books, 1969), 233.

75. Eastern Construction Company, Incorporated—History and Current Status, n.d. Box 28, Folder, ECCOI/Freedom Co 62. Bohannan Papers, Hoover Institution.

76. "They Shall Not Prevail," Claro Recto's address to the Chamber of Commerce of the Philippines, April 29, 1959. Box 43, Folder: 1258; Lansdale Papers.

77. Nick Cullather, *Illusions of Influence: The Political Economy of United States–Philippine Relations, 1942–1960* (Palo Alto, CA: Stanford University Press, 1994), 163.

78. Memorandum, Lansdale to Secretary of Defense, December 11, 1959. Box 42, Folder 1201; Lansdale Papers.

79. Miller, *Misalliance*, 204–5.

80. Quoted in Michael McClintock, *Instruments of Statecraft: U.S. Guerrilla Warfare, Counter-Insurgency, Counter-Terrorism, 1940–1990* (New York: Pantheon, 1992), 165.

81. Miller, *Misalliance*, 216.

82. Telegram, Manila to State, November 28, 1960. Box 49, Folder 1376; Lansdale Papers.

83. Telegram, Manila to State, January 3, 1961. Box 49, Folder 1376; Lansdale Papers.

84. Memorandum, Lansdale to McNamara, January 17, 1961. Box 43, Folder 1257; Lansdale Papers.

85. Letter, Lansdale to Banzon, April 23, 1962. Box 36, Folder 832; Lansdale Papers.

CHAPTER THREE

1. "Exercise 'Black Night,'" *Hawaii Lightning News,* March 26, 1965, 5.

2. "Jungle Warfare Training in the Canal Zone," prepared by Staff Historian, Assistant Chief of Staff, G-3, HQ USARSO, April 15, 1968, Military History Institute.

3. Kathy E. Ferguson and Phyllis Turnbull, *Oh, Say, Can You See? The Semiotics of the Military in Hawaiʻi* (Minneapolis: University of Minnesota Press, 1999), v. Other works on the militarization of Hawaiʻi include: Kyle Kajihiro, "The Militarizing of Hawaiʻi: Occupation, Accommodation, and Resistance," in *Asian Settler Colonialism: From Local Governance to the Habits of Everyday Life in Hawaiʻi,* eds. Candace Fujikane and Jonathan Y. Okamura (Honolulu: University of Hawaiʻi Press: 2008), 170–94; Juliet Nebolon, "'Life Given Straight to the Heart': Settler Militarism, Biopolitics, and Public Health in Hawaiʻi during World War II," *American Quarterly* 69, no. 1 (March 2017): 23–45.

4. Alfred Thayer Mahan, *The Influence of Sea Power Upon History, 1660–1783* (New York: Cambridge University Press, 2010 [1889]); General Macomb quoted in Ian Lind, "Ring of Steel: Notes on the Militarization of Hawaii," *Social Process in Hawaii* 31 (1984/1985): 25.

5. Hal Friedman, *Governing the American Lake: The U.S. Defense and Administration of the Pacific, 1945–1947* (East Lansing: Michigan State University Press, 2007), 4.

6. Letter, Farrant L. Turner to Lyndon B. Johnson, January 23, 1962. Box 48, Folder Special Correspondence: Frank E. Midkiff, Chamber of Commerce of Honolulu (1952), Henry S. Aurand Papers.

7. "Governor's Statement on Hawaiian Infantry Training Center," March 13, 1951. Box 339, Folder History of the Hawaiian Infantry Training Center; Organizational History Files, Military Historians' Office, RG 550.

8. "Hawaiʻi and the Armed Forces in 1951," paper submitted by Frank Midkiff to Henry Aurand, January 8, 1951. Box 48, Folder Special Correspondence: Frank E. Midkiff, Chamber of Commerce of Honolulu (1951), Aurand Papers.

9. Territorial Planning Director, Summary Report upon the Concentration of Military and Civilian Activities on Oahu, April 1958. Box 21, Folder Land Use and Kahoolawe; Hiram L. Fong Papers.

10. Quoted in George Cooper and Gavan Daws, *Land and Power in Hawaii: The Democratic Years* (Honolulu: University of Hawaiʻi Press, 1990), 5–8, 42.

11. Haunani-Kay Trask, "Settlers of Color and 'Immigrant' Hegemony: 'Locals' in Hawai'i," in *Asian Settler Colonialism,* eds. Fujikane and Okamura, 47. See also Dean Itsuji Saranillio, "Colliding Histories: Hawai'i Statehood at the Intersection of Asians 'Ineligible to Citizenship' and Hawaiians 'Unfit for Self-Government,'" *Journal of Asian American Studies* 13.3 (2010): 295.

12. Namaka to Eisenhower, July 12, 1957; Nakatsuka to Hagerty, January 6, 1956, both in Box 320, Folder Statehood for Hawaii (1), Central Files, DDE Papers as President, Dwight Eisenhower Presidential Library.

13. Dean Saranillio, "Seeing Conquest: Colliding Histories and the Cultural Politics of Hawai'i Statehood" (PhD diss., University of Michigan, 2009), 172.

14. On opposition against statehood, see Saranillio, "Seeing Conquest," 174.

15. Angela S. Krattiger, "Hawai'i's Cold War: American Empire and the Fiftieth State" (PhD diss., University of Hawai'i at Manoa, 2013), 28–29; Mililani B. Trask, "Hawai'i and the United Nations," in *Asian Settler Colonialism,* eds. Fujikane and Okamura, 67–70.

16. Chandan Reddy, *Freedom with Violence: Race, Sexuality, and the U.S. State* (Durham, NC: Duke University Press, 2011).

17. "Special Message on Federal Lands in Hawaii by Governor Quinn, to the First Legislature of the State of Hawaii, April 25, 1961," Hawaiian Collection, University of Hawai'i at Manoa Library.

18. "U.S. Pacific Chiefs on Alert Here," *Honolulu Advertiser,* August 5, 1964, A1; "Burns Strongly Backs Johnson on Vietnam War," *Honolulu Star-Bulletin,* July 30, 1965.

19. Shelby L. Stanton, *The Rise and Fall of an American Army: U.S. Ground Forces in Vietnam, 1965–1973* (New York: Presidio, 1985), 69–70; Quarterly Report, Office of the Assistant Chief of Staff, G-1, January–March 1960; Box 1, Folder Military Historian's Files–FY 1960; RG 550; *25th Infantry Division-Tropic Lightning in Vietnam, 1966–1967,* Hawaiian Collection; "'Tropic Lightning' Div. Answers 'Call to Arms,'" *Hawaii Lightning News,* January 7, 1966, 1.

20. Quoted in Marilyn Young, *The Vietnam Wars, 1945–1990* (New York: Harper Perennial, 1990), 139.

21. "25th Infantry Division-Tropic Lightning in Vietnam," news release, February 5, 1966, Box 101, Folder Tropic Lightning Helping Hand, John A. Burns Papers.

22. Weyand to Burns, January 12, 1966, Box 101, Folder Tropic Lightning Helping Hand, 1966–67, Burns Papers.

23. Statement by Burns, February 24, 1966, Box 101, Folder Tropic Lightning Helping Hand, Burns Papers.

24. News release, February 5, 1966.

25. "Massive Drive Ends Helping Hand," *Tropic Lightning News,* March 18, 1966, 3; Response by Burns, "Operation Helping Hand," March 5, 1966, Box 101, Folder Tropic Lightning Helping Hand, Burns Papers; "Operation Helping Hand," Cong. Rec. S4666 (daily ed. March 2, 1966) (statement of Sen. Fong).

26. "First Helping Hand Goods Arrive," *Tropic Lightning News,* March 4, 1966, 1.

27. Truong to Weyand, May 1966, Box 101, Folder Tropic Lightning Helping Hand, Burns Papers.

28. Laura Wexler terms this colonial gaze the "innocent eye." See Laura Wexler, *Tender Violence: Domestic Visions in an Age of U.S. Imperialism* (Chapel Hill: University of North Carolina Press, 2000), 6–7.

29. Quoted in Young, *Vietnam Wars,* 148.

30. Ibid., 333–34.

31. Nick Turse, *Kill Anything That Moves: The Real American War in Vietnam* (New York: Picador, 2013), 43.

32. ORLL 25th Inf. Div., 1 May–31 July 1966.

33. Territorial Planning Director, Summary Report; Stanton, *Rise and Fall of an American Army,* 69; DOD Report on the Study of Military Real Property, January 1960, Hawaiian Collection; Quarterly Reports, Office of the Assistant Chief of Staff, G-3, January–March 1960, Box 1, Folder Military Historian's Files, US Army Hawaii, RG 550.

34. "Twenty-Fifth Puts Its Mark on Vietnam," *Honolulu Advertiser,* January 8, 1967, A1–A.

35. "Training in Koolaus Pays Off for Twenty-Fifth," *Honolulu Advertiser,* May 3, 1966, A10.

36. ORLL, 25th ID, 1 January–30 April 1966, Box 22, Folder 25th Inf. Div. ORLL, Classified Organizational History Files, Military Historians' Office, RG 550; "Twenty-Fifth Puts Its Mark on Vietnam," *Honolulu Advertiser,* January 8, 1967, A1–A.

37. "Training in Koolaus Pays Off."

38. The use of land and villagers in Takae as a mock target for jungle-warfare training is discussed in the documentary *The Targeted Village* (directed by Chie Mikami, 2013).

39. Quarterly Historical Report, USARHAW, April–June 1967, Box 238, Classified Organizational History Files, RG 550.

40. "All-Hawaiian Co. Trains in 1st Bde.," *Fort Ord Panorama,* August 19, 1966. HQ, USATC, RG 553.

41. "Special Summer Camp Pictorial Spread," *The Hawaii Guardsmen,* September 1963, 15; Quarterly Historical Report, USARHAW, July–September 1965; Box 237; Classified Organizational History Files, RG 550; News Release, Department of Defense, Increased Readiness of Selected Army Reserve Components, September 30, 1965; Box 12, Folder Legislative—Armed Services—Air Force, Army, Coast Guard, Navy; Fong Papers.

42. "Eleventh Brigade to Mark Anniversary," *Honolulu Advertiser,* June 29, 1967, 13; Jungle and Guerrilla Warfare Training Center, Motion Picture Caption Sheet, June 14–15, 1967. Item number 10480105003, Bryan Grigsby Collection, Vietnam Center and Archives.

43. Quoted in "Trials: My Lai: A Question of Orders," *Time,* January 25, 1971; Robert Jay Lifton, *Home from the War: Vietnam Veterans: Neither Victims nor Executioners* (New York: Simon and Schuster, 1973), 48; "Schofield-Trained Troops Took Part in Massacre," *Honolulu Star-Bulletin,* November 28, 1969, A-2.

44. "White House Denounces Massacre," *Honolulu Star-Bulletin,* November 26, 1969, A-1.

45. "Inouye Says My Lai Shock May Stir Higher Morality," *Honolulu Star-Bulletin,* December 2, 1969, A-18.

46. "Friends in Miami Recall Calley as an Average Guy," *Honolulu Star-Bulletin,* December 4, 1969, B-6.

47. "Schofield-Trained Troops Took Part in Massacre."

48. Memorandum, J. B. Lampert to Clark Clifford, Reserve Call-up in Hawaii, April 13, 1968; White House Central File—Gen ST, Folder: ST 11 Hawaii (1 of 2); Papers of Lyndon Baines Johnson, President; "History of the 29th Brigade," Box 285, Folder: Unit History—29th Infantry Brigade; Organizational History Files; Military Historians' Office; RG 550.

49. Letter, Spark Matsunaga to Clark Clifford, October 11, 1968; Box 47, Folder Armed Forces—Military Duty—29th Brigade (1968); Spark M. Matsunaga Papers. Similar telegrams were exchanged between other Hawai'i congresspersons and military officials in the days and weeks following the announcement.

50. Correspondences, King Kwai and Hiram Fong, May 21, 1968 (with attached Aitken letter to the editor, *Honolulu Star-Bulletin,* May 21, 1968) (emphasis original); Box 12, Folder Legislative—Armed Services—Air Force, Army, Coast Guard, Navy; Fong Papers.

51. Erwin Marquit, "The Demobilization Movement of January 1946," *Society, Nature, and Thought* vol. 15, no. 1 (2002): 7–11.

52. "Hawaii Speaks Out on Vietnam," a Record of the April 11, 1967, Hearings of the Senate Military and Civil Defense Committee of the Hawai'i Legislature; Hawaiian Collection.

53. Quoted in Michael Ferber and Staughton Lynd, *The Resistance* (Boston: Beacon Press, 1971), 194.

54. "Student Defends Draft Card Burners," *Kaleo O Hawaii,* April 26, 1968, 4.

55. Stanford Masui, phone interview with author, July 2, 2010; News Release, Department of Army to Members of Congress, May 10, 1968; Box 12, Folder Legislative—Armed Services—Air Force, Army, Coast Guard, Navy; Fong Papers; "Awareness on Campus Increasing, Says Student," *Kaleo O Hawaii,* May 2, 1968, 4.

56. Stanford Masui, phone interview with author, July 2, 2010; News Release, Department of Army to Members of Congress, May 10, 1968; Box 12, Folder Legislative—Armed Services—Air Force, Army, Coast Guard, Navy; Fong Papers; "Awareness on Campus Increasing, Says Student," *Kaleo O Hawaii,* May 2, 1968, 4.

57. History of the 29th Brigade; Box 285, Folder Unit History—29th Infantry Brigade; Organizational History File, Military Historians' Office; RG 550; Masui, phone interview with author, July 2 and 6, 2010; Mobilization After-Action Report, June 24, 1968; Box 279, Folder 29th Inf. Bde, Unit History; Classified Organizational History Files; RG 550; Study, The 29th Infantry Brigade, 1 January 68–30 June 70; Box 265, Folder The 29th Infantry Bde (Separate), 1 January 68–30 June 70; Classified Organizational History Files; Military Historians' Office; RG 550.

58. Open Letter by Concerned Members of 29th Brigade, July 13, 1968 (emphasis original); Box 125, Folder 2; Mink Papers.

59. Open Letter by Concerned Members of 29th Brigade, October 7, 1968; Box 125, Folder 6; Mink Papers.

60. Study, The 29th Infantry Brigade, 1 January 68–30 June 70.

61. Senator Hiram Fong statement, *Congressional Record,* Senate (S9376), August 7, 1969; Box 125, Folder 6; Mink Papers.

62. "Gen. Schaefer's Reply," *Honolulu Star-Bulletin,* November 23, 1968; "'Fighting 29th' Sparks Mailbag Battle," *Honolulu Advertiser,* November 28, 1968; Box 47, Folder: Armed Forces—Military Duty—29th Brigade (1968); Matsunaga Papers.

63. Speech, Sam Sakamoto, *Puka Puka Parade* vol. XXI, no. 2 (October 1968).

64. Letter, Charles Miyamoto to Patsy Mink, December 18, 1968; Letter to the Editor, *Honolulu Advertiser,* December 2, 1968; Box 125, Folder 2; Mink Papers.

65. History of the 29th Brigade.

66. "Open Letter to Brothers and Sisters of Hawaii," *Hawaii Free Press,* vol. 1, no. 1, July 1969; Hawaiian Collection.

67. Noelani Goodyear-Ka'opua, Ikaika Hussey, and Erin Kahunawaika'ala Wright, eds., *A Nation Rising: Hawaiian Movements for Life, Land, and Sovereignty* (Durham, NC: Duke University Press, 2014), 8–9; Haunani-Kay Trask, "The Birth of the Modern Hawaiian Movement: Kalama Valley, O'ahu," *Hawaiian Journal of History* 21 (1987): 126–53.

68. Goodyear-Ka'opua, Hussey, and Wright, *Nation Rising,* esp. Davianna Pomaika'i McGregor and Ibrahim Aoude, "'Our History, Our Way!': Ethnic Studies for Hawai'i's People," 66–77; Jonathan Kamakawiwo'ole Osorio, "Hawaiian Souls: The Movement to Stop the U.S. Military Bombing of Kaho'olawe," 137–60. See also Trask, "Birth of the Modern Hawaiian Movement."

69. "Enjoy Hawaii: Home Staging-Ground for the Vietnam War in Indochina," *Liberated Barracks,* February 1972, 6–7.

70. Jim Albertini, phone interview with author, April 27, 2011.

71. Albertini, phone interview.

CHAPTER FOUR

1. Hwang Sŏkyŏng, *The Shadow of Arms,* translated by Chun Kyung-Ja (New York: Seven Stories Press, 2014).

2. The troop totals of allied military forces in Vietnam from 1964 to 1972 are as follows: South Korea, 343,044; Thailand, 37,664; Australia, 37,326; Philippines, 6,112; New Zealand, 2,497. Robert M. Blackburn, *Mercenaries and Lyndon Johnson's 'More Flags': The Hiring of Korean, Filipino, and Thai Soldiers in the Vietnam War* (Jefferson, NC: McFarland, 1994), 158.

3. Takashi Fujitani, *Race for Empire: Koreans as Japanese and Japanese as Americans during World War II* (Berkeley: University of California Press, 2011); Jodi Melamed, *Represent and Destroy: Rationalizing Violence in the New Racial Capital-*

ism (Minneapolis: University of Minnesota Press, 2011); Chandan Reddy, *Freedom with Violence: Race, Sexuality, and the U.S. State* (Durham, NC: Duke University Press, 2011); Naomi Murakawa, *The First Civil Right: How Liberals Built Prison America* (New York: Oxford University Press, 2014).

4. Jin-Kyung Lee, *Service Economies: Militarism, Sex Work, and Migrant Labor in South Korea* (Minneapolis: University of Minnesota Press, 2010).

5. On subimperialism as a function of the world system, see Thomas J. McCormick, *America's Half-Century: United States Foreign Policy in the Cold War and After* (Baltimore: Johns Hopkins University Press, 1995), 186–90. On subimperial desire, see Kuan-Hsing Chen, *Asia as Method: Toward Deimperialization* (Durham, NC: Duke University Press, 2010), especially chapter 1.

6. Letters, Ricardo Galang to Edward Lansdale, November 9, 1963, and April 18, 1963; Box 38, Folder 924, Lansdale Papers.

7. Memorandum, Edward Lansdale to Alexis Johnson, "Philippines III," February 13, 1963; Box 48, Folder 1352; Memorandum for the Record, "Visit with Macario Peralta," February 7, 1963; Box 97, Folder 4; Lansdale Papers.

8. Letter, Edward Lansdale to Edward Rowny, February 14, 1963; Box 49, Folder 1373; Lansdale Papers.

9. Rufus Phillips, *Why Vietnam Matters: An Eyewitness Account of Lessons Not Learned* (Annapolis, MD: Naval Institute Press, 2008), 123.

10. Rufus Phillips, A Report on Counter-Insurgency in Vietnam, August 31, 1962; Item Number 21940104003; Earl R. Rhine Collection (USOM/Office of Rural Affairs, Saigon).

11. "ECCOI, History and Current Status," n.d. Box 28, Folder ECCOI/Freedom Co 62; Memorandum, Frisco San Juan to Charles Bohannan, November 27, 1962; Box 28, Folder ECCOI/Freedom Co 62; Bohannan Papers, Hoover Institution.

12. Memorandum, Charles Bohannan to John M. Dunn, January 13, 1964; Box 42, Folder 1202; Lansdale Papers.

13. Memorandum, Rizalino Del Prado to Director, USOM, Saigon, April 7, 1965; Box 17, Folder Memo—R. G. Del Prado—Final Report USOM—April 7, 1965; Bohannan Papers.

14. Memorandum for the Record, "Visit with Macario Peralta," February 7, 1963.

15. Namhee Lee, *The Making of Minjung: Democracy and the Politics of Representation in South Korea* (Ithaca, NY: Cornell University Press, 2007), 28–29.

16. Tae Yang Kwak, "Anvil of War: The Legacies of Korean Participation in the Vietnam War" (PhD diss., Harvard University, 2006), 77.

17. Quoted in ibid, 85.

18. Letter, Henry Cabot Lodge to President, June 5, 1964; Document 200; *Foreign Relations of the United States, 1964–1968,* Volume I; Vietnam, 1964 (emphasis original); Telegram, Saigon Embassy to Department of State, May 6, 1964; Document 103; Box 4, Folder Vietnam memos, vol. VIII, 5/64 (1 of 2); NSF Vietnam Country File.

19. Telegram, President to Ambassadors, July 24, 1964; Document 45; Box 6, Folder Vol. XIII, Memos, 6/64–7/64; NSF Vietnam Country File. Emphasis original.

20. U.S. aid to South Korea dropped from $230 million annually in 1959–1963 to $110 million in 1964–1968. See Min Yong Lee, "The Vietnam War: South Korea's Search for National Security," in *The Park Chung Hee Era: The Transformation of South Korea,* eds. Byung-kook Kim and Ezra F. Vogel (Cambridge, MA: Harvard University Press, 2011), 407. Robert Komer quoted in Gregg Brazinsky, *Nation Building in South Korea: Koreans, Americans, and the Making of a Democracy* (Chapel Hill: University of North Carolina Press, 2009), 133.

21. Lee, *Service Economies,* 37–78.

22. Lee, *The Making of Minjung,* 32.

23. Jung-Hoon Lee, "Normalization of Relations with Japan," in *The Park Chung Hee Era,* eds. Kim and Vogel, 432.

24. Yi Tongwŏn quoted in Brazinsky, *Nation Building in South Korea,* 137.

25. Memorandum, State Department Bureau of Intelligence and Research, April 23, 1964; Document 27; Box 277, Folder Vol. I, Cables, 11/63–11/64; NSF Philippine Country File.

26. Blackburn, *Mercenaries and Lyndon Johnson's "More Flags,"* 158; Memorandum of Conversation, Macapagal and McNamara et al., October 6, 1964; Document 321; *FRUS, 1964–1968,* Vol. XXVI.

27. "3,000 Filipinos in Giant Anti-U.S. Rally; 1ˢᵗ Ever," *Chicago Daily Defender,* December 28, 1964, 1; "Filipino Is Slain by Marine Guard," *The Washington Post,* December 15, 1964, D10; "Court-Martial Finds U.S. Airman Guilty of Killing Filipino," *The New York Times,* February 26, 1965, 2; *The Daily Herald,* March 8, 1964, 4.

28. Memorandum of Conversation, Macario Peralta and William Blair Jr., December 22, 1964. Box 5, Folder Political Affairs & Rel. (Aid to South Viet-Nam); Entry 5309; Records Relating to the Philippines, 1964–66; Office of the Country Director of the Philippines; Bureau of Far Eastern Affairs; RG 59.

29. Memorandum, Napoleon Valeriano to Edward Lansdale, November 15, 1965; Box 59, Folder 1555; Lansdale Papers.

30. "Salons Split; Students Storm Capitol," *Daily Mirror,* February 11, 1966; "Vietnam-PI Aid," Newspaper Files, Lopez Memorial Museum.

31. Ibid.; "University Student Council, University of the Philippines—Manifesto," University Archives; University of Philippines Diliman Main Library; Cable, Manila to AID/Washington, "Report of the 21 February Anti-U.S. Demonstrations," March 2, 1966; The National Security Agency; Digital National Security Archives; "House Committee Reports Out Viet Bill," *The Manila Times,* March 17, 1966; "Mammoth Protest Rally on Viet Bill Next Week," *Daily Mirror,* March 17, 1966; "Vietnam-PI Aid," Newspaper Files.

32. Kwak, "Anvil of War," 106–7.

33. Blackburn, *Mercenaries and Lyndon Johnson's "More Flags,"* 78, 80.

34. According to Tae Yang Kwak, South Korea's earnings from American industrial and military sources totaled $617.2 million. Additionally, South Korean military personnel and civilian workers earned $473.7 million in wages during this period. Kwak, "Anvil of War," 159–60.

35. Letter, N MOI/Chieu Hoi to Charles Bohannan, April 26, 1966; Letter, Douglas Pike to Bohannan, May 24, 1966; Letter, Cabacunan to Smith, May 14, 1966; Letter, Smith to Bohannan, May 20, 1966; Charles Bohannan Personal Papers.

36. Letter, Charles to Bohannan, August 22, 1966; Letter, Gulla to Bohannan, September 9, 1966; Charles Bohannan Personal Papers. Emphasis original.

37. Walden Bello, *The Anti-Development State: The Political Economy of Permanent Crisis in the Philippines* (Quezon City, Philippines: Department of Sociology, University of the Philippines, Diliman, 2004).

38. Patricio N. Abinales and Donna J. Amoroso, *State and Society in the Philippines* (Lanham, MD: Rowman & Littlefield, 2005), 193–94; Neferti X. M. Tadiar, *Things Fall Away: Philippine Historical Experience and the Makings of Globalization* (Durham, NC: Duke University Press, 2009), 187.

39. Letter, Gulla to Bohannan, September 9, 1966.

40. Letter, Panganiban to Bohannan, August 16, 1967. Charles Bohannan Personal Papers.

41. "Volunteers Wanted for VN Action," *The Manila Times,* July 6, 1966.

42. Memorandum, Napoleon Valeriano to Edward Lansdale, November 15, 1965. Box 59, Folder 1555. Lansdale Papers.

43. "Hearings on Viet Bill End," *The Manila Times,* March 16, 1966.

44. Memorandum, Valeriano to Lansdale, November 15, 1965.

45. "U.S. Army Urged to Enlist R.P. Volunteers," *Daily Mirror,* April 16, 1966; Telegram, Manila to State Department, July 13, 1967; Document 7; Box 278, Folder Vol. III, Cables, 7/66–7/67 [1 of 2]; NSF Philippine Country File.

46. Memo, Edward Lansdale to William Blair Jr., February 17, 1967.

47. Telegram, Seoul to Department of State, July 10, 1965; Document 57; *FRUS,* 1964–1968, Volume XXIX.

48. Fujitani, *Race for Empire,* chapter 1.

49. Telegram, Seoul to Department of State, April 15, 1965. Box 46, Folder NODIS-LOR Vol. II (A), 3/65-0/65 (2 of 2); NSF Vietnam Country File, LBJ Library.

50. Lee, "Surrogate Military, Subimperialism, and Masculinity," 662.

51. Kwak, "Anvil of War," 183–85.

52. Seungsook Moon, "Regulating Desire, Managing the Empire: U.S. Military-Prostitution in South Korea, 1945–1970," in *Over There: Living with the U.S. Military Empire from World War II to the Present,* eds. Maria Hohn and Seungsook Moon (Durham, NC: Duke University Press, 2010), 58–63. On militarized and sexualized forms of migrant labor during the Park Chung-hee era, see Lee, *Service Economies.*

53. Chung Ro Yoon, "We Are Exporting Skilled Workers: Life of a Korean Worker Dispatched to Viet Nam and the Viet Nam War," *Journal BOL* (Winter 2007): 243–53. *The Stars and Stripes* is the official U.S. Army newspaper.

54. "Why Filipinos Refuse to Leave Saigon," *Graphic,* February 28, 1968; "Last Out of Vietnam," *Graphic,* October 22, 1969.

55. Memorandum, Edward Lansdale to Henry Cabot Lodge, June 15, 1966; Box 55, Folder 1483; Lansdale Papers.

56. "Filipinos Won't Be Strangers in Tay Ninh," *The Manila Times,* August 22, 1966.

57. "Filipino Mercenaries in Vietnam," *Graphic,* vol. 33, no. 27, December 28, 1966, 24–25, 29, 68.

58. Young, *The Vietnam Wars,* 212.

59. "The Mission of 1ˢᵗ PHILCAGV," *Weekly Nation.*

60. E. P. Patanne, "A Bunker Village in Tay Ninh," *Weekly Nation,* vol. 2, no. 44, June 26, 1967, 20–22.

61. Combined Committee Evaluation of the PHILCAGV, November 20, 1967; Box 169, Folder 1968 Free World—PHILCAG; Historians Background Material Files; Military History Branch; Secretary of the Joint Staff (MACJo3); Headquarters, MACV; RG 472.

62. "Filipino Mercenaries in Vietnam," 24–25, 29, 68.

63. Memorandum, Edward Lansdale to William Westmoreland, November 10, 1966; Box 56, Folder 1495; Lansdale Papers.

64. "Filipino Mercenaries in Vietnam," *Graphic.*

65. Lee, "Surrogate Military, Subimperialism, and Masculinity," 659.

66. Eun Seo Jo, "Fighting for Peanuts: Reimagining South Korean Soldiers' Participation in the Wŏllam Boom," *Journal of American-East Asian Relations* 21 (2014): 59.

67. Ibid., 80.

68. Youngju Ryu, "Korea's Vietnam: Popular Culture, Patriarchy, Intertextuality," *The Review of Korean Studies* 12, no. 3 (September 2009): 103.

69. Quoted in ibid.

70. Quoted in ibid.

71. Jonathan Schell, *The Military Half: An Account of Destruction in Quang Ngai and Quang Tin* (New York: Alfred A. Knopf, 1968), 8–9.

72. Heonik Kwon, *After the Massacre: Commemoration and Consolation in Ha My and My Lai* (Berkeley: University of California Press, 2006), 30.

73. Quoted in Diane and Michael Jones, "Allied Called Koreans—A Report from Vietnam," in *America's Rented Troops: South Koreans in Vietnam,* Frank Baldwin, Diane and Michael Jones (Philadelphia: American Friends Service Committee, 1975), 20–21.

74. Ibid., 23.

75. Ibid., 40.

76. Addendum to Combined Committee Evaluation of PHILCAGV, November 20, 1967; Box 169, Folder 1968 Free World—PHILCAG; Historian's Background Material Files; Military History Branch; Secretary of the Joint Staff (MACJo3); Headquarters, MACV; RG 472.

77. "The Big PHILCAG Swindle," *Weekly Graphic,* vol. 34, no. 33, February 7, 1968, 23–27 (emphasis original); "Come Home, Philcag!" *Weekly Graphic,* vol. 34, no. 35, February 21, 1968, 20–21,63.

78. "The Philcag Episode," *Weekly Graphic,* vol. 36, no. 27, December 10, 1969, 1–3, 64; "We Seem to Have Lost All Regard for Our National Sense of Honor," *Weekly Graphic,* January 17, 1968, quoted in "The Philcag Episode."

79. Hearings, U.S. Senate, Subcommittee on U.S. Security Arrangements and Commitments Abroad of the Committee on Foreign Relations, September 30–October 3, 1969; Fulbright quote, p. 276; "Philippines' Regime, Leaders Deny U.S. Paid for Troops," *The Evening Star,* November 19, 1969; "Marcos Denies U.S. Paid for Unit," *The New York Times,* November 20, 1969; Appendix I, pp. 3 and 6 of Report to the Subcommittee on U.S. Security Agreements and Commitments Abroad, by the Comptroller General of the United States, June 1, 1970; "The Philcag Episode," *Weekly Graphic.*

80. Hearings, U.S. Senate, Subcommittee on U.S. Security Arrangements and Commitments Abroad, 67.

81. "U.S. Bases Must Go" (emphasis original); "The Philcag Episode"; "Anti-U.S. Feelings Up in the Philippines," *The New York Times,* December 11, 1969, 17.

82. Lee, *The Making of Minjung,* 49–50.

83. Ibid., 44–46.

84. Youngju Ryu, "The Neighbor and Politics of Literature in 1970's South Korea: Yi Mungu, Hwang Sŏkyŏng, Cho Sehŭi," (PhD diss., UCLA, 2006), 3.

85. John Feffer, "The Other Vietnam Syndrome," *LA Review of Books,* September 8, 2014.

86. Ryu, "The Neighbor and Politics of Literature in 1970's South Korea," 126.

87. Lee, *The Making of Minjung,* 51.

CHAPTER FIVE

1. Judy Tzu-Chun Wu, *Radicals on the Road: Internationalism, Orientalism, and Feminism during the Vietnam Era* (Ithaca, NY: Cornell University Press, 2013), 150–53.

2. Pat Sumi interview with Ryan Masaaki Yokota, July 1, 1997.

3. Mike Nakayama and Nick Nagatani, interview with author, September 19, 2009; "Asian Americans for Peace, Peace Sunday, May 16," *Gidra,* April 1971, 8; "Peace Sunday: A Photographic Essay," *Gidra,* June 1971, 10–11.

4. Nakayama and Nagatani interview. On black and Japanese American settlement and social relations in Crenshaw, see Scott Kurashige, *The Shifting Ground of Race: Black and Japanese Americans in the Making of Multiethnic Los Angeles* (Princeton, NJ: Princeton University Press, 2008), 249–58.

5. David Roediger, "Gook: The Short History of an Americanism," *Monthly Review* 43, no. 10 (March 1992), 50–54.

6. Mike Nakayama speaking at the Winter Soldier Investigation in Detroit on February 2, 1971. Quoted in *Congressional Record,* 92nd Congress, 1st Session, Vol. 117, Part 8, 10012. April 6, 1971.

7. Doug Luna interview with Ken Mochizuki; Wing Luke Asian Pacific American Veterans Project, 1987.

8. Christian G. Appy, *Working-Class War: American Combat Soldiers and Vietnam* (Chapel Hill: University of North Carolina Press, 1993), 25–38.

9. Nakayama and Nagatani interview; Kenji Kudo phone interview with author, September 24, 2009; Tosh Nakano, interview with author, September 17, 2009; Yuzo Tokita, interview with author, October 6, 2009; James Arima, interview with author, August 25, 2009.

10. Karen Umemoto, "'On Strike!' San Francisco State College Strike, 1968–69: The Role of Asian American Students," *Amerasia Journal* 15 (1989): 3–41; Daryl J. Maeda, *Chains of Babylon: The Rise of Asian America* (Minneapolis: University of Minnesota Press, 2009), 40–72.

11. Richard Yee, interview with author, September 18, 2009.

12. Shimabukuro quoted in John Kerry and Vietnam Veterans Against the War, *The New Soldier* (New York: MacMillan, 1971), 42; Nakayama and Nagatani interview; James E. Westheider, *The Vietnam War* (Santa Barbara, CA: Greenwood Publishing Group, 2007), 50–51.

13. Kimberley L. Phillips, *War! What Is It Good For? Black Freedom Struggles and the U.S. Military from World War II to Iraq* (Chapel Hill: University of North Carolina Press, 2012), 217.

14. Operational Report for Quarterly Period Ending 31 October 1966, Department of the Army. Headquarters US Army School of the Americas, Fort Gulick, Canal Zone, Department of the Army. Military History Institute.

15. Robert Jay Lifton, *Home from the War: Vietnam Veterans: Neither Victims nor Executioners* (New York: Simon and Schuster, 1973), 16–18, 194, 197, 204–5.

16. Luna interview, 1987.

17. Jose Velasquez, interview with Ken Mochizuki, Wing Luke Asian Pacific American Veterans Project, 1986.

18. Chris Taga, phone interview with author, October 2, 2009.

19. Mochizuki, "The Asian American Vietnam Veteran," *The International Examiner,* vol. 13 no. 21, November 5, 1986.

20. Memorandum, Edward Lansdale to The Old Team, February 10, 1968; Box 59, Folder 1535. Lansdale Papers.

21. Richard Yee mentioned the death of his brother at the conclusion of the interview after the recording had stopped. Yee interview.

22. Tim O'Brien, *The Things They Carried* (New York: Broadway Books, 1990), 83.

23. The phrase "illegitimate historicity" is Vicente Rafael's. See Vicente L. Rafael, *White Love and Other Events in Filipino History* (Durham, NC: Duke University Press, 2000), 117.

24. Larry Wong interview with Ken Mochizuki, Wing Luke Asian Pacific American Veterans Project, 1987.

25. Quoted in Peter Nien-chu Kiang and Chalsa M. Loo, "Food in the Racial Experiences of Asian American Pacific Islander Vietnam Veterans," *Amerasia Journal* 32, 2 (2006): 13–14.

26. This example is one of the many NLF propaganda leaflets collected by Sgt. Maj. Herbert A. Friedman, compiled at http://www.psywarrior.com /VCLeafletsProp.html. Accessed July 19, 2012.

27. This anecdote about Nagatani was recounted by Pat Sumi in her interview with Ryan Yokota in 1997. Sumi interview with Yokota.

28. Nagatani and Nakayama interview.

29. In my interview with Nagatani, he did not share this experience or recall telling it to Sumi. I'm interested less in establishing the veracity of the story than in the way that Sumi recalled and shared the story and made meaning of it as an activist.

30. Nagatani and Nakayama interview.

31. Nikhil Pal Singh, *Black Is a Country: Race and the Unfinished Struggle for Democracy* (Cambridge, MA: Harvard University Press, 2004), 193–98.

32. Ibid., 184–93; Keith P. Feldman, *A Shadow over Palestine: The Imperial Life of Race in America* (Minneapolis: University of Minnesota Press, 2015), chapter 2.

33. Sumi interview with Yokota.

34. Singh, *Black Is a Country*, 198.

35. Sumi interview with Yokota.

36. Nakayama and Nagatani interview. For more on the Winter Soldier Investigation, see Richard R. Moser, *The New Winter Soldiers: GI and Veteran Dissent during the Vietnam Era* (New Brunswick, NJ: Rutgers University Press, 1996), 111; Wilbur J. Scott, *The Politics of Readjustment: Vietnam Veterans since the War* (New York: Aldine De Gruyter, 1993), 18–20. By Scott's account, 115 Vietnam veterans and 13 others were present at the testimony.

37. Nakayama and Nagatani interview; Nakayama quoted in *Congressional Record*, 92nd Congress, 1st Session, Vol. 117, Part 8, 10012. Note his name is misspelled as "Nakayamo."

38. Nakayama recalled five or six participants on the panel, representing blacks, Chicanos, Asian Americans, and American Indians; the transcripts entered into the *Congressional Record* listed ten individuals. Aside from Nakayama, the other Asian American was Scott Shimabukuro. *Congressional Record*, 92nd Congress, 1st Session, Vol. 117, Part 8, 10009.

39. See Maeda, *Chains of Babylon*, 73–96.

40. "Nam and USMC," by Mike Nakayama, *Gidra* (May 1971), 17. *Gidra*'s circulation figure is cited from Maeda, *Chains of Babylon*, 110; Nakayama and Nagatani interview. On the Indochinese Women's Conference, see Wu, *Radicals on the Road*, chapters 7–9.

41. "Draft Counsel," *AAPA Newspaper*, vol. 1, no. 2 (November–December 1968); "Draft Counselors Needed in Chinatown," *AAPA Newspaper*, vol. 1, no. 3 (December–January 1969); Box 1, Folders 1 and 2; "Chinatown-Manilatown Draft Help," pamphlet; Box 5, Folder 5; Collection 1805; Steve Louie Collection.

42. "Draft Counsel," *Getting Together*, vol. 1, no. 1, February 1970; Box 2, Folder 1; Collection 1805; Steve Louie Collection.

43. Ibid.; "Sam Choy," *Getting Together,* vol. 1, no. 2, April 1970 (emphasis original); Box 2, Folder 2; Collection 1805; Steve Louie Collection; Lifton, *Home from the War,* 215.

44. "AMMO," *Gidra,* August 1971, 19.

45. Nagatani and Nakayama interview; Kenji Kudo, phone interview with author, September 24 and 25, 2009.

46. Chris Taga interview.

47. Mike Yanagita, phone interview with author, September 29, 2009.

48. Nagatani and Nakayama interview.

49. Nagatani interview, September 23, 2009.

50. Kathy Nishimoto Masaoka, interview with author, July 7, 2016.

51. Nick Nagatani, "Action Talks and Bullshit Walks: From the Founders of Yellow Brotherhood to the Present," in *Asian Americans: The Movement and the Moment,* eds. Steve Louie and Glenn Omatsu (Los Angeles: UCLA Asian American Studies Center Press, 2001), 149–55.

52. "Statement from the Van Troi Anti-Imperialist Youth Brigade," *Gidra,* September 1972, 4–5; Nagatani and Nakayama interview.

53. "Statement from the Van Troi Anti-Imperialist Youth Brigade," *Gidra.*

54. "Statement from the Thai Binh Brigade," *Gidra,* September 1972, 6.

55. Kathy Masaoka interview, July 7, 2016; Karen L. Ishizuka, *Serve the People: Making Asian America in the Long Sixties* (London: Verso, 2016), 183–84; Karyn Mariko Smoot, "Unsettling the Gold Mountain: Asian Americans in Decolonial Resistance" (BA thesis, University of Oregon, 2013), 26–32.

56. Anders Corr, *No Trespassing! Squatting, Rent Strikes, and Land Struggles Worldwide* (Boston: South End Press, 1999), 156. See also Rolland Dewing, *Wounded Knee: The Meaning and Significance of the Second Incident* (New York: Irvington Publishers, 1985), 167; Nagatani and Nakayama also recounted it in their interview.

57. Nagatani and Nakayama interview.

58. "BAACAW, AMMO, and NY Asian Coalition Begin Medical Drive," *New Dawn,* vol. 2, no. 6, January 1973, 5.

59. "Asian Vets against the War," *New Dawn,* vol. 2, no. 7, February 1973, 6.

60. Nagatani and Nakayama interview.

61. Chalsa M. Loo, "Race-Related PTSD: The Asian American Vietnam Veteran," *Journal of Traumatic Stress* vol. 7, no. 4 (1994): 645, 650.

62. Jerry Lembcke, *The Spitting Image: Myth, Memory, and the Legacy of Vietnam* (New York: New York University Press, 1998).

CHAPTER SIX

1. "Crewmen Protest Coral Sea's Return to War," *San Francisco Chronicle,* October 12, 1971, 14; "Stop Our Ship" News Release; "Sanctuary for the Brothers of Coral Sea"; "City Action Regarding the U.S.S. Coral Sea"; "Statement by Crewmembers

of the USS Coral Sea, December 9, 1971," Carton 8, Folder 21; Pacific Counseling Service and Military Law Office Records (hereafter PCS-MLO).

2. "The Brass Hassles Filipinos Too," *The Whig*, November 1971, 3; NLG-MLO 3rd Monthly Report, February 1, 1972; Carton 4, Folder 23; PCS-MLO.

3. Robin D.G. Kelley, "How the West Was One: African Diaspora and the Remapping of U.S. History," in *Rethinking American History in a Global Age*, ed. Thomas Bender (Berkeley: University of California Press, 2002), 124.

4. Quoted in David Cortright, *Soldiers in Revolt: GI Resistance during the Vietnam War* (Chicago: Haymarket Books, 1975), 3.

5. Cortright, *Soldiers in Revolt*, 57. On the Bay Area and the GI movement, see Derek W. Seidman, "The Unquiet Americans: GI Dissent during the Vietnam War" (PhD diss., Brown University, 2010).

6. Cortright, *Soldiers in Revolt*, chapter 3; Seidman, "Unquiet Americans," chapters 2 and 3.

7. Background Information on the Pacific Counseling Service, n.d., Carton 1, Folder 1; PCS-MLO. U.S. Department of Justice, FBI Report on Alan Stanley Miller, June 28, 1968; Alan Miller personal papers.

8. DOD Directive No. 1325.6, September 12, 1969; Carton 10, Folder 13; PCS-MLO.

9. On the expansion of PCS on the West Coast, see Background Information on the Pacific Counseling Service; Carton 10, Folder 13; PCS-MLO. On GI-Civilian Alliance for Peace and the GI Movement in Tacoma, see Jessie Kindig, "Demilitarized Zone: The GI Movement at Fort Lewis during the Vietnam War" (MA thesis, University of Washington, 2009); Jessie Kindig, "GI Movement: Antiwar Soldiers at Fort Lewis," Antiwar and Radical History Project. Retrieved April 16, 2012 from http://depts.washington.edu/antiwar/gi_mvmt.shtml; Dale Borgeson, phone interview with author, February 4, 2012.

10. "Military Moratorium Sunday, Dec 14: Civilians and GIs March in Oceanside," *Attitude Check*, December 1969, 1; PCS Report, 1970; Carton 1, Folder 1; PCS-MLO. HCIS hearings, 6621; *New Dawn*, November 1972, 6.

11. HCIS hearings, 6490, 6742.

12. Thomas R.H. Havens, *Fire across the Sea: The Vietnam War and Japan, 1965–1975* (Princeton, NJ: Princeton University Press, 1987), 32–33, 54–67; Yuichiro Onishi, *Transpacific Antiracism: Afro-Asian Solidarity in 20th-Century Black America, Japan, and Okinawa* (New York: New York University Press, 2013), 155–56.

13. Letter, Alan Miller to Jane Fonda, January 6, 1972; Carton 7, Folder 44; PCS-MLO; Pamphlet, "Beheiren: An Introduction to the Japanese New Left Peace for Vietnam Committee"; Carton 6, Folder 19; PCS-MLO; Richard DeCamp, "The GI Movement in Asia," *Bulletin of Concerned Asian Scholars* vol. 4, no. 1 (Winter 1971): 110; Havens, *Fire across the Sea*, 55.

14. Beheiren pamphlet, November 5, 1970; Carton 6, Folder 19; PCS-MLO.

15. PCS release, "Hobbitt Open Soon," n.d; Carton 4, Folder 56; PCS-MLO.

16. Newsclip, Anti-War GIs Organized in the Pacific Area, 1971; Carton 9, Folder 44; PCS-MLO; NLG Letter, July 7, 1972; Carton 4, Folder 51; PCS-MLO.

17. President Nixon's Speech on "Vietnamization," November 3, 1969; Retrieved May 7, 2012 from http://vietnam.vassar.edu/overview/doc14.html.

18. Press Release, Japan Joint GI Conference, April 1972; Carton 5, Folder 53; PCS-MLO.

19. Marshall Green, "The Nixon Doctrine: A Blueprint for the 1970s." Department of State publication, January 1971; Speech by Green, "A Strategic Appraisal of the Pacific Area," Box 5, Folder 5; Marshall Green Papers.

20. Quoted in Green's statement before the Subcommittee on Foreign Operations, November 26, 1969, 3. Box 4, Folder 21; Green Papers.

21. Wesley Iwao Ueunten, "Rising Up from a Sea of Discontent: The 1970 Koza Uprising in U.S.-Occupied Okinawa," in *Militarized Currents: Toward a Decolonized Future in Asia and the Pacific*, eds. Setsu Shigematsu and Keith L. Camacho (Minneapolis: University of Minnesota Press, 2010), 103–8. Onishi, *Transpacific Antiracism*, 138.

22. Onishi, *Transpacific Antiracism*, 139–40, 157.

23. Quoted in Green's statement before the Subcommittee on Foreign Operations, November 26, 1969, 3.

24. Havens, *Fire across the Sea*, 205; PCS Report, January 4, 1972.

25. Ueunten, "Rising Up from a Sea of Discontent," 94–97.

26. Ibid, 95–96.

27. "Chibario! Okinawa's Struggle for Freedom," VVAW/WSO pamphlet, ca. 1972; Carton 5, Folder 52; PCS-MLO.

28. Dale Borgeson, phone interview with author, February 4, 2012.

29. People's House Progress Report, May–June 15, 1973, PCS-MLO.

30. Ibid.

31. Letter, Kabataang Makabayan to PCS, FTA, October 13, 1971; Carton 7, Folder 45; PCS-MLO.

32. DOD Report, "Jane Fonda Far East Trip: Nov–Dec 1971," reprinted in HCIS, 7099-7101.

33. Ibid.

34. Closure of Manila R&R Site, March 1970; Box 261, Folder Morale and Welfare, R&R, 1970; Historian's Background Material Files; RG 472.

35. Willard B. Gatewood Jr., *Black Americans and the White Man's Burden, 1898–1903* (Urbana: University of Illinois Press, 1975).

36. Excerpt of Special Study Mission to Asia of the Senate Foreign Affairs Committee, reprinted in *Congressional Record*, September 27, 1972. 92nd Congress, 2nd Session.

37. The National Lawyers Guild operated in the Philippines, Japan, and Okinawa under the Military Law Office (MLO). Proposal for Establishing NLG-MLO in Asia, Eric Seitz, 1971; Carton 4, Folder 23; Letter from Seitz to George Logan, January 22, 1971; Carton 2, Folder 28; Letter from Seitz to Angela Davis, May 21, 1971; Carton 1, Folder 56, PCS-MLO.

38. *The Whig*, November 1971, 2; PCS Work in Asia, 1972; Carton 4, Folder 13; PCS-MLO; Borgeson, phone interview with author, February 11, 2012; "Subic GI

Center Opens," *Seasick,* January 1972, 1; NLG-MLO 3ʳᵈ Monthly Report, February 1, 1972; Carton 4, Folder 23; PCS-MLO.

39. NLG-MLO 3ʳᵈ Monthly Report, February 1, 1972; Letter, Senator Ervin to Secretary Laird, March 17, 1972; Carton 1, Folder 56; NLG-MLO 4ᵗʰ Monthly Report, March 7, 1972; Carton 6, Folder 35; NLG-MLO 5ᵗʰ Monthly Report, April 27, 1972; Carton 6, Folder 35; Memorandum, PCS to Senators Alan Cranston, John Tunney, George McGovern, Mark Hatfield, April 24, 1972; Carton 6, Folder 21; Letter, Miller to Ronald Dellums, Alan Cranston, John Tunney, and George McGovern, May 1972; Carton 1, Folder 12; PCS-MLO.

40. Letter, Miller to Dellums, Cranston, Tunney, and McGovern, May 1972; Letter, J. Fred Buzhardt, DOD, to Sam Ervin Jr., June 19, 1972; Carton 2, Folder 30; PCS-MLO.

41. Borgeson, phone interview with author, February 11, 2012.

42. NLG-MLO 6ᵗʰ Monthly Report, May 27, 1972; Carton 6, Folder 35; PCS-MLO.

43. "GIs Expose U.S. Aggression from Philippines," June 1, 1972; Carton 6, Folder 23; PCS-MLO.

44. Naval Investigative Service Information Report, January 29, 1973; Subject: GI Center at San Antonio, R.P./Raid by Philippine Authorities; Alan Miller personal papers.

45. NLG-MLO Monthly Report, August–November 1972; Carton 4, Folder 23; PCS-MLO.

46. Ibid.; "Philippines Martial Law Symposium," *New Dawn,* vol. 2, no. 4, November 1972, 6; NLG-MLO Monthly Report, August to November, 1972.

47. Borgeson, phone interview with author, February 13, 2012.

48. Ibid. On the founding of the KDP, see Estella Habal, *San Francisco's International Hotel: Mobilizing the Filipino American Community in the Anti-Eviction Movement* (Philadelphia: Temple University Press, 2007), 70–71.

49. Borgeson, phone interview with author, February 13, 2012; Habal, *San Francisco's International Hotel,* 181.

50. PCS-Pamphlet 1974; "GI Organizers Needed!" PCS, May 1975.

CONCLUSION

1. Beth Bailey, *America's Army: Making the All-Volunteer Force* (Cambridge, MA: Harvard University Press, 2009); Deborah Cohen, "Fighting for 'Freedom': The End of Conscription and the Neoliberal Project of Citizenship in the United States," *Citizenship Studies* 10, no. 2 (2006): 167–83; Derek Seidman, "The Unquiet Americans: GI Dissent during the Vietnam War" (PhD diss., Brown University, 2010).

2. U.S. annual military spending rose from approximately $155 billion in 1980 to almost $300 billion in 1986. Carole K. Fink, *Cold War: An International History* (Boulder, CO: Westview Press, 2017), 201.

3. "Text of the Reagan Message to Congress on Foreign Policy," *New York Times,* March 15, 1986, 4.

4. Quoted in Andrew J. Bacevich, *The New American Militarism: How Americans are Seduced by War* (New York: Oxford University Press, 2005), 109.

5. Bailey, *America's Army,* 174.

6. Bacevich, *The New American Militarism,* 108–9.

7. Melani McAlister, *Epic Encounters: Culture, Media, and U.S. Interests in the Middle East, 1945–2000* (Berkeley: University of California Press, 2001), 240–41.

8. Ibid., 250.

9. Chalmers Johnson, *Blowback: The Costs and Consequences of American Empire* (New York: Henry Holt, 2000).

10. Blaine Harden, "Guam's Young, Steeped in History, Line Up to Enlist," *Washington Post,* January 27, 2008.

11. Liberation Day commemorates the U.S. Marines' liberation of Guam from the Japanese occupation during World War II. See Vicente M. Diaz, "Deliberating Liberation Day: Identity, History, Memory, and War in Guam," in *Perilous Memories: The Asia-Pacific War(s),* eds. T. Fujitani et al. (Durham, NC: Duke University Press, 2001), 155–80. On the gift of freedom, see Mimi Thi Nguyen, *The Gift of Freedom: War, Debt, and Other Refugee Passages* (Durham, NC: Duke University Press, 2012).

12. https://www.defense.gov/news/mavni-fact-sheet.pdf. Accessed May 15, 2007.

13. David Kilcullen describes counterinsurgency as "armed social work." See David Kilcullen, "Twenty-Eight Articles: Fundamentals of Company-Level Counterinsurgency," *Military Review* 83 (2006): 103–8.

14. Walden Bello, "From American Lake to a People's Pacific in the Twenty-First Century," in *Militarized Currents: Toward a Decolonized Future in Asia and the Pacific,* eds. Setsu Shigematsu and Keith Camacho (Minneapolis: University of Minnesota Press, 2010), 318–19.

BIBLIOGRAPHY

ARCHIVAL SOURCES

Bancroft Library, University of California, Berkeley:
  Pacific Counseling Service and Military Law Office Records

Charles E. Young Research Library, University of California, Los Angeles:
  Steve Louie Collection

Charles T. R. Bohannan Library, Manila:
  Charles Bohannan Personal Papers

Club 100 Veterans Archives, Honolulu:
  Puka Puka Parade Collection

Dwight D. Eisenhower Presidential Library:
  Henry S. Aurand Papers
  J. Lawton Collins Papers
  Joseph M. Dodge Papers
  Dwight D. Eisenhower Papers as President of the United States
  U.S. President's Committee on Information Activities Abroad Records
  U.S. President's Committee to Study the U.S. Military Assistance Program Records
  White House Office, National Security Council Staff, Papers
  White House Office, Office of the Special Assistant for National Security Affairs
    Records
  White House Office, Office of the Staff Secretary Records

Harry S. Truman Library and Museum:
  Public Papers of the President

Hawaiian Collection, University of Hawai'i at Manoa Library

Hawai'i Congressional Papers Collection, University of Hawai'i at Manoa Library:
  Hiram L. Fong Papers
  Spark M. Matsunaga Papers

Hawai'i State Archives, Honolulu:
  John A. Burns Papers
  William F. Quinn Papers

Hoover Institution Archives, Stanford University:
  Charles T. R. Bohannan Papers
  Marshall Green Papers
  Edward Geary Lansdale Papers

Library of Congress, Washington, D.C.:
  Patsy T. Mink Papers
  Veterans History Project

Lopez Memorial Museum, Pasig City:
  Newspaper Files

Lyndon Baines Johnson Presidential Library, Austin:
  National Security File, Korea Country File
  National Security File, Philippines Country File
  National Security File, Vietnam Country File
  White House Central File—Hawaii

Pacific Northwest Labor and Civil Rights Project, University of Washington:
  Antiwar and Radical History Project

Ramon Magsaysay Center, Manila:
  Newspaper Clippings

Rizal Library, Ateneo de Manila University:
  American Historical Collection

Tamiment Library, New York University:
  Newspapers Collection

The United States Army Military History Institute, Carlisle Barracks:
  Charles T. R. Bohannan Collection
  MACV Command Historian's Collection
  James A. Van Fleet Papers
  William C. Westmoreland Collection

University of Philippines-Diliman Main Library, Quezon City:
  Filipiana Special Collection
  University Archives

U.S. National Archives II, College Park:
  RG 59, General Records of the Department of State
  RG 330, Records of the Office of the Secretary of Defense
  RG 334, Records of the Interservice Agencies
  RG 469, Records of U.S. Foreign Assistance Agencies, 1948–1961

RG 472, Records of the United States Forces in Southeast Asia, 1950–1975
RG 550, Records of the United States Army, Pacific, 1944–1972
RG 553, Records of the United States Army Training and Doctrine Command
RG 554, Records of General Headquarters, Far East Command

The Vietnam Center and Archive Digital Collection:
Bryan Grigsby Collection
John O'Donnell Collection
Douglas Pike Collection
Earl R. Rhine Collection
Ogden Williams Collection

The Wing Luke Museum of the Asian Pacific American Experience, Seattle:
Asian Pacific American Veterans Project
Doug Luna Oral History Interview Transcript, 1986; 2008
Jose Velasquez Oral History Interview Transcript, 1987
Larry Wong, Oral History Interview Transcript, 1987

INTERVIEWS BY AUTHOR

Albertini, Jim. April 27, 2011, phone.
Arima, James. August 25, 2009, Bellevue, WA.
Borgeson, Dale. February 4, 11, 13, 2012, phone.
Kudo, Kenji. September 26, 27, 2009, phone.
Masaoka, Kathy. August 27, 2010, July 7, 2016, Los Angeles, CA.
Masui, Stanford. July 2, 10, 2010, phone; April 13, 2011, Honolulu, HI.
Miller, Alan. July 27, 2010, phone.
Nagatani, Nick. September 19, 2009, Los Angeles, CA; September 23, 2009, phone.
Nakano, Tosh. September 17, 2009, Los Angeles, CA.
Nakayama, Mike. September 19, 2009, Los Angeles, CA; October 1, 2009, phone;
    August 26, 2010, Los Angeles, CA.
Pablo, Josefina. January 24, 2010, phone.
Taga, Chris. October 2, 2009, phone.
Witeck, John. July 29, 2010, phone; April 13, 2011, Honolulu, HI.
Wong, Michael. February 20, 27, 2010, phone.
Yanagita, Mike. August 26, 2010, phone.
Yee, Richard. September 18, 2009, Los Angeles, CA.

NEWSPAPERS AND PERIODICALS

AAPA (Asian American Political Alliance) Newspaper
Afro-American (Baltimore)

Attitude Check (Vista, CA)
Chicago Daily Tribune
Chicago Defender
Cry Out (Clark Air Force Base)
Daily Mirror (Manila)
The Evening News (Manila)
Fort Ord Panorama
Getting Together (New York)
Gidra (Los Angeles)
Graphic (Manila)
Hawaii Free Press
The Hawaii Guardsmen
Hawaii Lightning News
Hawaii Pono Journal
Honolulu Advertiser
Honolulu Star-Bulletin
International Examiner (Seattle)
Kaleo O Hawaii (University of Hawai'i)
Liberated Barracks (Honolulu)
Manila Daily Bulletin
The Manila Times
New Dawn (San Francisco)
The New York Times
Omega Press (Koza, Okinawa)
Philippine Free Press (Manila)
Rafu Shimpo (Los Angeles)
San Francisco Chronicle
San Francisco Examiner
Saturday Evening Post
Seasick (Subic Bay Naval Base)
Semper Fi (Iwakuni)
Time Magazine
Tropic Lightning News
Washington Post
Weekly Nation (Manila)
The Whig (Clark Air Force Base)

GOVERNMENT PUBLICATIONS

Philippine Department of Foreign Affairs. *Ten Years of Philippine Progress*. Manila, 1956.

United States Comptroller General. "Review of U.S. Assistance to the Philippine Government in Support of the Philippine Civic Action Group." Report to the

Subcommittee on U.S. Security Agreements and Commitments Abroad, Committee of Foreign Relations, United States Senate. Washington, D.C.: U.S. Government Printing Office, 1971.

United States Congress. House. Committee on the Judiciary. "Naturalization of Alien Servicemen and Veterans." Report No. 223, 83d Congress, 1st Session. Washington, D.C.: U.S. Government Printing Office, 1953.

———. House. Dellums, The Honorable Ronald V. "Institutional Racism in the Military." *Congressional Record*. 118, pt. 6. 92d Congress, 2d Session. March 2, 1972.

———. House. Committee on Internal Security. "Investigation of Attempts to Subvert the United States Armed Forces." Hearings, 92d Congress, 2d Session. Washington, D.C.: U.S. Government Printing Office, 1972.

———. Senate. Committee on Armed Services. "Universal Military Training and Service Act." Report No. 117, 82d Congress, 1st Session. Washington, D.C.: U.S. Government Printing Office, 1951.

———. Senate. Internal Security Subcommittee, Senate Judiciary Committee. "The Anti-Vietnam Agitation and the Teach-In Movement: The Problem of Communist Infiltration and Exploitation." Staff Study, 89th Congress, 1st Session. Washington, D.C., October 25, 1965.

———. Senate. "United States Security Agreements and Commitments Abroad: Part 1: The Republic of the Philippines." Subcommittee on U.S. Security Agreements and Commitments Abroad, Committee on Foreign Relations. 91st Congress, 1st Session. Washington, D.C.: U.S. Government Printing Office, 1969.

United States Department of Defense. *Annual Report for Fiscal Year 1968*. Washington, D.C.: U.S. Government Printing Office, 1971.

———. Office of the Deputy Assistant Secretary of Defense for Equal Opportunity and Safety Policy. *Task Force on the Administration of Military Justice in the Armed Forces*. Washington, D.C.: U.S. Government Printing Office, 1972.

UNPUBLISHED MANUSCRIPTS

Borgeson, Dale. "Early Days of the Seattle KDP Chapter." February 12, 2012.

Frentzos, Christos G. "From Seoul to Saigon: U.S.-Korean Relations and the Vietnam War." PhD diss., University of Houston, 2004.

Kindig, Jessie. "Demilitarized Zone: The GI Movement at Fort Lewis during the Vietnam War." MA thesis, University of Washington, 2009.

Krattiger, Angela S. "Hawai'i's Cold War: American Empire and the Fiftieth State." PhD diss., University of Hawai'i at Manoa, 2013.

Kwak, Tae Yang. "The Anvil of War: The Legacies of Korean Participation in the Vietnam War." PhD diss., Harvard University, 2006.

Miller, Alan S. "G.I. Resistance in the American Military Services: The Pacific Counseling Service during the Vietnam Era." August 1, 1983.

Ryu, Youngju. "The Neighbor and Politics of Literature in 1970's South Korea: Yi Mungu, Hwang Sŏkyŏng, Cho Sehŭi." PhD diss., University of California Los Angeles, 2006.

Saranillio, Dean Itsuji. "Seeing Conquest: Colliding Histories and the Cultural Politics of Hawai'i Statehood." PhD diss., University of Michigan, 2009.

Seidman, Derek. "Unquiet Americans: GI Dissent during the Vietnam War." PhD diss., Brown University, 2010.

Smoot, Karyn Mariko. "Unsettling the Gold Mountain: Asian Americans in Decolonial Resistance." BA thesis, University of Oregon, 2013.

Woods, Colleen P. "Bombs, Bureaucrats, and Rosary Beads: The United States, the Philippines, and the Making of Global Anti-Communism, 1945–1960." PhD diss., University of Michigan, 2012.

PUBLISHED BOOKS AND ARTICLES

Abernethy, David B. *The Dynamics of Global Dominance: European Overseas Empires, 1415–1980*. New Haven, CT: Yale University Press, 2000.

Abinales, Patricio N., and Donna J. Amoroso. *State and Society in the Philippines*. Lanham, MD: Rowman & Littlefield, 2005.

Ahern, Thomas L., Jr. *Vietnam Declassified: The CIA and Counterinsurgency*. Lexington: The University Press of Kentucky, 2010.

Appy, Christian. *Working-Class War: American Combat Soldiers and Vietnam*. Chapel Hill: The University of North Carolina Press, 1993.

Atanasoski, Neda. *Humanitarian Violence: The U.S. Deployment of Diversity*. Minneapolis: University of Minnesota Press, 2013.

Azuma, Eiichiro. *Between Two Empires: Race, History, and Transnationalism in Japanese America*. New York: Oxford University Press, 2005.

———. "Brokering Race, Culture, and Citizenship: Japanese Americans in Occupied Japan and Postwar National Inclusion." *The Journal of American-East Asian Relations* 16 (Fall 2009): 183–211.

Bacevich, Andrew J. *The New American Militarism: How Americans Are Seduced by War*. New York: Oxford University Press, 2005.

Bailey, Beth. *America's Army: Making the All-Volunteer Force*. Cambridge, MA: Belknap, 2009.

Bailkin, Jordanna. *The Afterlife of Empire*. Berkeley: University of California Press, 2012.

Baldoz, Rick. *The Third Asiatic Invasion: Migration and Empire in Filipino America, 1898–1946*. New York: New York University Press, 2011.

Baldwin, Frank, Diane Jones, and Michael Jones. *America's Rented Troops: South Koreans in Vietnam*. N.p.: American Friends Service Committee, 1975.

Bascara, Victor. *Model-Minority Imperialism*. Minneapolis: University of Minnesota Press, 2008.

Bell, Roger. *Last among Equals: Hawaiian Statehood and American Politics.* Honolulu: University of Hawai'i Press, 1984.

Bello, Walden. *The Anti-Development State: The Political Economy of Permanent Crisis in the Philippines.* Quezon City: Department of Sociology, University of the Philippines, Diliman, 2004.

———. "From American Lake to a People's Pacific in the Twenty-First Century." In *Militarized Currents: Toward a Decolonized Future in Asia and the Pacific,* edited by Setsu Shigematsu and Keith L. Camacho, 318–19. Minneapolis: University of Minnesota Press, 2011.

Bender, Thomas E., and Jana K. Lipman. "Introduction: Through the Looking Glass: U.S. Empire through the Lens of Labor History." In *Making the Empire Work: Labor and United States Imperialism,* edited by Thomas E. Bender and Jana K. Lipman, 1–32. New York: New York University Press, 2015.

Benjamin, Walter. *Illuminations: Essays and Reflections.* New York: Random House, 2007.

Bernad, Miguel A. *Adventure in Viet-Nam: The Story of Operation Brotherhood, 1954–1957.* Manila: Operation Brotherhood International, 1974.

———. *Filipinos in Laos: The True Story of a Remarkable Asian People Partnership.* Manila: Operation Brotherhood International, 1974.

Bevacqua, Michael Lujan. "The Exceptional Life and Death of a Chamorro Soldier: Tracing the Militarization of Desire in Guam, USA." In *Militarized Currents: Toward a Decolonized Future in Asia and the Pacific,* edited by Setsu Shigematsu and Keith L. Camacho, 33–62. Minneapolis: University of Minnesota Press, 2010.

Blackburn, Robert M. *Mercenaries and Lyndon Johnson's "More Flags": The Hiring of Korean, Filipino and Thai Soldiers in the Vietnam War.* Jefferson, N.C.: McFarland, 1994.

Bonner, Raymond. *Waltzing with a Dictator: The Marcos and the Making of American Policy.* New York: Times Books, 1987.

Borden, William S. *The Pacific Alliance: United States Foreign Economic Policy and Japanese Trade Recovery, 1947–1955.* Madison: University of Wisconsin Press, 1984.

Bradley, Mark Philip. *Imagining Vietnam and America: The Making of Postcolonial Vietnam, 1919–1950.* Chapel Hill: University of North Carolina Press, 2000.

———. *Vietnam at War.* New York: Oxford University Press, 2009.

Bradley, Mark Philip, and Marilyn B. Young, eds. *Making Sense of the Vietnam Wars: Local, National, and Transnational Perspectives.* New York: Oxford University Press, 2008.

Brazinsky, Gregg. *Nation Building in South Korea: Koreans, Americans, and the Making of a Democracy.* Chapel Hill: University of North Carolina Press, 2007.

Briggs, Laura, Gladys McCormick, and J. T. Ways. "Transnationalism: A Category of Analysis." *American Quarterly* 60 (2008): 625–48.

Burk, James. "Citizenship Status and Military Service: The Quest for Inclusion by Minorities and Conscientious Objectors." *Armed Forces and Society* 21 (Summer 1995): 503–29.

Bush, Roderick. *The End of White World Supremacy: Black Internationalism and the Problem of the Color Line.* Philadelphia: Temple University Press, 2009.

Butler, Judith. *Precarious Life: The Powers of Mourning and Violence.* London: Verso, 2004.

Byrd, Jodi A. *The Transit of Empire: Indigenous Critiques of Colonialism.* Minneapolis: University of Minnesota Press, 2011.

Cacho, Lisa. *Social Death: Racialized Rightlessness and the Criminalization of the Unprotected.* New York: New York University Press, 2012.

Camacho, Keith L. *Cultures of Commemoration: The Politics of War, Memory, and History of the Mariana Islands.* Honolulu: University of Hawai'i Press, 2011.

Camacho, Keith L., and Laurel A. Monnig. "Uncomfortable Fatigues: Chamorro Soldiers, Gendered Identities, and the Question of Decolonization in Guam." In *Militarized Currents: Toward a Decolonized Future in Asia and the Pacific,* edited by Setsu Shigematsu and Keith L. Camacho, 147–80. Minneapolis: University of Minnesota Press, 2010.

Camp, Jordan T. *Incarcerating the Crisis: Freedom Struggles and the Rise of the Neoliberal State.* Berkeley: University of California Press, 2016.

Canaday, Margot. *The Straight State: Sexuality and Citizenship in Twentieth-Century America.* Princeton, N.J.: Princeton University Press, 2009.

Capozzola, Christopher. "Minutemen for the World: Empire, Citizenship, and the National Guard." In *Colonial Crucible: Empire in the Making of the Modern American State,* edited by Alfred W. McCoy and Francisco A. Scarano, 421–30. Madison: University of Wisconsin Press, 2009.

Carafano, James Jay. "Mobilizing Europe's Stateless: America's Plan for a Cold War Army." *Journal of Cold War Studies* 1 (Spring 1999): 61–85.

Carter, April. "Liberalism and the Obligation of Military Service." *Political Studies* 46 (1998): 68–81.

Chambers, John Whiteclay. *To Raise an Army: The Draft Comes to Modern America.* New York: Free Press, 1987.

Chang, Kornel. *Pacific Connections: The Making of the U.S.-Canadian Borderlands.* Berkeley: University of California Press, 2012.

Chapman, Jessica M. *Cauldron of Resistance: Ngo Dinh Diem, the United States, and 1950s Southern Vietnam.* Ithaca, NY: Cornell University Press, 2013.

Chavez, Ernesto. *Mi Raza Primero! Nationalism, Identity, and Insurgency in the Chicano Movement in Los Angeles, 1966–1978.* Berkeley: University of California Press, 2002.

Chen, Kuan-Hsing. *Asia as Method: Toward Deimperialization.* Durham, NC: Duke University Press, 2010.

Cheng, Cindy I-Fen. *Citizens of Asian America: Democracy and Race during the Cold War.* New York: New York University Press, 2013.

Chong, Sylvia Shin Huey. *The Oriental Obscene: Violence and Racial Fantasies in the Vietnam Era*. Durham, NC: Duke University Press, 2012.

Choy, Catherine Ceniza. *Empire of Care: Nursing and Migration in Filipino American History*. Durham, NC: Duke University Press, 2003.

Churchill, Thomas. *Triumph over Marcos: A Story Based on the Lives of Gene Viernes & Silme Domingo, Filipino American Cannery Union Organizers, Their Assassination, and the Trial That Followed*. Seattle: Open Hand Publishing, 1995.

Cohen, Deborah. "Fighting for 'Freedom': The End of Conscription and the Neoliberal Project of Citizenship in the United States." *Citizenship Studies* 10, no. 2 (2006): 167–83.

Cohen, Eliot A. *Citizens and Soldiers: The Dilemmas of Military Service*. Ithaca, NY: Cornell University Press, 1985.

Constantino, Renato. *The Making of a Filipino: A Story of Philippine Colonial Politics*. Quezon City, Philippines: Malaya Books, 1969.

Cooper, Frederick, and Ann Laura Stoler, eds. *Tensions of Empire: Colonial Cultures in a Bourgeois World*. Berkeley: University of California Press, 1997.

Cooper, George, and Gavan Daws. *Land and Power in Hawaii: The Democratic Years*. Honolulu: University of Hawai'i Press, 1985.

Corr, Anders. *No Trespassing! Squatting, Rent Strikes, and Land Struggles Worldwide*. Boston: South End Press, 1999.

Cortright, David. *Soldiers in Revolt: GI Resistance during the Vietnam War*. Chicago: Haymarket Books, 2005.

Craig, Campbell, and Fredrik Logevall. *America's Cold War: The Politics of Insecurity*. Cambridge, MA: Belknap, 2009.

Cullather, Nick. *Illusions of Influence: The Political Economy of United States–Philippine Relations, 1942–1960*. Palo Alto, CA: Stanford University Press, 1994.

Cumings, Bruce. *Origins of the Korean War: Liberation and the Emergence of Separate Regimes, 1945–1947*. Princeton, NJ: Princeton University Press, 1981.

———. *Korea's Place in the Sun: A Modern History*. New York: W. W. Norton, 2005.

———. *Dominion from Sea to Sea: Pacific Ascendency and American Power*. New Haven, CT: Yale University Press, 2009.

———. *The Korean War: A History*. New York: Modern Library, 2010.

Dang, Janet. "The Wounds of War and Racism: Groundbreaking Study Now Examining Vietnam's Effect on Asian American Troops." *AsianWeek*, December 3–9, 1998.

Daum, Andreas W., Lloyd C. Gardner, and Wilfried Mausbach, eds. *America, the Vietnam War, and the World: Comparative and International Perspectives*. New York: Cambridge University Press, 2003.

Davis, Sasha. *The Empires' Edge: Militarization, Resistance, and Transcending Hegemony in the Pacific*. Athens: The University of Georgia Press, 2015.

DeCamp, Richard. "The GI Movement in Asia." *Bulletin of Concerned Asian Scholars* 4 (Winter 1971): 109–18.

De Genova, Nicholas, "Introduction: Latino and Asian Racial Formations at the Frontiers of U.S. Nationalism." In *Racial Transformations: Latinos and Asians*

Remaking the United States, edited by Nicholas De Genova, 1–22. Durham, NC: Duke University Press, 2005.

De Nike, Howard J. *Mission (Un)Essential: Contemplations of a Civilian Lawyer in the Vietnam War.* Berlin: Harald Kater Publishers, 2000.

Denning, Michael. *The Cultural Front: The Laboring of American Culture in the Twentieth Century.* London: Verso, 1997.

De Vera, Arleen. "Without Parallel: The Local 7 Deportation Cases, 1949–1955." *Amerasia Journal* 20, no. 2 (1994): 1–25.

Dewing, Rolland. *Wounded Knee: The Meaning and Significance of the Second Incident.* New York: Irvington Publishers, 1985.

Diaz, Vicente M. "Deliberating 'Liberation Day': Identity, History, Memory, and War in Guam." In *Perilous Memories: The Asia-Pacific War(s),* edited by T. Fujitani, Geoffrey M. White, and Lisa Yoneyama, 155–80. Durham, NC: Duke University Press, 2001.

Dower, John W. *War without Mercy: Race and Power in the Pacific War.* New York: Pantheon, 1986.

———. *Embracing Defeat: Japan in the Wake of World War II.* New York: W. W. Norton, 1999.

Drinnon, Richard. *Facing West: The Metaphysics of Indian-Hating and Empire-Building.* Minneapolis: University of Minnesota Press, 1980.

Dudziak, Mary L. *Cold War Civil Rights: Race and the Image of American Democracy.* Princeton, NJ: Princeton University Press, 2000.

Du Bois, W. E. B. *The Souls of Black Folk.* New York: Johnson, 1968.

———. *Color and Democracy: Colonies and Peace.* New York: Harcourt, Brace, and Company, 1945.

Duus, Masayo Umezawa. *Unlikely Liberators: The Men of the 100th and 442nd.* Honolulu: University of Hawai'i Press, 1987.

Elbaum, Max. *Revolution in the Air: Sixties Radicals Turn to Lenin, Mao, and Che.* London: Verso, 2002.

Ellsberg, Daniel. *Secrets: A Memoir of Vietnam and the Pentagon Papers.* New York: Penguin, 2002.

Enloe, Cynthia. *Bananas, Beaches, and Bases: Making Feminist Sense of International Politics.* Berkeley: University of California Press, 2000.

Espiritu, Augusto. "Journeys of Discovery and Difference: Transnational Politics and the Union of Democratic Filipinos." In *The Transnational Politics of Asian Americans,* edited by Christian Collet and Pei-te Lien, 38–55. Philadelphia: Temple University Press, 2009.

Espiritu, Yen Le. *Homebound: Filipino American Lives across Cultures, Communities, and Countries.* Berkeley: University of California Press, 2003.

———. "The 'We-Win-Even-When-We-Lose' Syndrome: U.S. Press Coverage of the Twenty-Fifth Anniversary of the 'Fall of Saigon.'" *American Quarterly* 58 (June 2006): 329–52.

———. *Body Counts: The Vietnam War and Militarized Refugees.* Berkeley: University of California Press, 2014.

Fanon, Frantz. *Toward an African Revolution.* New York: Grove, 1979.

———. *The Wretched of the Earth.* New York: Grove, 2005 [1961].

Farish, Matthew. *The Contours of America's Cold War.* Minneapolis: University of Minnesota Press, 2010.

Feffer, John. "The Other Vietnam Syndrome." *LA Review of Books,* September 8, 2014.

Feldman, Keith P. *A Shadow over Palestine: The Imperial Life of Race in America.* Minneapolis: University of Minnesota Press, 2015.

Ferber, Michael, and Staughton Lynd. *The Resistance.* Boston: Beacon Press, 1971.

Ferguson, Kathy E., and Phyllis Turnbull. *Oh, Say, Can You See? The Semiotics of the Military in Hawai'i.* Minneapolis: University of Minnesota Press, 1999.

Figley, Charles R., and Seymour Leventman. *Strangers at Home: Vietnam Veterans since the War.* New York: Praeger, 1980.

Fishkin, Shelley Fisher. "Crossroads of Cultures: The Transnational Turn in American Studies; Presidential Address at the American Studies Association, November 12, 2004." *American Quarterly* 57 (2005): 17–57.

Foley, Michael S. *Confronting the War Machine: Draft Resistance during the Vietnam War.* Chapel Hill: The University of North Carolina Press, 2003.

Franklin, H. Bruce. *M.I.A. or Mythmaking in America.* New York: Lawrence Hill, 1992.

Friedman, Andrew. *Covert Capital: Landscapes of Denial and the Making of U.S. Empire in the Suburbs of Northern Virginia.* Berkeley: University of California Press, 2014.

Friedman, Hal M. *Governing the American Lake: The U.S. Defense and Administration of the Pacific, 1945–1947.* East Lansing: Michigan State University Press, 2007.

Fujikane, Candace, and Jonathan Y. Okamura, eds. *Asian Settler Colonialism: From Local Governance to the Habits of Everyday Life in Hawai'i.* Honolulu: University of Hawai'i Press, 2008.

Fujimoto, Hiroshi. "Japan and the War in Southeast Asia, 1965–67." In *International Perspectives on Vietnam,* edited by Lloyd C. Gardner and Ted Gittinger, 176–85. College Station: Texas A&M University Press, 2000.

Fujino, Diane C. *Heartbeat of Struggle: The Revolutionary Life of Yuri Kochiyama.* Minneapolis: University of Minnesota Press, 2005.

———. *Samurai among Panthers: Richard Aoki on Race, Resistance, and a Paradoxical Life.* Minneapolis: University of Minnesota Press, 2012.

Fujitani, T., Geoffrey M. White, and Lisa Yoneyama, eds. *Perilous Memories: The Asia-Pacific War(s).* Durham, NC: Duke University Press, 2001.

Fujitani, Takashi. "Right to Kill, Right to Make Live: Koreans as Japanese and Japanese as Americans during WWII." *Representations* 99 (Summer 2007): 13–39.

———. *Race for Empire: Koreans as Japanese and Japanese as Americans during World War II.* Berkeley: University of California Press, 2011.

Fujita-Rony, Dorothy B. *American Workers, Colonial Power: Philippine Seattle and the Transpacific West, 1919–1941.* Berkeley: University of California Press, 2003.

Fukumura, Yoko, and Martha Matsuoka. "Redefining Security: Okinawan Women's Resistance to U.S. Militarism." In *Women's Activism and Globalization: Linking Local Struggles and Global Politics,* edited by Nancy A. Naples and Manisha Dasai. London: Routledge, 2002.

Gaddis, John Lewis. *Strategies of Containment: A Critical Appraisal of Postwar American National Security Policy.* New York: Oxford University Press, 1982.

Gaerlan, Barbara S. "The Movement in the United States to Oppose Martial Law in the Philippines, 1972–1991. An Overview." *Pilipinas* 33 (1999): 75–98.

Gatewood,Willard B., Jr. *Black Americans and the White Man's Burden, 1898–1903.* Urbana: University of Illinois Press, 1975.

Gibby, Bryan R. *Will to Win: American Military Advisors in Korea, 1946–1953.* Tuscaloosa: University of Alabama Press, 2012.

Gilmore, Ruth Wilson. *Golden Gulag: Prisons, Surplus, Crisis, and Opposition in Globalizing California.* Berkeley: University of California Press, 2007.

Gilroy, Paul. *The Black Atlantic: Modernity and Double Consciousness.* Cambridge, MA: Harvard University Press, 1995.

Goff, Stanley, and Robert Sanders. *Brothers: Black Soldiers in the Nam.* Novato, CA: Presidio Press, 1982.

Goldstein, Alyosha. "Introduction: Toward a Genealogy of the U.S. Colonial Present." In *Formations of United States Colonialism,* edited by Alyosha Goldstein. Durham, NC: Duke University Press, 2014.

Gonzalez, Vernadette Vicuña. "Military Bases, 'Royalty Trips,' and Imperial Modernities: Gendered and Racialized Labor in the Postcolonial Philippines." *Frontiers* 28 (2007): 28–59.

———. *Securing Paradise: Tourism and Militarism in Hawai'i and the Philippines.* Durham, NC: Duke University Press, 2013.

Goodyear-Ka'opua, Noelani, Ikaika Hussey, and Erin Kahunawaika'ala Wright, eds. *A Nation Rising: Hawaiian Movements for Life, Land, and Sovereignty.* Durham, NC: Duke University Press, 2014.

Gordon, Avery F. *Ghostly Matters: Haunting and the Sociological Imagination.* Minneapolis: University of Minnesota Press, 1997.

Green, Michael Cullen. *Black Yanks in the Pacific: Race in the Making of American Military Empire after World War II.* Ithaca, NY: Cornell University Press, 2010.

Gregory, Derek. *The Colonial Present: Afghanistan, Palestine, Iraq.* Malden, MA: Blackwell, 2004.

Habal, Estella. *San Francisco's International Hotel: Mobilizing the Filipino American Community in the Anti-Eviction Movement.* Philadelphia: Temple University Press, 2007.

Hall, Stuart, et al. *Policing the Crisis: Mugging, the State, and Law and Order.* London: MacMillan, 1978.

Haney Lopez, Ian F. *White by Law: The Legal Construction of Race.* New York: New York University Press, 1996.

Havens, Thomas R. H. *Fire across the Sea: The Vietnam War and Japan, 1965–1975.* Princeton, NJ: Princeton University Press, 1987.

Hernandez, Kelly Lytle. *Migra! A History of the U.S. Border Patrol*. Berkeley: University of California Press, 2010.

Hershberger, Mary. *Traveling to Vietnam: American Peace Activists and the War*. Syracuse, NY: Syracuse University Press, 1998.

Ho, Fred, ed. *Legacy to Liberation: Politics and Culture of Radical Asian Pacific America*. New York: Big Red Media, 2000.

Hobson, Emily K. *Lavender and Red: Liberation and Solidarity in the Gay and Lesbian Left*. Berkeley: University of California Press, 2016.

Hohn, Maria, and Seungsook Moon, eds. *Over There: Living with the U.S. Military Empire from World War Two to the Present*. Durham, NC: Duke University Press, 2010.

Horne, Gerald. *Race War! White Supremacy and the Japanese Attack on the British Empire*. New York: New York University Press, 2004.

HoSang, Daniel Martinez. *Racial Propositions: Ballot Initiatives and the Making of Postwar California*. Berkeley: University of California Press, 2010.

Hoskins, Janet, and Viet Thanh Nguyen, eds. *Transpacific Studies: Framing an Emerging Field*. Honolulu: University of Hawai'i Press, 2014.

Hsu, Madeline Y. *The Good Immigrants: How the Yellow Peril Became the Model Minority*. Princeton, NJ: Princeton University Press, 2015.

Hunt, Andrew. *The Turning: A History of Vietnam Veterans against the War*. New York: New York University Press, 2001.

Hunt, David. *Vietnam's Southern Revolution: From Peasant Insurrection to Total War*. Amherst: University of Massachusetts Press, 2008.

Hunt, Michael H. *Ideology and U.S. Foreign Policy*. New Haven, CT: Yale University Press, 1987.

Hwang, Sok-yong. *The Shadow of Arms*. Translated by Chun Kyung-ja. New York: Seven Stories Press, 2014.

Imada, Adria L. *Aloha America: Hula Circuits through the U.S. Empire*. Durham, NC: Duke University Press, 2012.

Immerwahr, Daniel. *Thinking Small: The United States and the Lure of Community Development*. Cambridge, MA: Harvard University Press, 2015.

Ireland, Brian. *The US Military in Hawai'i: Colonialism, Memory and Resistance*. London: Palgrave MacMillan, 2011.

Ives, Christopher K. *U.S. Special Forces and Counterinsurgency in Vietnam: Military Innovation and Institutional Failure, 1961–1963*. New York: Routledge, 2007.

Jacobs, James B., and Leslie Anne Hayes. "Aliens in the U.S. Armed Forces: A Historico-Legal Analysis." *Armed Forces and Society* 7 (Winter, 1981): 187–208.

Jacobs, Seth. *America's Miracle Man in Vietnam: Ngo Dinh Diem, Religion, Race, and U.S. Intervention in Southeast Asia, 1950–1957*. Durham, NC: Duke University Press, 2005.

Jacobson, Matthew Frye. *Barbarian Virtues: The United States Encounters Foreign Peoples at Home and Abroad, 1876–1917*. New York: Hill and Wang, 2000.

Jager, Sheila Miyoshi. *Brothers at War: The Unending Conflict in Korea*. New York: W. W. Norton, 2014.

Jeffords, Susan. *The Remasculinization of America: Gender and the Vietnam War.* Bloomington: Indiana University Press, 1987.

Jo, Eun Seo. "Fighting for Peanuts: Reimagining South Korean Soldiers' Participation in the Wŏllam Boom." *Journal of American-East Asian Relations* 21, no. 1 (2014): 57–87.

Johnson, Chalmers. *Blowback: The Costs and Consequences of American Empire.* New York: Henry Holt, 2000.

———. *The Sorrows of Empire: Militarism, Secrecy, and the End of the Republic.* New York: Henry Holt, 2004.

Jung, Moon-Ho. *Coolies and Cane: Race, Labor, and Sugar in the Age of Emancipation.* Baltimore: Johns Hopkins University Press, 2006.

———. "Seditious Subjects: Race, State Violence, and the U.S. Empire." *The Journal of Asian American Studies* 14 (June 2011): 221–47.

———. "Introduction: Opening Salvo." In *The Rising Tide of Color: Race, State Violence, and Radical Movements across the Pacific,* edited by Moon-Ho Jung, 4–35. Seattle: University of Washington Press, 2014.

Jung, Moon-Kie. *Reworking Race: The Making of Hawaii's Interracial Labor Movement.* New York: Columbia University Press, 2005.

Kajihiro, Kyle. "The Militarizing of Hawai'i: Occupation, Accommodation, and Resistance." In *Asian Settler Colonialism,* edited by Candace Fujikane and Jonathan Y. Okamura, 170–94. Honolulu: University of Hawai'i Press, 2008.

Kaplan, Amy. *The Anarchy of Empire in the Making of U.S. Culture.* Cambridge, MA: Harvard University Press, 2002.

———. "Black and Blue on San Juan Hill." In *Cultures of United States Imperialism,* edited by Amy Kaplan and Donald E. Pease. Durham, NC: Duke University Press, 1993.

Kaplan, Amy, and Donald E. Pease, eds. *Cultures of United States Imperialism.* Durham, NC: Duke University Press, 1993.

Kent, Noel J. *Hawaii: Islands under the Influence.* New York: Monthly Review Press, 1983.

Kelley, Robin D. G. *Race Rebels: Culture, Politics, and the Black Working Class.* New York: The Free Press, 1994.

———. *Freedom Dreams: The Black Radical Imagination.* New York: Beacon, 2002.

———. "How the World Was One: The African Diaspora and the Re-Mapping of U.S. History." In *Rethinking American History in a Global Age,* edited by Thomas Bender, 123–47. Berkeley: University of California Press, 2002.

Kerkvliet, Benedict J. *The Huk Rebellion: A Study of Peasant Revolt in the Philippines.* Berkeley: University of California Press, 1977.

Khalili, Laleh. *Time in the Shadows: Confinement in Counterinsurgencies.* Stanford, CA: Stanford University Press, 2013.

Kiang, Peter Nien-chu. "About Face: Recognizing Asian & Pacific American Vietnam Veterans in Asian American Studies." *Amerasia Journal* 17 (1991): 22–40.

Kim, Byung-Kook, and Ezra F. Vogel, eds. *The Park Chung Hee Era: The Transformation of South Korea.* Cambridge, MA: Harvard University Press, 2011.

Kim, Jodi. *Ends of Empire: Asian American Critique and the Cold War.* Minneapolis: University of Minnesota Press, 2010.

Klein, Christina. *Cold War Orientalism: Asia in the Middlebrow Imagination, 1945–1961.* Berkeley: University of California Press, 2003.

Knoll, Erwin, and Judith N. McFadden. *War Crimes and the American Conscience.* New York: Holt, Rinehart and Winston, 1970.

Korean House for International Solidarity. "Dream for Peace and Reconciliation: Korean Soldiers in Vietnam and the Scar of War." *Korea Report 21* vol. 1, no. 1 (2000).

Kramer, Paul A. *The Blood of Government: Race, Empire, the United States, and the Philippines.* Chapel Hill: University of North Carolina Press, 2006.

———. "Power and Connection: Imperial Histories of the United States in the World." *American Historical Review* 116 (December 2011): 1348–91.

Krebs, Ronald R. *Fighting for Rights: Military Service and the Politics of Citizenship.* Ithaca, NY: Cornell University Press, 2006.

Kurashige, Lon. *Japanese American Celebration and Conflict: A History of Ethnic Identity and Festival in Los Angeles, 1934–1990.* Berkeley: University of California Press, 2002.

Kurashige, Scott. *The Shifting Grounds of Race: Black and Japanese Americans in the Making of Multiethnic Los Angeles.* Princeton, NJ: Princeton University Press, 2008.

Kwon, Heonik. *After the Massacre: Commemoration and Consolation in Ha My and My Lai.* Berkeley: University of California Press, 2006.

———. *The Other Cold War.* New York: Columbia University Press, 2010.

———. "The Transpacific Cold War." In *Transpacific Studies: Framing an Emerging Field,* edited by Janet Hoskins and Viet Thanh Nguyen, 64–84. Honolulu: University of Hawai'i Press, 2014.

Labor Research Association. *U.S. and the Philippines: The Economic, Social and Political Aspects of the Fight for Full Freedom and National Development.* Lansing, MI: International Publishers, 1958.

LaFeber, Walter. *The New Empire: An Interpretation of American Expansion, 1860–1898.* Ithaca, NY: Cornell University Press, 1963.

Lake, Marilyn, and Henry Reynolds. *Drawing the Global Colour Line: White Men's Countries and the International Challenge of Racial Equality.* Cambridge, UK: Cambridge University Press, 2008.

Lansdale, Edward Geary. *In the Midst of Wars: An American's Mission to Southeast Asia.* New York: Harper & Row, 1972.

Larsen, Stanley Robert, and James Lawton Collins, Jr. *Allied Participation in Vietnam.* Washington, D.C.: Department of the Army, 1975.

Latham, Michael E. *Modernization as Ideology: American Social Science and "Nation-Building" in the Kennedy Era.* Chapel Hill: University of North Carolina Press, 2000.

Lawrence, Mark Atwood. *Assuming the Burden: Europe and the American Commitment to War in Vietnam.* Berkeley: University of California Press, 2005.

Lawrence, Mark Atwood, and Fredrik Logevall, eds. *The First Vietnam War: Colonial Conflict and Cold War Crisis.* Cambridge, MA: Harvard University Press, 2007.

Lederer, William J., and Eugene Burdick. *The Ugly American.* New York: W. W. Norton, 1958.

Lee, Chi-Op, and Stephen M. Tharp. *Call Me 'Speedy Lee': Memoirs of a Korean War Soldier.* Seoul: Wonmin Publishing House Company, 2001.

Lee, Erika, and Naoko Shibusawa. "What Is Transnational Asian American History?" *Journal of Asian American Studies* 8 (October 2005): vii–xvii.

Lee, Jin-kyung. "Surrogate Military, Subimperialism, and Masculinity: South Korea in the Vietnam War, 1965–1973." *positions:east asia cultures critique* 17, no. 3 (2009): 655–82.

———. *Service Economies: Militarism, Sex Work, and Migrant Labor in South Korea.* Minneapolis: University of Minnesota Press, 2010.

Lee, Jung-Hoon. "Normalization of Relations with Japan." In *The Park Chung Hee Era: The Transformation of South Korea,* edited by Byung-kook Kim and Ezra F. Vogel, 430–56. Cambridge, MA: Harvard University Press, 2011.

Lee, Min Yong. "The Vietnam War: South Korea's Search for National Security." In *The Park Chung Hee Era: The Transformation of South Korea,* edited by Byung-kook Kim and Ezra F. Vogel, 403–29. Cambridge, MA: Harvard University Press, 2011.

Lee, Namhee. *The Making of Minjung: Democracy and the Politics of Representation in South Korea.* Ithaca, NY: Cornell University Press, 2007.

Leffler, Melvyn P. *A Preponderance of Power: National Security, the Truman Administration, and the Cold War.* Palo Alto, CA: Stanford University Press, 1992.

Lekus, Ian. "Queer Harvests: Homosexuality, the U.S. New Left, and the Venceremos Brigades to Cuba." *Radical History Review* 89 (Spring 2004): 57–91.

Lembcke, Jerry. *The Spitting Image: Myth, Memory, and the Legacy of Vietnam.* New York: New York University Press, 2000.

Leventman, S., and P. Camacho. "The 'Gook' Syndrome: The Vietnam War as a Racial Encounter." In *Strangers at Home,* edited by C. R. Figley and S. Leventman, 55–70. New York: Praeger, 1980.

Lifton, Robert Jay. *Home from the War: Vietnam Veterans: Neither Victims nor Executioners.* New York: Simon and Schuster, 1973.

Lind, Ian. "Ring of Steel: Notes on the Militarization of Hawaii." *Social Process in Hawaii* 31 (1984/1985): 25–47.

Linn, Brian McAllister. *Guardians of Empire: The U.S. Army and the Pacific, 1902–1940.* Chapel Hill: University of North Carolina Press, 1997.

Lipman, Jana. *Guantanamo: A Working-Class History between Empire and Revolution.* Berkeley: University of California Press, 2009.

Lipsitz, George. "'Frantic to Join . . . the Japanese Army': The Asia Pacific War in the Lives of African American Soldiers and Civilians." In *Politics of Culture in the Shadow of Capital,* edited by Lisa Lowe and David Lloyd, 324–53. Durham, NC: Duke University Press, 1997.

Logevall, Fredrik. "'There Ain't No Daylight': Lyndon Johnson and the Politics of Escalation." In *Making Sense of the Vietnam Wars,* edited by Mark Philip Bradley and Marilyn B. Young, 91–108. New York: Oxford University Press, 2008.

Loo, Chalsa M. "Race-Related PTSD: The Asian American Vietnam Veteran." *Journal of Traumatic Stress* 7 (1994): 637–56.

Louis, Steve, and Glenn Omatsu, eds. *Asian Americans: The Movement and the Moment.* Los Angeles: UCLA Asian American Studies Center Press, 2001.

Lowe, Lisa. *Immigrant Acts: On Asian American Cultural Politics.* Durham, NC: Duke University Press, 1997.

———. *The Intimacies of Four Continents.* Durham, NC: Duke University Press, 2014.

Lowe, Lisa, and David Lloyd, eds. *The Politics of Culture in the Shadow of Capital.* Durham, NC: Duke University Press, 1997.

Maeda, Daryl J. *Chains of Babylon: The Rise of Asian America.* Minneapolis: University of Minnesota Press, 2009.

Mahan, Alfred Thayer. *The Influence of Sea Power upon History, 1660–1783.* Cambridge, UK: Cambridge University Press, 2010 [1889].

Mamdani, Mahmood. *Citizen and Subject: Contemporary Africa and the Legacy of Late Colonialism.* Princeton, NJ: Princeton University Press, 1996.

———. *Good Muslim, Bad Muslim: America, the Cold War, and the Roots of Terror.* New York: Pantheon, 2004.

Mariscal, George, ed. *Aztlán and Vietnam: Chicano and Chicana Experiences of the War.* Berkeley: University of California Press, 1999.

Marquit, Erwin. "The Demobilization Movement of January 1946." *Nature, Society, and Thought* 15, no. 1 (2002): 5–39.

Mast, Robert H., and Anne B. Mast, eds. *Autobiography of Protest in Hawai'i.* Honolulu: University of Hawai'i Press, 1996.

Masuda, Hajimu. *Cold War Crucible: The Korean Conflict and the Postwar World.* Cambridge, MA: Harvard University Press, 2015.

Matsuda, Matt K. *Pacific Worlds: A History of Seas, Peoples, and Cultures.* New York: Cambridge University Press, 2012.

McAlister, Melani. *Epic Encounters: Culture, Media, and U.S. Interests in the Middle East, 1945–2000.* Berkeley: University of California Press, 2001.

McClain, Charles J. "Tortuous Path, Elusive Goal: The Asian Quest for American Citizenship." *Asian Law Journal* 2 (May 1995): 33–60.

McClintock, Michael. *Instruments of Statecraft: U.S. Guerrilla Warfare, Counter-Insurgency, Counter-Terrorism, 1940–1990.* New York: Pantheon, 1992.

McCormick, Thomas J. *America's Half-Century: United States Foreign Policy in the Cold War and After.* Baltimore: Johns Hopkins University Press, 1995.

McCoy, Alfred W. *Policing America's Empire: The United States, the Philippines, and the Rise of the Surveillance State.* Madison: The University of Wisconsin Press, 2009.

McGregor, Davianna Pomaika'i. "Statehood: Catalyst of the Twentieth-Century Kanaka 'Oiwi Cultural Renaissance and Sovereignty Movement." *Journal of Asian American Studies* 13 (October 2010): 311–26.

McGregor, Davianna Pomaikaʻi and Ibrahim Aoude. "'Our History, Our Way!': Ethnic Studies for Hawaiʻi's People." In *A Nation Rising: Hawaiian Movements for Life, Land, and Sovereignty,* edited by Noelani Goodyear-Kaʻopua, Ikaika Hussey, and Erin Kahunawaikaʻala Wright, 66–77. Durham, NC: Duke University Press, 2014.

Mehta, Uday Singh. *Liberalism and Empire: A Study in Nineteenth-Century British Thought.* Chicago: University of Chicago Press, 1999.

Melamed, Jodi. *Represent and Destroy: Rationalizing Violence in the New Racial Capitalism.* Minneapolis: University of Minnesota Press, 2011.

Memmi, Albert. *The Colonizer and the Colonized.* New York: Beacon Press, 1991 [1957].

Miller, Edward. *Misalliance: Ngo Dinh Diem, the United States, and the Fate of South Vietnam.* Cambridge, MA: Harvard University Press, 2013.

Millett, Allan R. "Captain James A. Hausman and the Formation of the Korean Army, 1945–1950." *Armed Forces and Society* 23, no. 4 (Summer 1997): 503–39.

MIS Veterans Club of Hawaiʻi. *Secret Valor: MIS Personnel, World War II, Pacific Theater, Pre-Pearl Harbor to September 8, 1951.* Honolulu: MIS Veterans Club of Hawaiʻi, 1993.

Molina, Natalia. *How Race Is Made in America: Immigration, Citizenship, and the Historical Power of Racial Scripts.* Berkeley: University of California Press, 2013.

Moon, Seungsook. *Militarized Modernity and Gendered Citizenship in South Korea.* Durham, NC: Duke University Press, 2005.

———. "In the U.S. Military but Not Quite of It: Contesting the Imperial Power in a Discourse of KATUSAS." In *Over There: Living with the U.S. Military Empire from World War II to the Present,* edited by Maria Hohn and Seungsook Moon, 231–57. Durham, NC: Duke University Press, 2010.

———. "Regulating Desire, Managing the Empire: U.S. Military Prostitution in South Korea, 1945–1970." In *Over There: Living with the U.S. Military Empire from World War II to the Present,* edited by Maria Hohn and Seungsook Moon, 38–77. Durham, NC: Duke University Press, 2010.

Moser, Richard. *The New Winter Soldiers: GI and Veteran Dissent during the Vietnam Era.* New Brunswick, NJ: Rutgers University Press, 1996.

Moyd, Michelle R. *Violent Intermediaries: African Soldiers, Conquest, and Everyday Colonialism in German East Africa.* Athens: Ohio University Press, 2014.

Mueller, Eric L. *Free to Die for Their Country: The Story of the Japanese American Draft Resisters in World War II.* Chicago: University of Chicago Press, 2001.

Murakawa, Naomi. *The First Civil Right: How Liberals Built Prison America.* New York: Oxford University Press, 2014.

Nakano, Satoshi. "Nation, Nationalism, and Citizenship in the Filipino World War II Veterans Equity Movement, 1945–1999." *Hitotsubashi Journal of Social Studies* 32 (2000): 33–53.

Nashel, Jonathan. *Edward Lansdale's Cold War.* Amherst: University of Massachusetts Press, 2005.

Nebolon, Juliet. "'Life Given Straight from the Heart': Settler Militarism, Biopolitics, and Public Health in Hawai'i during World War II." *American Quarterly* 69 (March 2017): 23–45.

Ngai, Mae M. *Impossible Subjects: Illegal Aliens and the Making of Modern America.* Princeton, NJ: Princeton University Press, 2005.

Nguyen, Mimi Thi. *The Gift of Freedom: War, Debt, and Other Refugee Passages.* Minneapolis: University of Minnesota Press, 2012.

Nguyen, Viet Thanh. *Nothing Ever Dies: Vietnam and the Memory of War.* Cambridge, MA: Harvard University Press, 2016.

Nguyen, Viet Thanh, and Janet Hoskins. "Introduction: Transpacific Studies: Critical Perspectives on an Emerging Field." In *Transpacific Studies: Framing an Emerging Field,* edited by Viet Thanh Nguyen and Janet Hoskins, 1–38. Honolulu: University of Hawai'i Press, 2014.

O'Brien, Tim. *The Things They Carried.* New York: Mariner Books, 2009.

Odo, Franklin. *No Sword to Bury: Japanese Americans in Hawaii during World War II.* Philadelphia: Temple University Press, 2004.

Okihiro, Gary Y. *Cane Fires: The Anti-Japanese Movement in Hawaii, 1865–1945.* Philadelphia: Temple University Press, 1991.

———. *Margins and Mainstreams: Asians in American History and Culture.* Philadelphia: Temple University Press, 1994.

Omatsu, Glenn. "The 'Four Prisons' and the Movements for Liberation." In *The State of Asian America: Activism and Resistance in the 1990s,* edited by Karin Aguilar-San Juan, 19–70. Boston: South End Press, 1994.

Omi, Michael, and Howard Winant. *Racial Formation in the United States.* 2nd ed. New York: Routledge, 1994.

Onishi, Yuichiro. *Transpacific Antiracism: Afro-Asian Solidarity in 20th-Century Black America, Japan, and Okinawa.* New York: New York University Press, 2013.

Oropeza, Lorena. *Raza Si! Guerra No! Chicano Protest and Patriotism during the Viet Nam War.* Berkeley: University of California Press, 2005.

Osorio, Jonathan Kamakawiwo'ole. "Hawaiian Souls: The Movement to Stop the U.S. Military Bombing of Kaho'olawe." In *A Nation Rising: Hawaiian Movements for Life, Land, and Sovereignty,* edited by Noelani Goodyear-Ka'opua, Ikaika Hussey, and Erin Kahunawaika'ala Wright, 137–60. Durham, NC: Duke University Press, 2014.

Paik, A. Naomi. *Rightlessness: Testimony and Redress in U.S. Prison Camps since World War II.* Chapel Hill: University of North Carolina Press, 2016.

Park, Joon Young. *Korea's Return to Asia: South Korean Foreign Policy, 1965–1975.* Seoul: Jin Heong Press, 1985.

Peery, Nelson. *Black Fire: The Making of an American Revolutionary.* New York: The New Press, 1994.

Phillips, Kimberly L. *War! What Is It Good For? Black Freedom Struggles and the U.S. Military from World War II to Iraq.* Chapel Hill: University of North Carolina Press, 2011.

Phillips, Rufus. *Why Vietnam Matters: An Eyewitness Account of Lessons Not Learned.* Annapolis, MD: Naval Institute Press, 2008.

Prashad, Vijay. *Everybody Was Kung Fu Fighting: Afro-Asian Connections and the Myth of Cultural Purity.* New York: Beacon, 2001.

———. *The Darker Nations: A People's History of the Third World.* New York: The New Press, 2008.

Pulido, Laura. *Black, Brown, Yellow & Left: Radical Activism in Los Angeles.* Berkeley: University of California Press, 2006.

Quinsaat, Jesse. "An Exercise on How to Join the Navy and Still Not See the World." In *Letters in Exile,* edited by Jesse Quinsaat et al., 96–110. Los Angeles: UCLA Asian American Studies Center Press, 1976.

Rafael, Vicente. *White Love and Other Events in Filipino History.* Durham, NC: Duke University Press, 2000.

Renda, Mary. *Taking Haiti: Military Occupation and the Culture of U.S. Imperialism, 1915–1940.* Chapel Hill: University of North Carolina Press, 2000.

Robinson, Cedric J. *Black Marxism: The Making of the Black Radical Tradition.* 2nd ed. Chapel Hill: University of North Carolina Press, 2000.

———. *Black Movements in America.* London: Routledge, 1997.

Robinson, Michael E. *Korea's Twentieth-Century Odyssey: A Short History.* Honolulu: University of Hawai'i Press, 2007.

Rodriguez, Robyn Magalit. *Migrants for Export: How the Philippine State Brokers Labor to the World.* Minneapolis: University of Minnesota Press, 2010.

Roediger, David R. "Gook: The Short History of an Americanism." *Monthly Review* 43 (March 1992): 50–54.

Rostow, Walt W. *An American Policy in Asia.* New York: Technology Press of Massachusetts Institute of Technology, 1955.

Ruth, Richard A. *In Buddha's Company: Thai Soldiers in the Vietnam War.* Honolulu: University of Hawai'i Press, 2011.

Ryu, Youngju. "Korea's Vietnam: Popular Culture, Patriarchy, Intertextuality." *The Review of Korean Studies* 12, no. 3 (2009): 101–23.

———. *Writers of the Winter Republic: Literature and Resistance in Park Chung Hee's Korea.* Honolulu: University of Hawai'i Press, 2015.

Said, Edward. *Orientalism.* New York: Vintage Books, 1979.

Sakai, Naoki. "On Romantic Love and Military Violence: Transpacific Imperialism and U.S.-Japan Complicity." In *Militarized Currents: Toward a Decolonized Future in Asia and the Pacific,* edited by Setsu Shigematsu and Keith L. Camacho, 205–22. Minneapolis: University of Minnesota Press, 2010.

Salyer, Lucy E. "Baptism by Fire: Race, Military Service, and U.S. Citizenship Policy, 1918–1935." *The Journal of American History* 91 (December 2004): 847–76.

Sandars, C. T. *America's Overseas Garrisons: The Leasehold Empire.* New York: Oxford University Press, 2000.

Saranillio, Dean Itsuji. "Colonial Amnesia: Rethinking Filipino 'American' Settler Empowerment in the U.S. Colony of Hawai'i." In *Asian Settler Colonialism,* edited by Candace Fujikane and Jonathan Y. Okamura, 256–78. Honolulu: University of Hawai'i Press, 2008.

———. "Colliding Histories: Hawai'i Statehood at the Intersection of Asians 'Ineligible to Citizenship' and Hawaiians 'Unfit for Self-Government.'" *Journal of Asian American Studies* 13 (October 2010): 283–309.

Schell, Jonathan. *The Military Half: An Account of Destruction in Quang Ngai and Quang Tin*. New York: Alfred A. Knopf, 1968.

Schirmer, Daniel B., and Stephen Rosskamm Shalom, eds. *The Philippines Reader: A History of Colonialism, Neocolonialism, Dictatorship, and Resistance*. Boston: Southend Press, 1987.

Scott, James C. *Domination and the Arts of Resistance: Hidden Transcripts*. New Haven, CT: Yale University Press, 1990.

Scott, Stanley L. "The Military Aid Program." *Annals of the American Academy of Political and Social Science* 278 (November 1951): 47–55.

Scott, Wilbur. *The Politics of Readjustment: Vietnam Veterans since the War*. New York: Aldine de Gruyter, 1993.

———. *Vietnam Veterans since the War: The Politics of PTSD, Agent Orange, and the National Memorial*. Norman: University of Oklahoma Press, 2004.

Seigel, Micol. "Beyond Compare: Comparative Method after the Transnational Turn." *Radical History Review* 91 (Winter 2005): 62–90.

Self, Robert O. *American Babylon: Race and the Struggle for Postwar Oakland*. Princeton, NJ: Princeton University Press, 2003.

Shalom, Stephen. *The United States and the Philippines: A Study of Neo-colonialism*. Quezon City, Philippines: New Day Publishers, 1986.

Shepard, Todd. *The Invention of Decolonization: The Algerian War and the Remaking of France*. Ithaca, NY: Cornell University Press, 2006.

Sherry, Michael S. *In the Shadow of War: The United States since the 1930s*. New Haven, CT: Yale University Press, 1995.

Sherwood, John Darrell. *Black Sailors, White Navy: Racial Unrest in the Fleet during the Vietnam War Era*. New York: New York University Press, 2007.

Shibusawa, Naoko. *America's Geisha Ally: Reimagining the Japanese Enemy*. Cambridge, MA: Harvard University Press, 2006.

Shibutani, Tamotsu. *The Derelicts of Company K: A Sociological Study of Demoralization*. Berkeley: University of California Press, 1978.

Shigematsu, Setsu, and Keith L. Camacho, eds. *Militarized Currents: Toward a Decolonized Future in Asia and the Pacific*. Minneapolis: University of Minnesota Press, 2010.

Shizuka, Karen L. *Serve the People: Making Asian America in the Long Sixties*. London: Verso, 2016.

Silva, Noenoe K. *Aloha Betrayed: Native Hawaiian Resistance to American Colonialism*. Durham, NC: Duke University Press, 2004.

Simbulan, Roland G. *The Bases of Our Insecurity: A Study of the US Military Bases in the Philippines*. Manila: BALAI Fellowship Inc., 1985.

Simpson, Bradley R. *Economists with Guns: Authoritarian Development and U.S.-Indonesian Relations, 1960–1968.* Palo Alto, CA: Stanford University Press, 2008.

Singh, Nikhil Pal. *Black Is a Country: Race and the Unfinished Struggle for Democracy.* Cambridge, MA: Harvard University Press, 2004.

———. "Racial Formation in an Age of Permanent War." In *Racial Formation in the Twenty-First Century,* edited by. Daniel Martinez HoSang, Oneka LaBennett, and Laura Pulido, 276–301. Berkeley: University of California Press, 2011.

Smith-Norris, Martha. *Domination and Resistance: The United States and the Marshall Islands during the Cold War.* Honolulu: University of Hawai'i Press, 2016.

Stanton, Shelby L. *The Rise and Fall of an American Army: U.S. Ground Forces in Vietnam, 1965–1973.* New York: Presidio, 1985.

Statler, Kathryn C. *Replacing France: The Origins of American Intervention in Vietnam.* Lexington: The University Press of Kentucky, 2007.

Statler, Kathryn C., and Andrew L. Johns, eds. *The Eisenhower Administration, the Third World, and the Globalization of the Cold War.* Lanham, MD: Rowman & Littlefield, 2006.

Stoler, Ann Laura. *Carnal Knowledge and Imperial Power: Race and the Intimate in Colonial Rule.* Durham, NC: Duke University Press, 2002.

———, ed. *Haunted by Empire: Geographies of Intimacy in North American History.* Durham, NC: Duke University Press, 2006.

———, "Colonial Archives and the Arts of Governance." *Archival Science* 2, no. 2 (2002): 87–109.

Szonyi, Michael. *Cold War Island: Quemoy on the Front Line.* New York: Cambridge University Press, 2008.

Tadiar, Neferti X. M. *Things Fall Away: Philippine Historical Experience and the Makings of Globalization.* Durham, NC: Duke University Press, 2009.

Trask, Haunani-Kay. "The Birth of the Modern Hawaiian Movement: Kalama Valley, O'ahu." *Hawaiian Journal of History* 21 (1987): 126–53.

Turner, Fred. *Echoes of Combat: The Viet Nam War in American Memory.* New York: Doubleday, 1992.

Turse, Nick. *Kill Anything That Moves: The Real American War in Vietnam.* New York: Metropolitan Books, 2013.

Uchida, Jun. *Brokers of Empire: Japanese Settler Colonialism in Korea, 1876–1945.* Cambridge, MA: Harvard University Press, 2011.

Ueunten, Wesley Iwao. "Rising Up from a Sea of Discontent: The 1970 Koza Uprising in U.S.-Occupied Okinawa." In *Militarized Currents: Toward a Decolonized Future in Asia and the Pacific,* edited by Setsu Shigematsu and Keith L. Camacho, 91–124. Minneapolis: University of Minnesota Press, 2010.

Umemoto, Karen. "'On Strike!' San Francisco State College Strike, 1968–69: The Role of Asian American Students." *Amerasia Journal* 15 (1989): 3–41.

Valentine, Douglas. *The Phoenix Program: America's Use of Terror in Vietnam.* New York: Morrow, 1990.

Valeriano, Napoleon D., and Charles T. R. Bohannan. *Counter-Guerilla Operations: The Philippine Experience*. Westport, CT: Praeger Security International, 2006 [1962].

Vietnam Veterans Against the War. *The Winter Soldier Investigation: An Inquiry into American War Crimes*. Boston: Beacon Press, 1972.

Von Eschen, Penny M. *Race against Empire: Black Americans and Anticolonialism, 1937–1957*. Ithaca, NY: Cornell University Press, 1997.

———, *Satchmo Blows Up the World: Jazz Ambassadors Play the Cold War*. Cambridge, MA: Harvard University Press, 2003.

Welchel, Toshio. *From Pearl Harbor to Saigon: Japanese American Soldiers and the Vietnam War*. London: Verso, 1999.

Westad, Odd Arne. *The Global Cold War: Third World Interventions and the Making of Our Times*. New York: Cambridge University Press, 2007.

Westheider, James E. *Fighting on Two Fronts: African Americans and the Vietnam War*. New York: New York University Press, 1999.

———, *The Vietnam War*. Santa Barbara, CA: Greenwood Publishing Group, 2007.

Wexler, Laura. *Tender Violence: Domestic Visions in an Age of U.S. Imperialism*. Chapel Hill: University of North Carolina Press, 2000.

Wilder, Gary. *Freedom Time: Negritude, Decolonization, and the Future of the World*. Durham, NC: Duke University Press, 2015.

Williams, William Appleman. *The Tragedy of American Diplomacy*. New York: W. W. Norton, 1959.

Wong, K. Scott. *Americans First: Chinese Americans and the Second World War*. Philadelphia: Temple University Press, 2005.

Wood, Ellen Meiksins. *Empire of Capital*. London: Verso, 2003.

Wu, Ellen D. *The Color of Success: Asian Americans and the Origins of the Model Minority*. Princeton, NJ: Princeton University Press, 2013.

Wu, Judy Tzu-Chun. *Radicals on the Road: Internationalism, Orientalism, and Feminism during the Vietnam Era*. Ithaca, NY: Cornell University Press, 2013.

Yi, Kil J. "The U.S.-Korean Alliance in the Vietnam War: The Years of Escalation, 1964–68." In *International Perspectives on Vietnam*, edited by Lloyd C. Gardner and Ted Gittinger, 154–75. College Station: Texas A&M University Press, 2000.

Yoneyama, Lisa. *Cold War Ruins: Transpacific Critique of American Justice and Japanese War Crimes*. Durham, NC: Duke University Press, 2016.

Yoon, Chung Ro. "We Are Exporting Skilled Workers: Life of a Korean Worker Dispatched to Viet Nam and the Viet Nam War." *Journal BOL* (Winter 2007): 243–53.

Young, Marilyn. *The Vietnam Wars, 1945–1990*. New York: Harper Perennial, 1990.

Yuh, Ji-Yeon. *Beyond the Shadow of Camptown: Korean Military Brides in America*. New York: New York University Press, 2002.

AMERICAN CROSSROADS

Edited by Earl Lewis, George Lipsitz, George Sánchez, Dana
Takagi, Laura Briggs, and Nikhil Pal Singh

INDEX

Abrams, Creighton, 124
Acheson, Dean, 49, 54
Afghanistan, 190
African Americans, 2, 12, 31, 38, 138, 140, 143, 148, 151, 176. *See also* black communities
Afro-Asian Conference, 56
Air America, 57
Aitken, Robert, 94
Alameda Naval Complex, 162, 165
Albertini, Jim, 100, 102
Aleutians, 79
Algeria: Algiers, 52
Ali, Muhammad, 2
Allied Forces, 41–43, 120, 123–124, 171, 185, 212n2; occupation of Japan, 21
All-Volunteer Force (AVF), 187–188
Alverado, Manuel, 91
American Civil Liberties Union, 181
American Friends Service Committee, 165; *America's Rented Troops*, 125
American Indian Movement, 159
American Indians, 138, 143, 159, 219n38
American Psychiatric Association, 160, 188
American Servicemen's Union, 169
American Youth Congress, 28
Amphibious Base, 44
Andersen Air Base, 29
Andric, Tom, 180
anticolonialism, 5–6, 8–10, 12, 14–15, 20–22, 30, 36, 42, 51–52, 55–56, 73–74,

78, 115, 118, 125, 128–129, 140, 148, 165, 177, 187. *See also* anti-imperialism; decolonization
anticommunism, 8, 22, 27, 33, 35, 46–47, 54, 56, 65, 67, 75, 105, 110, 126, 132
anti-imperialism, 13, 15, 30, 54, 99, 102, 131, 135–136, 147, 149, 157, 159, 161–164, 168, 172, 175, 182, 184. *See also* anticolonialism
anti-Normalization Treaty movement, 112–115, 128
antiracism, 8, 12, 147, 149, 161, 165, 168, 177
Appy, Christian, 138
Aquino, Benigno, 180
Arellano, Oscar, 58, 61
Arima, James, 139
Armed Forces of the Philippines (AFP), 70, 72, 118, 121. *See also* Philippine Army
Arnold, Archibald, 20
"Asia for Asians," 8, 15, 17–48, 51–52, 64, 72, 104, 111, 133, 187–188. *See also* pan-Asianism
Asian American Political Alliance (AAPA), 151–152
Asian Americans, 4–5, 12–13, 16, 183–186, 219n38; in Vietnam War, 15–16, 134–161, 165. *See also* Chinese Americans; Filipino Americans; Japanese Americans; Korean Americans
Asian Americans for Peace, 135, 151
Asian Movement for Military Outreach (AMMO), 154–159

251

138, 186; racial, 2–4, 8, 13, 75, 78–79, 83, 137, 189

Liberal Party (Philippines), 114, 175

Liberated Barracks (organization), 100

Liberated Barracks (publication), 99

Liberation Day (Guam), 190, 224n11

Life magazine, 25

Lifton, Robert Jay: *Home from the War*, 142

Livingston, David, 30, 199n45

Lodge, Henry Cabot, 110, 120

Lodge Act, 40

Long Beach State College, 147

Los Angeles City College, 143

L'Overture, Toussaint, 53

Lowe, Lisa, 14, 196n37

Lubow, Bart, 182

Luna, Doug, 138–140, 142, 144

Macapagal, Diosdado, 104, 107, 112–114, 117

MacArthur, Douglas, 20–21, 79

Magsaysay, Ramon, 56, 58, 71, 73, 75, 107

Mahan, Alfred Thayer, 79

Makoto, Oda, 169, 172

Malaya, 5–6, 50, 126

Malcolm X, 148

Manglapus, Raul, 56

Manila Bulletin, 75

Manila Chronicle, 179–180

Manila Pact, 54, 57

Manila Times, 117, 122

Marcos, Ferdinand, 104, 114, 116–118, 127, 175–177, 179–183

Marianas, 5–6, 7*fig.*, 78–79, 191

Marshall, George C., 37

Marshall Islands, 5–7*fig.*, 78, 191

Marxism, 98, 188

Marxist-Leninism, 153

Masaoka, Mike, 157

Masoka, Kathy Nishimoto, 156, 159

Masui, Stanford, 95–96*fig.*

Mata, Ernesto, 121

McCarthy, Joseph, 34

McConaughy, Walter P., 45

McCormick, Thomas, 8

McKeldin, William, 60–61, 63

McNamara, Robert, 42, 75, 113, 127, 138

medicine, 55, 65–66, 85, 104, 122–123, 159;

healthcare workers, 11, 15, 51, 57–64, 58, 111, 117, 121, 186, 190; public health, 63–65, 77, 84, 172

Medina, Ernest, 91–92

methodology, of book, 8, 14

Micronesia, 190

Military Bases Agreement, 72

Military Intelligence Service Language School, 33

Miller, Allan, 166–167, 175, 178–179

mirror imaging, 41–42

Miyamoto, Charles, 98

model minority discourse, 12, 137

More Flags program, 104

Movement for a Democratic Military (MDM)

Muccio, John, 24

Mutual Defense Assistance Act, 35

Mutual Defense Assistance program (MDAP), 18, 35–36, 41–46

Mutuc, Amelito, 107, 109

Mydans, Carl, 25–26*fig.*

My Lai Jungle Training Center, 99–100

My Lai massacre, 90–93, 99–100, 125, 128, 142

NAACP, 148

Nagatani, Nick, 1–2, 11, 13, 139–140, 146–149, 153, 155–157, 159, 219n27, 219n29, 220n56

Nakatsuka, Lawrence, 81

Nakayama, Mike, 1–2, 11, 13, 136–141, 147–155, 152*fig.*, 159–160, 219n38, 220n56

Namaka, David, 81

Nasser, Gamal Abdel, 109

National Bureau of Investigation (Philippines), 75

National Committee to Restore Civil Liberties in the Philippines (NCRCLP), 182

nationalism, 4, 11, 17, 34, 62, 68–69, 73–75, 82, 117–118, 133, 148–149, 175, 177, 188; anticolonial, 15, 48–49, 51, 104, 125, 128, 132; capitalism and, 52; colonialism and, 5, 57, 105, 114, 179

Nationalists (China), 35, 45, 110. *See also* China: Republic of China

National Lawyers Guild (NLG), 177–182

Philippine Rural Reconstruction
  Movement (PRRM): National
  Headquarters and Training Center, 116
Philippines, 7*fig.*, 17, 133, 191; Angeles City,
  143, 178; antiwar activism in, 29–31, 106,
  114–115, 126–128, 134, 162–164, 170,
  175–184; Bataan, 31; Cotabato, 71;
  decolonization/anticolonialism, 6,
  10–11, 15, 18, 21–22, 49, 54–55, 73–74,
  100, 115, 187; Japanese occupation of, 66,
  120; Luzon, 22–23, 49–50, 83;
  Malacañang Palace, 114; Manila, 29,
  54–61, 66, 69–70, 75, 106, 116–118, 122,
  152, 175, 177–180; martial law, 163–164,
  175–184; Olongapo, 178; San Luis, 71;
  Tarlac, 31; US imperialism and, 3–5,
  11–12, 15–16, 23, 36, 48–76, 79, 103–110,
  112–118, 120–123, 126–128, 161, 163–164,
  170, 182–183, 185–187. *See also* Filipinos
Philippine Scouts, 39, 41, 66
Philippines National Economic
  Council, 73
Philippines-Ryukyus Command, 31
Philippine Veterans Legion (PVL), 66, 69
Phillips, Rufus, 62–64, 107–108
Pike, Douglas, 116
Pine Ridge Indian Reservation, 159
Pioneer Center, 155
Portugal: imperialism of, 5
postcolonialism, 4, 9, 11, 27, 52, 54–55, 58,
  68, 73, 103, 111, 115, 121–123, 134, 185. *See
  also* decolonization
Post-traumatic Stress Disorder (PTSD),
  142, 160, 188. *See also* war-related
  trauma
Presbyterians, 165–166
Presidio, 165
Progressive Era, 55
Provisional Revolutionary Government of
  the Republic of South Vietnam (PRG),
  148, 159
psychological warfare (psywar), 51–52, 58,
  72, 108
Psychological Warfare Training Center, 72
Puerto Rico, 5, 138, 148

Quakers, 125
Quinn, William, 82

race, 1, 16, 28, 38, 43, 112, 124, 133, 136, 138,
  141, 144, 145, 148–149, 151, 155, 160,
  167, 169; citizenship and, 40, 141, 154;
  imperialism and, 5, 8–13, 16, 22, 31–34,
  36, 48, 52, 56, 64, 71, 81–94, 98, 140,
  161, 164–165, 173, 177, 185–189;
  postraciality, 12; racial intimacy, 56,
  71, 109, 113, 121–123, 146; racial
  liberalism, 2–4, 8, 13, 75, 78–79, 83,
  137, 189. *See also* integration (racial);
  race war; segregation (racial);
  whiteness
race war, 8–9, 71, 77–102, 108, 124, 134,
  137–138, 140, 142, 146–147
racism, 2, 12, 18, 22, 43–44, 103, 148–151,
  153, 186–187; imperialism and, 8–9, 52;
  in military, 13, 15, 92, 95, 137–138, 140–
  141, 143, 145, 154–155, 167–168, 173, 176,
  184; of US capitalism, 2, 183. *See also*
  antiracism; Japanese Internment; Jim
  Crow; race war; segregation; segregation
  (racial); white supremacy
RAND Corporation, 86
Reagan, Ronald, 132, 188–189, 191
Recto, Claro M., 56–57, 71, 73–74
Red Guard Party, 148
"Red menace," 25
Refugee Relief Act, 45, 47
refugees, 24, 47, 51, 55, 58–60, 64, 68, 117,
  122. *See also* asylum
Reserve Officers' Training Corps (ROTC),
  118, 139
The Resistance, 95
Revolutionary Development program, 122
Rhee, Syngman, 24–27, 34, 42
Ridgeway, Matthew, 38
Rimlands War, 8
Robeson, Paul, 52
Robinson, Cedric, 9
Roediger, David, 137
Romulo, Carlos P., 54, 72, 74
Roosevelt, Theodore, 20
Rowny, Edward, 107
Royal Indian Navy, 30
Royall, Kenneth, 28
Rusk, Dean, 113
Russo-Japanese War, 20
Ryukyus, 79